Federalism, Bureaucracy, and Public Policy

CANADIAN PUBLIC ADMINISTRATION
SERIES

COLLECTION ADMINISTRATION PUBLIQUE
CANADIENNE

J. E. Hodgetts, *General Editor/Directeur général*
Roch Bolduc, *Directeur associé/Associate Editor*

The Institute of Public Administration of Canada
L'Institut d'administration publique du Canada

This series is sponsored by the Institute of Public
Administration of Canada as part of its constitutional
commitment to encourage research on contemporary
issues in Canadian public administration and public
policy, and to foster wider knowledge and understanding amongst practitioners and the concerned citizen.
There is no fixed number of volumes planned for the
series, but under the supervision of the Research
Committee of the Institute, the General Editor,
and the Associate Editor, efforts will be made to
ensure that significant areas will receive appropriate
attention.

L'Institut d'administration publique du Canada
commandite cette collection dans le cadre de ses
engagements statutaires. Il se doit de promouvoir la
recherche sur des problèmes d'actualité portant sur
l'administration publique et la détermination des poli-
tiques publiques ainsi que d'encourager les praticiens
et les citoyens intéressés à les mieux connaître et à les
mieux comprendre. Il n'a pas été prévu de nombre de
volumes donné pour la collection mais, sous la direction du Comité de recherche de l'Institut, du Directeur
général, et du Directeur associé, l'on s'efforce d'ac-
corder l'attention voulue aux questions importantes.

Canada and Immigration:
Public Policy and Public Concern
Freda Hawkins

The Biography of an Institution:
The Civil Service Commission of Canada, 1908–1967
J. E. Hodgetts, William McCloskey, Reginald
Whitaker, V. Seymour Wilson

An edition in French has been published under the
title *Histoire d'une institution: La Commission de la*
Fonction publique du Canada, 1908–1967,
by Les Presses de l'Université Laval

Old Age Pensions and Policy-Making in Canada
Kenneth Bryden

Provincial Governments as Employers:
A Survey of Public Personnel Administration
in Canada's Provinces
J. E. Hodgetts and O. P. Dwivedi

Transport in Transition:
The Reorganization of the Federal Transport Portfolio
John W. Langford

Initiative and Response:
The Adaptation of Canadian Federalism to
Regional Economic Development
Anthony G. S. Careless

Canada's Salesman to the World:
The Department of Trade and Commerce, 1892–1939
O. Mary Hill

Health Insurance and Canadian Public Policy:
The Seven Decisions that Created the Canadian
Health Insurance System
Malcolm G. Taylor

Federalism, Bureaucracy, and Public Policy

The Politics of Highway Transport Regulation

RICHARD J. SCHULTZ

The Institute of Public Administration of Canada
L'Institut d'administration publique du Canada

McGill–Queen's University Press
Montreal

© The Institute of Public Administration of Canada/
L'Institut d'administration publique du Canada 1980

ISBN 0-7735-0360-9 (cloth)
ISBN 0-7735-0362-5 (paper)

Legal deposit third quarter 1980
Bibliothèque Nationale du Québec

Printed and bound in Canada by
T. H. Best Printing Company Limited

To my mother and the
memory of my father

Contents

Preface

This book undertakes the study of a victim—a policy that fell foul of that ubiquitous feature of the contemporary Canadian political scene, intergovernmental negotiations. The victim in question is Part III of the National Transportation Act of 1967, which, though a major section of the act, has not been implemented after more than a decade, and my initial purpose is to explain why. The book's major objectives, however, are broader in that it attempts to employ the analysis of the fate of Part III to examine some of the dynamics of both intergovernmental and intragovernmental relations in Canada. Two different, although not necessarily exclusive, models are used in the analysis of the policy process. The first is the "unitary actor" model, which is common to the study of Canadian intergovernmental relations; the second, which is far less common, is the "bureaucratic politics" model. It is this latter, much neglected model, that most convincingly explains the shelving of Part III.

After analysing the lengthy negotiations between the two levels of government on the issue, the study examines the complex internal bargaining *within* the federal government in order to assess its impact on the negotiations *between* governments. In focusing on the diversity of goals and resources within a government and in arguing that conflict and competition are inherent in bureaucratic life, the study challenges some of the common assumptions held by advocates of the unitary actor model about the nature of the policy process within a parliamentary system. Although no attempt is made to generalize from the particular issue, the study does isolate some of the factors which suggest in particular that central agencies may not exercise the degree of control commonly ascribed to them and, more significantly, that power and influence are much more widely dispersed and diffused within our parliamentary system than is usually acknowledged.

In undertaking this study, I have incurred a great number of debts.

The most important by far is owed to over fifty individuals who agreed to be interviewed, several of them repeatedly, during 1973 and 1974. These persons were drawn from the federal government, seven of the ten provinces, and three interest groups. In addition, a number of people outside the governmental or industry circles, yet knowledgeable of the issue, were also interviewed. Several of the central participants, at both the federal and provincial levels, as well as one interest group official, permitted me to examine their extensive personal files. The interviews were conducted on the understanding that there would be no direct attribution to individuals, but for the record, it should be noted that they included the president and vice president of the CTC, all but one member of the CTC's Motor Vehicle Committee, every senior CTC official who was involved, with a single exception, and every senior official in the Department of Transport up to the senior assistant deputy minister—the most senior departmental official involved. In addition, as a major supplement to the interviews, I was given access to the relevant files of both the CTC and DOT, as well as to the files of the Federal-Provincial Advisory Council on Motor Carrier Regulation. Without the willing cooperation of all these individuals, this study could not have been completed.

I would also like to thank Tom Hockin, Douglas Verney, and especially Fred Fletcher, all colleagues at York University, for their assistance with an earlier version of the study. J. E. Hodgetts, the general editor of this series, has also offered valuable advice and, perhaps more important, has been most patient. I am also indebted to two anonymous referees who provided extensive and useful comments on an earlier draft.

The Canada Council, the federal Department of Transport, and the McGill Centre for the Study of Regulated Industries provided essential financial assistance. I particularly wish to thank Ruth Griffin of Glendon College and Cathy Duggan of McGill University for their excellent secretarial assistance. The study has also greatly benefited from the editorial skills of Barbara Herchmer of Toronto and Joan Harcourt of Kingston. I wish to thank Richard Shaw for his assistance with the index.

Earlier versions of Chapter 7 and part of Chapter 8 appeared in Peter Meekison's *Canadian Federalism: Myth and Reality* (3rd ed.) and Thomas Hockin's *Apex of Power* (2nd ed.). I wish to thank Methuen of Canada and Prentice-Hall of Canada respectively for permission to publish revised versions of this material.

Finally, my wife, Barbie, deserves special mention for, once again, her tolerance, patience, and good humour, while this and other projects were in process, have been crucial to their completion. Although I may not show it well, or often enough, I am grateful to her.

Chronology of Key Dates

1954 Winner Decision of the Judicial Committee of the Privy Council; Motor Vehicle Transport Act enacted.

1961 Report of the MacPherson Royal Commission on Transportation.

1966 August—Introduction of National Transportation Act.

1967 February—NTA receives Royal Assent.

1969 December 2–3—Federal-Provincial Conference of Ministers responsible for Motor Carrier Regulation; creation of Joint Technical Committee of Officials—first meeting December 3.

December 15—Revised Ontario proposal sent by federal chairman of Joint Technical Committee to provinces for comment.

1970 May 15—Part III of NTA proclaimed.
November 2—Second meeting of Joint Technical Committee.

1971 May 15—Federal-Provincial Conference of Ministers responsible for Motor Carrier Regulation: creation of Advisory Council on Motor Carrier Regulation.

June 8—First meeting of Advisory Council in Ottawa.

July 22—Second meeting of Advisory Council in Ottawa.

August 22–23—Third meeting of Advisory Council in Halifax; creation of two sub-groups on Regulations and Regulatory Structure.

September 23–24—Regulations Sub-Group meets in Edmonton.

September 28–29—Regulatory Structure Sub-Group meets in Toronto.

October 13–15—Regulation Sub-Group meets in Edmonton.

November 15–19—Fourth meeting of Advisory Council in Winnipeg.

1972 January 17–21—Fifth meeting of Advisory Council in Ottawa.
     April—Advisory Council reports.
     June—MOT–CTC Task Force on Part III created.
1973 May—Task Force collapses: no report issued.
1980 Part III still not implemented.

Commonly Used Abbreviations

CTA Canadian Trucking Associations

CTC Canadian Transport Commission

DOT Department of Transport

MVTA Motor Vehicle Transport Act

MVTC Motor Vehicle Transport Committee

NTA National Transportation Act

OHTB Ontario Highway Transport Board

PCO Privy Council Office

QTA Quebec Trucking Association

Chapter One

INTRODUCTION

The National Transportation Act (NTA) of 1967 promised radical changes in Canadian transportation regulation.[1] All major regulatory functions were assigned to a single agency, a reversal of previous policies and decisions. The railways, for the first time in Canadian history, were to be significantly deregulated. Finally, the federal government, with sole and almost sole authority for air and rail regulation respectively, proposed to extend its regulatory responsibilities to include the highway transport industry. This would be accomplished by rescinding the delegation to the provinces of federal authority to regulate the extraprovincial motor carrier industry.[2]

This last change, contained in Part III of the NTA, did not attract as much attention in 1967 as did the other two, but it was nonetheless an integral part of the new regulatory regime. Indeed, direct federal regulation of the highway transport industry, especially the trucking component, was thought to be essential to the successful implementation of the new national transportation policy. By 1967, the trucking industry was a central part of the Canadian transportation system, so central in fact that its growth was credited with setting in motion "the process which culminated in passage of the National Transportation Act."[3] The primary responsibility of the new multimodal regulatory agency, the Canadian Transport Commission (CTC), was "co-ordinating and harmonizing the operations of all carriers" under federal jurisdiction. If the commission was to fulfil its mandate, implementation of Part III was a prerequisite. Furthermore, attainment of the goals of the new policy, which stipulated that "regulation of all modes of transport will not be of such a nature as to restrict the ability of any mode to compete freely with any other mode of transport," made it imperative that federal regulation replace the existing costly and fragmented provincial regulatory systems.

Despite its significance to the NTA, a decade later Part III has not

1

been implemented and the provinces continue to regulate the extraprovincial motor carrier industry. Yet the nature of provincial regulation with its confusion, contradictions, and lack of uniformity represents the very type of regulatory chaos the NTA was intended to correct. It is a system that, rather than facilitating and furthering its competitive potential, is a fundamental impediment, distorting and inhibiting the industry. In view of the significance of the motor carrier industry to the national transportation system, the philosophy of the NTA, the mandate given the CTC, and the inadequacies of the provincial regulatory system, it is important to ask why Part III has not been implemented.

The most immediate answer, according to successive federal ministers of transport, is that Part III fell victim to federal-provincial conflict.[4] When the NTA was before Parliament, the federal government made a commitment to consult the provinces before implementing Part III. Six years of intergovernmental consultations and negotiations followed, during which the federal government encountered fundamental provincial opposition to such implementation. This provincial opposition was so intensive that, despite the fact that the federal government has exclusive jurisdiction over the extraprovincial motor carrier industry, no acceptable method of implementation was agreed upon.

How does one explain the outcomes of federal-provincial negotiations? It is this broader question which underlies our concern with the fate of Part III. The importance of the question should be readily apparent. The dominant characteristic of contemporary Canadian federalism is not the division of powers between two levels of government, described by one observer as, "separate and co-ordinate."[5] Rather, to paraphrase Richard Neustadt's description of the American presidential system, what we have today in Canada is a system of separate levels of government sharing powers. It is an accepted, although often decried, fact of political life in Canada that the federal and provincial governments are obliged to collaborate in the making of public policy. Such collaboration is necessitated by what M. J. C. Vile describes as the "mutually dependent political relationship" that characterizes the relations between the two levels of government in modern federal systems.[6] Accordingly, a central feature of policy-making in Canada today is the necessity for policy-makers at one level of government to "influence, bargain with and persuade" those at the other levels.[7] If policy-making is so inextricably interwoven with the politics of the federal system, it is imperative, for an understanding of the nature of the policy process, that we have a full appreciation of those factors that have an impact in shaping the outcomes of intergovernmental negotiations.

This study will employ two alternative methods currently used in developing explanations for the outcomes of intergovernmental negotiations in Canada. The first is the most popular among Canadian analysts and is rooted in fundamental assumptions about the nature and distribution of power in a parliamentary system and its impact on the federal system. The second method is one that is far less common in Canadian studies, in part because the evidence necessary to its employment is, or at least has been, difficult to obtain in a system characterized by a very high degree of secrecy about the inner workings of decision-making processes. An even more important reason for its lack of favour is that it challenges some of those very assumptions that are central to the dominant mode of analysis.

The first method concentrates its search for explanations of the outcomes of intergovernmental negotiations on the interactions between governments. Underlying this method of analysis is a model of governmental decision-making which conceives of governments as internally homogeneous, coherent entities—in other words, as "unitary actors." The alternative method contends that the common emphasis on what happens between governments may fail to do justice to the complex intragovernmental process that can precede, accompany, and follow negotiations between governments. This model singles out the forces that give rise to such a process. Furthermore, such a model maintains that the intragovernmental process may substantially affect the negotiations between governments and therefore cannot be disregarded in the development of explanations of the outcomes.

GOVERNMENT AS "UNITARY ACTOR"

According to this method (or, in a non-rigorous sense, model) of analysis, attention should be focused on the interactions between what are, in terms of both structures and goals, essentially fundamentally unified actors. Although numerous examples of the use of such a model could be cited, the work of Richard Simeon stands out as the most explicit, and refined, example of its use. In his *Federal-Provincial Diplomacy*, Simeon states that, in his framework for analysing intergovernmental negotiations, "Canada's eleven governments are the actors. For most purposes each will be considered as a single unit."[8] What is important for our purposes is Simeon's reason for adopting such an approach, for it hinges on fundamental assumptions about the nature of power within the parliamentary system.

Simeon's starting point is the assumption that "the institutional arrangements of the constituent governments are a fundamental factor shaping intergovernmental relations in Canada."[9] After surveying several such arrangements, Simeon concludes that the most crucial institutional arrangement is one that is often considered to be a defining characteristic of the parliamentary system, namely, strong central control. The centralization of power in the parliamentary system has two dimensions with respect to intergovernmental relations. The first is that the actors in the negotiations are limited to the executives of the different governments at the expense of the legislatures. As Simeon states, "one of the consequences . . . of Cabinet dominance . . . is that premiers and prime ministers can firmly commit their own governments, since there is very little chance of their being repudiated by a recalcitrant legislature."[10]

Although there can be little dispute about this first conclusion, it is the second dimension of the assumption that is more fundamental to Simeon's use of the unitary-actor model. This dimension contends that the intergovernmental process is dominated by a select few among the various executives because "the participants are not scattered through the system . . .; rather they are concentrated and limited largely to provincial premiers, senior cabinet ministers and senior officials on the one hand and their federal counterparts on the other."[11] The parliamentary system is thus characterized by a centralization of power both by the executive vis-à-vis the legislature and within the executive by senior cabinet ministers and central officials vis-à-vis program departments. This is in marked contrast to an earlier period of federal-provincial negotiations when, as Donald Smiley claims, program departments dominated central agencies.[12]

The result of strong central control, according to Simeon, is "a characteristic form of decision-making, one narrowly focused in direct relations between distinct governments which have relatively few links with each other except through direct contacts between their political leaders."[13] There are two related consequences of this "characteristic form of decision-making." The first is that, unlike in the earlier period described by Smiley, horizontal relations between ministers and officials with similar interests will be inhibited by central officials and their goals and values. Such relations will be inhibited because domination by a few central executives "makes it less likely that alliances in policy-making will cut across governmental lines."[14] Secondly, because of the decentralization, conflicts are channelled "through to cabinets and senior central officials of the governments," with the result that conflicts over policy become expressed as conflicts between governments and institutional status and prestige concerns become merged with "more substantive program differences."[15] This has direct implications for other potential actors in the negotiations, particularly interest groups, because the centralized intergovernmental bargaining process and the increased importance attached to status and prestige by individual governments "tends to freeze out interest groups."[16]

It is the assumption that the dominant actors are few and united within individual governments that leads to the concentration on the interactions between governments in the subsequent analysis. If governments are unified, for the reasons advanced, then it is only what happens between them that is relevant to explaining the outcomes. Consequently, after ascertaining the contending goals or objectives of the governments as actors, explanations are developed by analysing the resources, the constraints, the strategies, and the tactics of the individual actors. The objective of such an analysis is to arrive at an assessment of the effectiveness of the different actors as negotiators and the factors influencing such effectiveness. With such an approach, explanations for outcomes are contingent upon the effectiveness "ratings" assigned to the individual actors.

The "Bureaucratic Politics" Model

Adherents of this second model of analysis claim that governments may not exhibit the high degree of unity assumed by the unitary actor model; that decision-making, instead of being dominated by a few central actors, may exhibit a much more complex political process. Moreover, the issue is not simply one of "internal" politics, for everyone assumes such politics to exist in all large organizations, public or private. The issue, rather, is more significant, and requires an assessment of the impact of the internal decision-making process on the outcomes of negotiations between governments. The "bureaucratic politics" model, as it is now commonly known, does exactly this and we will employ it in our search for the explanation for the fate of Part III of the NTA. Because it has been less commonly employed in Canadian studies, it would seem appropriate to outline at somewhat greater length its underlying rationale, premises, and central concerns.

For students of bureaucratic politics, there is a fundamental weakness in the unitary actor model, in that

it obscures the persistently neglected fact of bureaucracy: the "maker" of government policy is not one calculating decision-maker, but rather a conglomerate of large organizations and political actors who differ substantially about what their government should do on any particular issue and who compete in attempting to affect both governmental decisions and the actions of their government.[17]

The central focus of the bureaucratic politics framework is "on the individuals within governments, and the interactions among them, as determinants of the actions of government."[18] A crucial assumption of this framework is that governments have diverse goals and means. Conflict and competition among individual officials is endemic and pervasive in a bureaucracy because of the different roles such individuals must perform. From their roles officials develop "competitive, not homogenous interests."[19] Such interests must be reconciled and this is attempted through a complex bargaining process in which the participants possess different sources of power. The fact that no one individual can dominate the other participants is what necessitates this internal bargaining.

There are two types of conflict within bureaucratic structures that are relevant to the bureaucratic politics framework. The first is that which exists within individual government departments or agencies, the second is that between such departments or agencies. With respect to the former, Wamsley and Zald maintain: "One of the most revealing of analytic concerns about internal policy is the degree of consensus on goals that exists within an organization. Few organizations have complete internal unity on purpose or functional niche."[20] Anthony Downs has suggested that within an organization a lack of consensus on goals and means can arise from a variety of sources:

(1) from competing subunits seeking to move the organization in a direction that results in their aggrandizement, (2) from the ambiguity of the organization's statutory mandate that encourages differing interpretations, (3) from the machinations or intervention of external actors who seek to change its direction or niche, (4) from heterogeneity or disparateness within the elite cadre stemming from diverse recruitment channels and socialization processes, (5) from elite factions with external ties to a profession or functional specialty, (6) from the placement of a political executive with "new ideas" over high-ranking civil servants of long tenure, (7) from operations that cover wide areas that are complex, vague or diverse.[21]

The potential for conflict within governments is compounded when different departments or agencies are involved in the policy-making process. There are many reasons for assuming that a competitive relationship exists in such a situation. Indeed, Downs has postulated a "Law of Interorganizational Conflict" for such situations which states that "every large organization is in partial conflict with every other social agent it deals with."[22] Governmental bodies such as departments develop a degree of "territorial sensitivity" and are always vigilant lest their "policy space" is invaded.[23] Government departments and agencies often have overlapping responsibilities and this is conducive to the creation of intense rivalries between them. It can also be assumed that conflict is automatic between operating departments and central agencies that attempt to coordinate such departments and develop "common policies." Several departments and agencies may be compelled to participate in developing a policy on a single issue and may be responsible for different sets of activities necessary for the formulation and implementation of the policy in question. In such an interdependent situation, the various participants bring to bear on the issue different interests, perspectives, and values. In essence, the situation within a bureaucracy is that conflict is inherent among individuals who are performing a variety of roles both within their "base" organization and with respect to other organizations.

The bureaucratic politics framework incorporates an understanding of the conflict and competition that is inherent in bureaucratic life by focusing its analysis on the positions occupied or roles performed by the various officials. It is because of the differences in roles or positions performed by the individual participants in the policy-making process that issues are seldom seen to be clear-cut and straightforward. Rather, issues have many faces and, in the process of adopting a policy on any one issue, officials are affected by a multitude of interests, principal among which are governmental, organizational, and personal. Officials are influenced by what they think is best for their government but this is not their only, or perhaps even their primary, consideration. As Allison and Halperin suggest, many officials are concerned with the impact of an issue on the "health of their organization." Organizational health "is seen to depend on maintaining influence, fulfilling its mission, and securing the necessary capabilities. The latter two interests lead to concern for maintaining autonomy and organizational morale, protecting the organization's essence, maintaining or expanding roles or missions, and maintaining or increasing budgets."[24]

Individual interests also have an important influence on officials' perception of issues. Downs contends that individual officials are motivated by a complex set of goals, some of which are highly personal, and may include power, prestige, pride, and professionalism. It cannot be assumed that officials are simply and always motivated by a single personal interest.[25] In this regard, Peter Self's challenge to Downs' emphasis on "bureaucratic free enterprise" is valuable more as a qualification of Downs' more dogmatic assertions of the importance of "administrative egoism" than as a successful refutation of its existence in countries other than the United States.[26] The assumption of the bureaucratic politics model is not that officials are exclusively or even primarily motivated by self-interest but that it is one component of the variety of interests that influence them.

As a result of the diverse interests that may be affected by government policy, the officials concerned will compete to influence the policy adopted. Unlike Simeon's emphasis on the "hierarchical controls" at the disposal of the central agencies, the bureaucratic politics model assumes that decisions on policy are the result of a complex bargaining process involving all the officials affected. Policy results from "the pulling and hauling that is politics."[27] The argument is not that all actors are equal or that a hierarchy does not exist, for such an argument misrepresents "both constitutional and political reality."[28]

The bureaucratic politics model assumes that, while hierarchical controls do exist, they do not ensure that the preferences of the central agencies, or indeed that superiors within an organization, will automatically prevail. Rather, the model assumes that bargaining is necessary within governments because all the participants possess some resources, however unequal. To offset hierarchical controls, participants may possess independent sources of power or "bargaining advantages." One such source of power suggested by Wamsley and Zald is the "essentiality of function" that characterizes different subunits of bureaucracies responsible for performing specialized functions.[29] Allison suggests that among other bargaining advantages that various actors may possess are:

> actual control over resources necessary to carry out action; expertise
> and control over information that enables one to define the
> problem, identify options, and estimate feasibilities; control over
> information that enables chiefs to determine whether and in what form
> decisions are being implemented; . . . and access to and persuasiveness
> with players who have bargaining advantages from the above.[30]

Possession and skilful use of these and other bargaining advantages can preclude any attempt by central agencies, or for that matter, any single set of actors, to impose a policy on any other actors.

According to the bureaucratic politics model, given the extent of conflict and the distribution of independent sources of power, policy emerges as the outcome or, to use Allison's term, the "resultant," of a complex internal bargaining process. Government actions are conceptualized as "resultants" because "what happens is not chosen as a solution to a problem but rather results from compromise, conflict and confusion of officials with diverse interests and unequal influence."[31] Government actions emerge as "collages" and to understand the nature of these collages one must undertake an examination of the following:

Choices by one player (e.g. to authorize action by his department, to make a speech, or to refrain from acquiring certain information), resultants of minor games (e.g., the wording of a cable or the decision on departmental action worked out among lower-level players), resultants of central games (e.g., decision, actions, and speeches bargained out among central players), and "foul-ups" (e.g., choices are not made because they are not recognized or are raised too late, misunderstandings).[32]

To understand or explain "why one pattern of governmental behavior emerged," Allison argues that "it is necessary to identify the games and players, to display the coalitions, bargains and compromises and to convey some feel for the confusion."[33]

Aside from the intrinsic importance of studying the bureaucratic policy process, the argument here is that this process is particularly important because of its impact on the negotiations between governments. It can be important, in the first place, because of the specific policy that results from the internal bargaining. That this policy may not be the coherent, clearly defined policy that is implied by the unitary-actor model with its assumptions of central control is suggested by the following summary of the work of one student of bureaucratic politics:

the bureaucratic political process can produce "no policy at all", stalemate; "compromised policy", with the direction hardly evident; or "unstable policy" where "changes in the *ad hoc* grouping of elites point policy first in one and then in another direction." It can result in "contradictory policy", where different government organizations pursue conflicting courses; "paper policy", officially promulgated without the support needed for effective implementation; or "slow policy", since competition and consensus-building take time.[34]

The significance of such a variety of policy outcomes to the intergovernmental bargaining process can be suggested by means of the concept of "signals." As Allison states in his discussion of Schelling's *The Strategy of Conflict*, "the explicit statements and tactical moves of nations constitute strategic signals. Adversaries watch and interpret each other's behaviour, each aware that his own actions are being interpreted and each acting with a consciousness of the expectations he creates."[35] The impact of bureaucratic politics on such signals is suggested by Morton Halperin who "depicts bureaucrats who are so deeply engrossed in intragovernmental manoeuvring that the actions which result are seldom clear signals to other countries."[36] The lack of clear signals can have serious repercussions on the intergovernmental bargaining if it affects the strategies and tactics of other governments.

Internal bargaining merits study for another reason—it often occurs simultaneously with intergovernmental negotiations. One cannot assume that one set of negotiations begins when the other ends. Often the intra- and intergovernmental negotiations proceed in tandem. Intergovernmental negotiations that are extended and result in proposal and counter-proposal often require the respective negotiators to reassess their positions, adopt new objectives, pursue alternative strategies. When such a reassessment occurs, it may produce internal bargaining afresh with actors not satisfied with the initial result, once again pressing their case or at least attempting to attain modifications more in line with their perceived interests. Members of the internal coalition may be constantly on the defensive during the intergovernmental negotiations lest their ox be gored in any trade-off, while the interests of the other members of the coalition remain intact.

Intragovernmental bargaining, moreover, should not be seen as necessarily having a final solution, as a once-and-for-all-time knock-down fight with a clear winner emerging. Such bargaining should be understood as a many round encounter with each round providing yet another opportunity for the combatants to gain points on their opponents. Every opportunity provided to reopen the intragovernmental bargaining may have serious repercussions on the intergovernmental negotiations because of the costs involved. In such a situation, one result may be that negotiators for a government may more readily accept a compromise than their objective position would indicate in order to avoid the necessity of reopening the internal bargaining process.

"Bureaucratic politics," according to one analyst, "is the process by which people inside government bargain with one another on complex public policy questions."[37] The objective of the preceding discussion is to provide a basic outline of the concepts of the framework and its central assumptions. The bureaucratic politics framework assumes that the policy adopted by a government is the result of an intense bargaining process within the government. Such bargaining is the result of the various interests that are affected by an issue. The diversity of interests, it is argued, is the result of the diversity of roles performed within governments. The central argument is that the negotiations that take place *within* a government may be a significant determinant of the results of the negotiations *between* governments.

REGULATORY AGENCIES AND BUREAUCRATIC POLITICS

If researchers were searching for an obvious point in the institutional structure in the Canadian parliamentary system where conventional notions of strong central control might be attenuated, regulatory agencies provide just such a point. The roles of regulatory agencies and their position in the parliamentary institutional system provide one of the more neglected areas of Canadian research. This is most unfortunate for they have become an increasingly important instrument in accomplishing public policy objectives. For our more immediate purposes, regulatory agencies are of direct relevance to the central issues underlying the debate over the merits of the two models employed in this study inasmuch as they are, in Hodgett's phrase, "structural heretics" in the parliamentary system because of their non-departmental form.[38] Their officers have both an independent status, unlike that of traditional departments, and a statutory freedom for action and manoeuvre, that is, in large part, unique.

The assumption that strong central control is a defining characteristic of a parliamentary system is contingent upon the concept of ministerial responsibility of either a collective or individual nature. It is ministerial responsibility, whatever its earlier purposes, that is the cornerstone of executive domination of the legislature and correspondingly of coordination, centralization, and unification of the executive branch of government. Regulatory agencies, or at least those that are granted a degree of independence, do "violence to the constituted system of ministerial responsibility" to the extent that they are free from ministerial control.[39] For our purposes, the grant of some degree of independence to a regulatory agency may be important insofar as it undermines the dominant or superior position of the few actors whose pre-eminence is central to the unitary actor model. On issues which involve, in some meaningful way, regulatory agencies, governments may not be able to act in the unified manner claimed by the unitary actor model, because they cannot control the agencies to the degree or in the manner they purportedly can control individual departments and their officials.

Part III of the NTA was an issue in which an independent regulatory agency, the newly created Canadian Transport Commission, was a central actor. Accordingly, a study of the fate of Part III provides, in Lijphart's terms, at the minimum a "deviant" case study which challenges conventional generalizations and possibly a "hypothesis-generating" case study from which further research endeavours may be derived.[40] The value of a study of Part III will be considered in the concluding chapter.

PART III AND INTEREST GROUPS

Although not related to the central conceptual concerns of this study, the fate of Part III offers an opportunity to examine the policy process and its intergovernmental variant from another perspective, a sort of case study within a case study. That perspective is the role of interest groups in intergovernmental negotiations. The conflict over Part III involved interest group activities, particularly of one group, the trucking industry, and analysis of such activities permits a testing of both the conclusion drawn by Simeon cited earlier that interest groups tend to be ineffective and frozen out of the negotiations and, more broadly, some general conclusions about the relationships between interest group activity and the operations of federal systems.

OUTLINE OF THE STUDY

The basic objective of this study in attempting to account for the fate of Part III is to test the contribution the two particular models of analysis can make to our understanding of the intergovernmental policy process. To do this, each one will be employed separately to study the negotiations. In chapters 3 and 4, the unitary actor model is used and an explanation for the fate of Part III is sought in an analysis of the interactions between the governments and the strategies, resources, and tactics that shaped and influenced these interactions. In chapters 5 and 6, the bureaucratic politics model is used and the focus of the analysis is on the complex process that ensued within the federal government.[41] The goal in these two chapters is to determine the nature, and assess the significance, of the internal bargaining on the fate of Part III.

It is admittedly somewhat of a distortion of reality to treat the intergovernmental and intragovernmental bargaining as if they were completely discrete phenomena, but such an approach is considered necessary. Although it should be obvious that the study will conclude that due attention must be paid in the study of intergovernmental negotiations to intragovernmental factors, the analysis will not be so directly self-serving. Every effort has been made not to present a strawman in the use of the unitary actor model; rather, the strongest case possible is made to demonstrate that it can be used to explain the outcome of the negotiations. That it cannot do so is the result of intrinsic weaknesses of the model and not of a deliberately distorted analysis.

Chapter Two

Part III: The Issues

If the Canadian experience is a reliable guide, transportation issues are invariably political issues. As with so many issues, the federal system significantly influences the political nature of transportation. It was to be expected, therefore, that Part III would provoke a battle between the federal and provincial governments. The clash involved more than a constitutional tug of war in which the federal government sought to reclaim a function that had been controlled by the provinces for a number of years. Much more basic was the conflict between the federal perspective of the motor carrier industry as an integral component of the national transportation system and the provincial view of that industry as the only mode of transportation under provincial jurisdiction that could be employed to accomplish provincial policy objectives.

It would seem appropriate that a survey of the politics of Part III begin with a discussion of the relevant constitutional provisions. In this context, Charles Aikin's comment in a discussion of the change in emphasis in recent studies of federalism is relevant. "Design, of course, is descriptive," asserted Aikin, "for it makes clear what the results of process are. But design is more than description; it is also a force in and of itself."[1] Aikin's point is well taken because in some studies there is a tendency to underestimate the relevance of constitutional provisions to an understanding of the relations between the constituent units of a federal system and to concentrate instead on the "politics" of such relations. Such a focus is understandable, given the obvious ability of governments to overcome what appear at first glance to be insurmountable constitutional roadblocks. Nevertheless, one should not ignore the importance of constitutional provisions in establishing, if only initially, the parameters of intergovernmental conflict nor discount the role that "readings" of the constitution may have in shaping the attitudes and predispositions of policy-makers to questions of public policy.[2] The controversy over Part III clearly demonstrates that intergovernmental conflict can develop even when jurisdiction is not in dispute. Equally important is the fact that the origins of the conflict over Part III can be traced back to a much earlier period before the jurisdictional questions were clarified, the ambiguous legacy of which had an enormous impact on the actions of decision-makers.

There is no doubt that when Part III was drafted the federal government had jurisdiction over the extraprovincial motor carrier transport industry. The question had been resolved in 1954 by the Winner case. Prior to 1954 the question of who possessed the constitutional authority to regulate the extraprovincial motor transport industry had been several times disputed. In 1937, for example, Senator Dandurand, government house leader in the Senate, introduced a bill to establish a board of transport commissioners with the authority to regulate railways, ships, aircraft, and motor vehicles.[3] A number of provinces, including Ontario and Quebec, objected to the inclusion of the motor vehicle section on the grounds that the federal government did not have jurisdiction in this area. The strong opposition from the provinces, and from the newly formed Canadian Trucking Associations, was instrumental in the defeat of the legislation.

C. D. Howe, Minister of Transport, described the 1937 legislation as being "friendless," and deleted the offensive section when he reintroduced the bill to create the Board of Transport Commissioners in 1938. His explanation of the revised bill is indicative of the confusion that existed regarding jurisdiction.

Howe justified the deletion on the grounds that his legal advisers had informed him that federal authority was limited to the individual trucks which crossed provincial or international boundaries or went through certain national parks. Federal jurisdiction extended, therefore, to only 2 percent of all road transport and would not be particularly meaningful under such circumstances. Given this fact and the strenuous opposition from the provinces, the government decided to delete the motor carrier section.[4]

The legal advice given the minister had serious implications for federal policy in the motor transport field. As a result of the decision not to proceed with federal legislation, no foundation was established for the time when the federal government would be required to establish a regulatory system for the industry. Despite the fact that the federal government had been advised by the Rowell-Sirois Commission in 1940[5] and the Turgeon Royal Commission on Transportation in 1951[6] that some federal action was necessary to coordinate the national transportation system, including the motor carrier industry, the federal government did nothing, assuming that its jurisdiction was too limited to be effective.

The judicial decisions in the Winner case, therefore, came as quite a shock to everyone concerned. The case involved a bus company operating from the United States through New Brunswick to Nova Scotia. The New Brunswick Motor Transport Board refused to permit the company to pick up or discharge passengers within New Brunswick under the terms of its license to travel through the province. The Winner Company argued that the New Brunswick Board had no authority to so restrict its operations. Although the board was upheld in the New Brunswick Court of Appeal, the Supreme Court of Canada overturned the decision. Crucial to the Supreme Court's decision, however, was its contention that a distinction could be made between the extraprovincial and intraprovincial parts of the undertaking, with the federal government having jurisdiction over the former and the provinces over the latter. All parties appealed the Supreme Court's decision, Winner because of the separation of the two parts of its operations, and Ontario, Alberta, Prince Edward Island, and New Brunswick because of the granting of jurisdiction over the extraprovincial operations to the federal government.

The ultimate outcome in 1954 was that the Judicial Committee of the Privy Council, in its last decision as the final court of appeal for Canada,[7] ruled that not only did the federal government have jurisdiction over extraprovincial motor transport under Section 92(10)(a) of the British North America Act[8] but also that the intraprovincial operations of a company engaged in extraprovincial transport could not be separated, as the Supreme Court of Canada had ruled. Such operations were "one and indivisible" and accordingly were under the exclusive jurisdiction of the federal government.[9] As a result of the Winner decision, federal officials estimated that 50 percent, rather than 2 percent, of all commercial highway transport in Canada came under their jurisdiction.

Federal jurisdiction, however, existed only on paper. The federal government, because it consistently had maintained that it did not have effective jurisdiction over highway transport, had no administrative tribunal, no staff, and no set of regulations with which to regulate the industry. The Winner decision resulted in a regulatory vacuum for 50 percent of the motor transport industry. In view of this situation, the federal government opted for the easiest alternative available to it. Rather than enacting a comprehensive act to regulate that portion of the motor transport industry under its jurisdiction, the federal government decided to leave the regulation of all forms of motor transport in the hands of the provinces. It achieved this objective with the support of the provinces obtained at a federal-provincial conference only two months after the Privy Council delivered its judgement. By means of the Motor Vehicle Transport Act (MVTA), the federal government delegated its authority to regulate the motor transport industry to the provincial regulatory agencies. The relevant section of the act stated that:

> Where in any province a licence is by law of the province required for the operation of a local undertaking, no person shall operate an extra-provincial undertaking in that province unless he holds a licence issued under the authority of this Act.

> The Provincial Transport Board in each province may at its discretion issue a licence to a person upon the like terms and conditions and in the like manner as if the extra-provincial undertaking operated in the province were a local undertaking.[10]

The administrative result of the passing of the MVTA was thus *status quo ante* the Winner decision.

The minister of transport defended the federal government's actions in the following manner:

> Why did we proceed to act in the way in which we have? . . . We felt that we did not have the necessary experience nor the necessary staff or personnel to deal with this kind of traffic. After all, the provinces have been dealing with this traffic for years; it is their business; and all they will be doing by this enabling legislation will be to extend the powers which they possess under provincial legislation to cover extra-provincial undertakings. Then we do not have the staff; we do not have the board . . . and the establishment of such a board would mean: extra costs, extra personnel, extra staff not only in Ottawa, but in every province in this country.[11]

Mr. Chevrier did not say that the faulty legal advice of federal officials was in a large part responsible for the federal failure to provide the foundations prior to 1954 for a federal regulatory system.

The federal government's decision to delegate its responsibility for the regulation of extraprovincial motor transport industry to provincial officials was to have serious repercussions, particularly when the trucking industry developed into a far more important part of the national transportation system than it had been in 1954. The industry had grown considerably between 1937 and 1954 and all evidence suggested even greater growth. At some point the federal government would have to assume its responsibilities for what was becoming a significant component of the national transportation system. The Motor Vehicle Transport Act of 1954 was at best a stop-gap measure, although the federal response demonstrated how little this fact was appreciated.

The consequences of the MVTA were not immediately evident. Although it was recognized in a study in 1956, for example, that some interprovincial coordination was necessary in the regulation of the motor carrier industry, it was suggested that growth in the long-haul traffic (beyond 1500 miles) was unlikely.[12] Federal policy towards the industry appears to have been predicated during this period on the acceptance of this assumption of limited growth in the industry.

The MacPherson Royal Commission on Transportation, which reported in 1961, challenged not only the assumptions underlying federal policy towards the motor carrier industry but also much of the conventional wisdom of national transportation policy.[13] The central argument of the MacPherson Report was that existing public policies regarding transportation were based on invalid assumptions. Existing policies, it was argued, were based on the assumption that monopoly characterized the transportation market, while in reality there was extensive intermodal competition. It is not necessary for the purpose of this study to provide a detailed commentary on the report. It is important, however, to consider the Royal Commission's assessment of the changes in the motor carrier industry and the implications of these changes for public policy.

A central argument of the report was that the motor carrier industry, especially trucking, was now a major competitor of the railways. D. W. Carr, a consultant to the commission, documented the fact that in the 1950s the trucking industry, contrary to earlier assumptions, had begun to compete vigorously with the railways for long-haul or transcontinental traffic. The following figures demonstrate the extent of the growth of the trucking industry in comparison with the railways:

	Rail	*Highway*
	(thousands of tons)	
1942	155,646	130,194
1947	175,566	160,659
1952	185,056	226,364
1957	197,010	293,925

As Carr pointed out, in the fifteen-year period from 1942 to 1957, "the railway share of Canada's total inter-city tonnage (this includes rail, highway, water, air, and pipeline) fell from 46.2% to 30.7% [but] highway tonnage rose from 38.7% to 45.7%."[14] The trucking industry was

17

able to lure traffic away from the railways for a number of reasons, such as cheaper costs, speed of service, technological development, flexibility, and the ability to provide specialized services. One should also not underestimate the impact of railway strikes such as occurred in 1950. The growth of the industry between 1947 and 1952 suggests that a great deal of the traffic carried by the truckers during the 1950 strike did not "go home" once the strike was settled.

The significance for public policies of the growth of competition in the transportation market is expressed in the following statement from the commission's report:

> The essence of the position we have taken with respect to national transportation policy is that it is no longer possible, as it was in the monopolistic era of transportation, to treat a particular mode of transport in relative isolation from others. It is, to us, manifest that in the present situation of competitive co-existence, the attainment of an efficient and balanced transport system will require that careful attention be paid to the effects of policies relating to one carrier upon all those other carriers which have become an integral part of the system. The transportation structure, in other words, must be looked at in *toto*. Only a national transportation policy which adopts such an approach would, we believe, be properly equipped in the new competitive environment to meet the present needs and difficulties of Canada's increasingly complex system and thereby enable the system to fulfill national policy objectives and at the same time to develop along commercial and market-oriented lines.[15]

The implications for the trucking industry and the existing regulatory system under the Motor Vehicle Transport Act of 1954 were succinctly stated by Carr: "In the long run, it seems no more likely that the provinces can carry the full responsibilities of developing and regulating large-scale inter-provincial trucking operations effectively than it was possible for them to carry the burden of railway building and regulation they attempted 50 to 70 years ago."[16] Trucking, it was argued, was now an integral component of the national transportation system. The conclusion was obvious: "substantial federal initiative and participation" was required.[17]

Other factors were also at work in the 1960s undermining the existing regulatory system. There were a number of court cases which demonstrated that the Motor Vehicle Transport Act suffered from several serious legal defects. In one decision in the Ontario courts in 1964, it was ruled that there was nothing in the MVTA which would make it an offence to operate contrary to the terms and conditions of a licence once the licence was granted.[18] In another decision in 1965, the Manitoba Court of Appeal ruled that because the MVTA did not include the words "out of" in the section covering the granting of licences, a carrier did not have to have a licence from the Manitoba regulatory agency to operate only "out of" Manitoba.[19] Perhaps the most important case to threaten the MVTA was the Coughlin case, which involved an appeal to the Supreme Court of Canada challenging the basis of the MVTA. The appeal was on the grounds that the legislation was invalid because it involved an attempt by one government to delegate its legislative jurisdiction to the other level of government.[20]

The significance of these court cases cannot be underestimated in terms of their impact on the regulatory system. The first two cases cited were considered to constitute serious restrictions on the ability of the provincial regulatory agencies to regulate the extraprovincial transportation industries, so much so that the provinces of Ontario, Manitoba, and Alberta had written to the federal government requesting amendments to the MVTA to correct the deficiencies. The Coughlin case was by far the most serious challenge to the existing system. Indeed, if Coughlin were to be upheld, the existing system would be invalidated. The result would be a legal vacuum comparable to that created by the Winner decision. As it was, the existing legal morass surrounding the MVTA led the trucking industry in a brief to the federal minister of transport in 1965 to complain in exasperation:

> This state of uncertainty, when considered with the lack of uniformity
> in the applicable provincial statutes, has presented any carrier
> attempting to know his fundamental rights and obligations under
> the Motor Vehicle Transport Act with an impossible task. The result
> is that the industry simply accepts varying interpretations of their
> rights as propounded by the various provincial authorities.[21]

The potential for abuse and for arbitrary treatment was an obvious cause for concern in industry circles.

A further criticism of the regulatory system suggested in the above comment from the trucking industry was its fragmentary nature. There were ten boards acting under ten sets of regulations and procedures with little cooperation between provinces. This fragmentation appeared inevitable because the MVTA instructed the provincial agencies to treat extraprovincial carriers as if they were local undertakings. In a 1965 submission to the federal government, the trucking industry stated: "Within several years of the passage of the Act it became apparent to the trucking industry that a statute which told provincial boards to wear a federal hat and go away and control routes and rates 'in like manner' to existing local laws was an unworkable system of regulation."[22] Similar criticisms had been made by other observers.[23] Few, however, were as blunt and comprehensive as that articulated by the affected industry:

> we ... emphasize that as an efficient method of administering control over the extra-provincial trucking industry, the Motor Vehicle Transport Act is a failure. Instead of promoting orderly healthy development of ... industry, the Act has actually fostered conflicting and inconsistent regulatory policies by the ten federal controlling bodies (the provincial transport boards). The Act has militated against uniform and long-run continuity in extra-provincial regulatory policy. It has encouraged, rather than removed, parochialism in a geographical sense. It is an Act which today is removed from the realities of extra-provincial trucking development of the past decade.[24]

The criticisms voiced by the trucking industry are important for two basic reasons. First, the industry had long been a supporter of provincial regulation. As such, it had been repeatedly requesting that the provincial authorities correct the deficiencies by means of interprovincial cooperation. The failure of the provinces to adopt remedial action had led the trucking industry in frustration to the federal government. This was to be extremely significant in the federal-provincial negotiations that were to ensue.[25] The second reason for the importance of the industry's criticisms was the emphasis on the extra costs to the industry because of the fragmented regulatory system. This was important in the context of the new national transportation policy being developed by the federal government.

It is beyond the scope of this study to explain the federal government's decision to introduce the NTA when and in the manner it did.[26] What is necessary is an explanation for the inclusion of a motor carrier section. One basic reason has already been alluded to, namely, the legal defects of the existing statute. The threat posed by the Coughlin case was of even greater concern to federal policy-makers for, as stated, if Coughlin were upheld, the MVTA would be unconstitutional and a regulatory vacuum would once again exist. Within the federal government, it was thought that a distinct possibility existed that this would happen.[27]

Far more important than the legal defects, existing or potential, of the MVTA, was the importance of the trucking industry to the national transportation system and, accordingly, to the philosophy of the new national transportation policy set out in the NTA. The act was prefaced by a declaration of "national transportation policy" calling for "an economic,

20

efficient and adequate transportation system." Such a system was predicated on intermodal competition that could only be attained if the "regulation of all modes of transport will not be of such nature as to restrict the ability of any mode of transport to compete freely with any other mode of transport."[28]

Critics of the regulatory system established by the MVTA had argued that the existing lack of uniformity and coordination was fragmenting a major competitive sector of the transportation system in Canada. Moreover, such fragmentation had resulted in greatly increased costs for the trucking industry. The implication of such criticisms was that the existing regulatory system constituted a basic violation and contradiction of the central tenets of the NTA. The conflict between the philosophy of the NTA and the reality of regulation under the MVTA could not be ignored in view of the significance of the competitive impact of the trucking industry.

An equally important consideration was the responsibility given to the CTC to "co-ordinate and harmonize" all transport regulation under federal jurisdiction in order to satisfy the policy objectives of the NTA.[29] That this function was central to the creation of the CTC is suggested by the following statement by one of the draftsmen of the legislation in defence of the decision to create a single, multifunctional regulatory body:

> Examination indicated that the various regulatory agencies were,
> in part, using different approaches. This would hamper the competitive
> relationship which was to be the foundation for new transporta-
> tion policy. Difference in regulation could mean that some modes
> were held back in terms of possible competitive relationships with
> others because of greater regulatory restrictions or other imposed
> public limitations. The government therefore decided that a single
> approach to the regulation of all transportation must be developed.[30]

Given the existing regulatory system, the philosophy of the NTA, and the mandate of the CTC, the rhetorical nature of J. W. Pickersgill's question is obvious: "How can we be sure that we are making the best use of all available modes of transportation, if one mode of national transport is subject to varying rules, regulations and requirements of up to ten different agencies of ten different governments?" Pickersgill answered by stating that "the present system of regulation is unlikely to result in the best use of all available modes of transport on a national scale."[31] Pickersgill provided the single most important reason for the inclusion of Part III in the NTA: "It does not seem possible to realize these objectives [of the NTA] . . . unless the extra-provincial operations of commercial motor carriers are eventually brought under direct federal jurisdiction."[32]

Part III, therefore, was important to federal policy-makers for several related reasons. By far the most important was their belated recognition that the motor carrier industry was a major competitive force in the national transportation system. Its competitive strength was being hamstrung by the existing regulatory system in contradiction to the new national policy. Indeed, without implementation of Part III, the objectives of the National Transportation Act were not attainable. Subsidiary reasons for the enactment of Part III were the serious concerns that a regulatory vacuum could again result if the challenges before the courts to the MVTA were successful, and the legal defects that had become apparent in the MVTA.

Despite the fact that the federal government possessed the legislative instrument with which to exercise its constitutional responsibility, it was apparent that several hurdles would have to be overcome before Part III could be implemented effectively. Most of these hurdles required provincial cooperation. The federal government still did not have the manpower or experience with which to regulate the industry. In the seventeen years following the enactment of the MVTA, the federal government hired only one "highways economist" and he was not hired until 1964. The federal government recognized that provincial cooperation was essential if Part III was to be implemented effectively, for they alone had the necessary personnel and experience.

Thus far only the federal perspective on the issue of Part III has been discussed. What was the provincial perspective? While there were a number of shared provincial concerns over Part III, there was little consensus, and this is not unusual given the different provincial perceptions, situations, and priorities. They were in agreement on only the most general issues. Most provincial authorities were prepared to concede that the threat posed by Part III was of their own making because of their failure to ameliorate the regulatory system through interprovincial mechanisms. Nevertheless, the provinces were in basic agreement that the federal government should not completely pre-empt provincial regulators from a field where provincial authorities had traditionally had exclusive control.

The provincial fear of complete pre-emption was the result of a number of factors. Although the federal government had jurisdictional authority to regulate extraprovincial motor carriers, such carriers would be using provincially owned highways; therefore, there was general concern that Part III should not interfere with the provincial power. A second concern was that even after Part III was implemented, the provinces would still be responsible for regulating that part of the industry which engaged solely in intraprovincial operations. Those companies would be in direct competition with the federally regulated companies which also engaged in intraprovincial operations. The provinces were concerned that federal and provincial regulations should not conflict to the detriment of the strictly provincial operators.

The provinces were also reluctant to surrender a responsibility that had been theirs for so many years. No authority wishes to lose part of its effective jurisdiction if this results in a loss of status and prestige. Not all the provinces, however, were to be equally affected and this is important in explaining the limited agreement among the provinces on the extent of their opposition to Part III. Some of the provincial regulatory agencies were multifunctional, such as the Nova Scotia Board of Commissioners of Public Utilities, while others, like the Ontario Highway Transport Board, regulated only motor carriers. Thus, Part III posed a far greater threat to Ontario than it did to Nova Scotia.

A related factor was the extent to which the industry came under the jurisdiction of a particular provincial regulatory agency. In some provinces there was very little extraprovincial motor carrier traffic, while in others there was a great deal. Again the situation of Ontario stands out.[33] The potentially dramatic effects of Part III on Ontario were documented by a study commissioned by the province. This estimated that 75 to 90 percent of Ontario's for-hire trucking industry would come under federal control.[34] The firms affected accounted for 95 percent of the for-hire revenue in Ontario, even though 75 percent of the tonnage from which the 95 percent of the revenue was derived moved wholly within Ontario. This latter figure underscores Ontario's concern over the federal government assuming the regulation of the intraprovincial operations of extraprovincial trucking firms. The feared impact on Ontario explains to a large extent its opposition from the outset to Part III. But all provincial authorities shared a general concern over their loss of status, especially since they felt only they had the experience and competence to regulate the industry. Accordingly, one of the provincial objectives was to seek some form of agreement whereby this provincial expertise could be used. If this could be accomplished, it would diminish their loss of status.

Provincial apprehension over the implementation of Part III involved more than a loss of status or a desire to maintain jurisdictional responsibility, although such concerns ensured that a federal-provincial dispute would occur. Far more important was the clash over the use of motor carrier transport to satisfy regional as opposed to national policy objectives. For the federal government Part III represented a recognition that

23

the motor carrier industry was a vital part of the national transportation system. As such, it was believed the industry should be placed under federal regulation to attain the objectives set out in the NTA. At the time the federal posture towards the industry was being re-examined, the provinces in varying degrees were becoming increasingly interested in regional development and in the trucking industry as a tool for such development.[35] The Ontario-commissioned study reflected this attitude: "The significant role of trucking in overland freight transportation within, to, and from Ontario would appear to justify considering motor carriers as a candidate for becoming a development tool. The economic regulation of motor carriers consistent with development objectives could provide the framework within which motor carriers can become an effective tool."[36] Part III posed a fundamental challenge to the provinces. If implemented completely, it would mean that "the federal government may, at its discretion, effectively control the entire commercial trucking industry in Canada."[37]

Central to the provincial concern over the challenge posed by Part III to any provincial development strategy was the fact that, for the most part, the trucking industry was the only mode of transport regulated by the provinces. Rail, air, and water modes are, with few limited exceptions, under exclusive federal jurisdiction. Naturally the provinces would oppose the loss of the only mode of transportation which they could regulate, especially in light of the role they envisaged for trucking in regional economic development.

The concern over the loss of regulatory authority over the motor carrier industry was intensified by provincial dissatisfaction with available mechanisms for input into the federal decision-making process in an area where provincial policy objectives had been identified. To a degree, therefore, Part III was symptomatic of a general trend in the 1960s, in which provinces were demanding to participate in the formulation of policies within federal jurisdictional areas.[38] A particular concern was the adequacy of the role available to the provinces vis-à-vis the CTC.

The provinces found their only role was that of intervener on specific applications before the commission. Some provinces were to argue that, from experiences with the CTC in other regulatory matters, such a limited role was "degrading," in that they were treated in the same manner as any other participant. The provinces thought it insulting to be treated as "just another pressure group." What was to exacerbate provincial dissatisfaction with their role was that the distribution of responsibility for policy within the federal government precluded an easy approach to policy discussions.

Part III, therefore, for some provinces, became tied to the adequacy of the role of intervener in regulatory proceedings for furthering their policy objectives. As negotiations proceeded, this issue became the dominant concern of some provinces as they sought to define the stakes to include potential trade-offs involving federal regulation of the extraprovincial motor carrier industry in return for provincial participation in the federal regulatory process.

The issues presented by Part III were substantial in that both jurisdictional and functional concerns of government were involved. Part III was important on its own merits, inasmuch as its justification was to remedy the fragmentation that had developed in the regulation of the extraprovincial motor carrier industry. But Part III was also important in that it came to represent a classical conflict within a federal state: a clash between national and regional policy objectives. The federal government sought to regulate the industry in order to fulfil the national transportation policy of "an economic, efficient and adequate transportation system." The provinces, although in varying degrees, perceived the industry in terms of its potential as a tool for regional economic development. Part III thus created an intergovernmental conflict because both levels of government desired to regulate the industry to accomplish separate, and potentially conflicting, objectives. The conflict was intensified because the provinces had been the sole regulators for several decades.

Chapter Three

The Federal-Provincial Negotiations: 1966–1970

Part III of the National Transportation Act gave no new powers to the federal government. The Winner decision of 1954 had established that regulation of extraprovincial motor carriers was clearly within federal jurisdiction. Nevertheless, despite its unquestionable, exclusive jurisdiction, the federal government had committed itself to consultation with the provinces before implementing Part III. From 1966 until 1972 consultations and negotiations included two conferences of ministers of transport, one conference of officials, and a series of informal meetings with provincial representatives. The negotiations culminated in a year-long study by a Federal-Provincial Advisory Council on Motor Carrier Regulation that issued its report in April 1972. Despite these protracted negotiations, Part III has yet to be implemented. The provinces appear to have been the "victors"; the federal objective has been frustrated.

In this and the succeeding chapter, an explanation for this outcome is developed on the assumption that the governments involved in the negotiations were single, unified actors. The analysis then searches for an explanation in the interactions between the governments as the actors, the critical assumption being that the outcomes of intergovernmental bargaining are determined by factors related to how the actors interact with one another. The analysis looks for the determinants for the outcomes in the strategies pursued, the tactics employed, the resources exploited, and the constraints confronted by the actors. The central question is: how effectively did the governments use their resources, strategies, and specific tactics in the pursuit of their goals?

A problem with the model as employed by Simeon is that little attention is directed to the linkages between the numerous variables included in his analysis. The relationships between the various factors is crucial if one is to analyse the dynamics of the interactions between governments rather than simply provide a descriptive, static analysis of this interaction. A solution to this problem may be found if the negotiations are thought of as "games of strategy," to use Schelling's phrase. Such games are "those in which the best course of action for each player depends on what the other players do. The term is intended to focus on the interdependence of the adversaries' decisions and on their expectations about each other's behaviour."[1] The central argument of the following analysis is that in "games of strategy," when one employs the unitary-actor model, the communications process between adversaries is a crucial variable. One basic measure, therefore, of negotiating prowess is the ability to communicate to one's adversaries one's own strengths and, conversely, to point up their weaknesses. Accordingly, the analysis must focus on the exchange of signals between the participants in the negotiations as they transmit their demands, their responses, and their warnings in their attempts to influence the perceptions and behaviour of the other participants.[2] In the following analysis, we start with the static variables that are basic to the government-as-unitary-actor model, such as defining the problem of the different actors, and identifying their basic resources, describing their broad strategies and specific tactical plans. Once we have completed this "descriptive inventory," we can turn to an analysis of the interactions between the actors. Such an analysis will attempt to explain why the provinces were the victors in this round of conflict and will do so by assessing the effectiveness of the different protagonists in the struggle over the implementation of Part III.

It is too simplistic to define the federal government's goal as "the implementation of Part III" and that of the provinces as "the prevention of its implementation." The objectives at both levels were more complicated than this. For the federal government, the problem was how to implement Part III with the cooperation of the provinces, because from the outset it had realized that unilateral federal action would not succeed. For the provinces, the problem was that there was no common perspective on the nature of the issue but rather ten different positions, each reflecting apprehension over the extent of implementation of Part III. Prior to the negotiations, the provinces articulated their general concern with Part III's ramifications for their regulatory systems, but were not able to develop a common proposal for salvaging at least part of their threatened regulatory authority.

Basic to the respective definitions of the problem and the objectives of the participants was their assessment of the resources they could bring to bear in the negotiations and the constraints they would encounter. The federal government's major political resources was its unquestionable constitutional authority. Other resources were the National Transportation Act and the Canadian Transport Commission which, respectively, provided the philosophy and basic instrument for federal regulation. The justification for instituting federal regulation was that pressure groups, especially from the trucking industry, were demanding the implementation of Part III.[3] Thus, the resources of the federal government included the constitutional authority, the philosophy, the policy instrument, and a public demand for action.

Despite these impressive resources, the federal government was still substantially constrained in its options. Its transportation experience was primarily in the rail, marine, and air modes, and not in motor carriers. This lack of experience was reflected in the fact that although the federal government had the NTA philosophy to guide it in regulating the motor carrier industry, it was basically unsure of how to translate the philosophy into a concrete regulatory framework. In addition, the federal government possessed neither the facilities nor the manpower to implement federal regulation. The provinces had both and, if the federal government were to avoid duplication, it was essential that their active cooperation be enlisted. In recognition of these various constraints, the federal government had promised during the debate on the NTA that it would implement Part III only after the fullest consultation with the provinces, with their complete cooperation. This public commitment in itself had become a constraint on the federal government.

The provinces knew that they did not like Part III; they did not know how to oppose its implementation. The provinces were convinced, notwithstanding what would be some dubious constitutional interpretations by Quebec, that the federal government was holding the upper hand because its jurisdiction in the field had been established. No province was prepared, therefore, to challenge Part III on constitutional grounds. Thus, an important feature of the negotiations at the outset was the provincial perception that their resources were minimal, their constraints overwhelming, and their options severely limited.

The federal government based its strategy and tactics for attaining its objectives on a realistic assessment of its resources and constraints. The basic federal objective was to convince the provinces of the necessity to implement Part III and to persuade them to cooperate actively to accomplish this end. The federal strategy was to emphasize the practical necessity for Part III rather than its constitutional prerogatives. Federal strategy thus required, above all, that the provinces trust the good faith of the federal government. The success of the negotiations would be determined as much by how the federal government negotiated as by the substance of its position. To further this strategy, the federal govern-

ment planned to employ a number of tactics, three of which were fundamental. The first was to allay any provincial suspicions about its intentions. No hard lines were to be adopted; no doors closed. The central
federal tactic was to "carry along" the provinces. The second basic tactic
was to exploit the provincial fears about the scope of implementation of
Part III in order to make them more amenable to cooperating. The final
basic tactic was to solicit provincial assistance in the drafting of the
regulations necessary for the implementation of Part III. The provinces
would be asked to help "flesh out" what was essentially only skeletal
legislation. Given federal strategy and tactics, it was recognized that
communication of its motives and intentions to the provinces would be
a crucial determinant of the success of federal objectives.

In part because they had no clear conception of their objectives and
were inclined to emphasize the severe constraints they faced, the provinces assumed that they were bargaining from weakness and consequently
they came to negotiate more as supplicants than as challengers to the
federal government—although Ontario and Quebec would adopt a more
aggressive posture than the others. All the provinces were on the defensive. They wanted to salvage at least part of their regulatory authority
and were not confident that they would be able to do so. It was only well
into the negotiations that the provinces were to reassess the respective
bargaining positions of the governments and come to appreciate that they
need not be as defensive as they had assumed.

The basic thrust of the unitary-actor model is that the explanation for
the outcomes of negotiations between governments is to be found in an
analysis of the interactions between governments. The preceding summary of objectives, resources, strategies, and tactics was necessary in
order to provide the background to such negotiations. The focus of the
unitary-actor model, however, is on the interplay of these variables in
the course of the dynamics of the interactions between governments. It
is to these interactions that we now turn in our search for an explanation
for the fate of Part III. An important feature of these interactions, which
will quickly become apparent from the ensuing analysis, is that the process of intergovernmental negotiations itself becomes an important determinant of the outcome of such negotiations. In this respect, Part III
was no different from many other issues in many areas of intergovernmental concern, in that, for a time, process transcended substance as
the central issue in the intergovernmental negotiations.

PRELIMINARY SOUNDINGS, 1966–1969

Although the negotiations did not begin in earnest until late 1969, after the introduction of the NTA, the federal government engaged in a series of informal exchanges with the provinces and affected private groups to prepare the way for them. These exchanges are important for an understanding of the negotiations because they were a central part of the federal strategy. There was an extended effort by the federal government to communicate to the provinces its intention to proceed in a determined fashion to implement Part III. Equally important as the federal declaration of its intention to act was the effort to elicit a willingness to cooperate from the provinces. One aspect of this communications process was straightforward. The federal government went repeatedly to the provinces to discuss problems and proposals for implementing Part III. The federal signals were direct and clear: it had the authority and it intended to act.

The federal government also attempted to supplement its direct messages to the provinces by indirect messages. Federal officials "showed the colours" at various meetings and conventions of truckers, shippers, and manufacturers, at which they affirmed their intention to implement Part III and solicited advice on how to do so. The federal government was not simply gathering private input, although this was important; it was using these meetings to send additional, supportive messages of its intentions to the provinces.

A crucial aspect of the federal government's efforts in this period was its style of transmitting its intentions. It sought to establish its *bona fides* with the provinces and, therefore, was specific only on its intentions, but not on its planned methods to implement Part III. It sought to allay any fears the provinces might have had that the federal intention was merely to push the provinces aside in order to implement arbitrarily federal regulation. The federal government went to great lengths in this period to signal to the provinces its desire to carry them along in support of federal regulation.

This early round of exchanges was important also because it enabled the federal government to ascertain the main provincial concerns about implementation. If the federal government's strategy was to sell Part III to the provinces, it had to determine the provincial position in order to anticipate what concessions would be necessary to gain provincial support. A significant result of this gauging of the provincial response was that the federal government learned that the provinces had no unified position. The federal government also learned that only two provinces, Ontario and Quebec, were adamantly opposed to Part III but, despite their opposition, that neither appeared to have any counter-proposal.

The exchanges began in late 1966 after Prime Minister Pearson had written to the provincial premiers suggesting "exploratory" discussions between federal and provincial officials.[4] Federal officials were pleased with the apparent success of the meetings that were subsequently held with eight of the provinces. In these eight provinces there appeared to be general agreement that the trucking industry was poorly served by the existing regulatory system and that a principal reason for this was the provinces' failure to provide interprovincial cooperation. The federal officials concluded that the chief provincial concern was not with Part III *per se*, but with its scope. The provinces appeared resigned to some federal initiative but were concerned that the federal government might completely supplant the provincial regulators.[5]

Any illusions that the federal government may have entertained about the ease of the negotiations, as a result of the discussions with the first eight provinces, were shattered by the responses of Ontario and Quebec. The Quebec government criticized the federal government on both substantive and procedural grounds. On the matter of substance, Premier Johnson wrote:

I shall not try to hide from you that, whatever may be the promises of future consultation, the Government of Quebec looks most unfavourably upon the fact that the federal government wishes to acquire the right to exempt an undertaking from the provincial boards so as to place it under the authority of the Canadian Transport Commission. Already, in 1954, Quebec had objected to the discretionary powers the federal government reserved itself under Section 5 of the Motor Vehicle Transport Act; in our opinion, this was holding back with one hand what one was giving with the other. It seems now that our opinion was well founded. Indeed, the whole arrangement of 1954 is presently being questioned.[6]

The interpretation Quebec gave to the Motor Vehicle Transport Act was that the federal power of regulation had not been simply delegated to the provincial regulatory board which, when acting under the MVTA, was acting as a federal board. Rather, Quebec maintained that under the MVTA the federal government had transferred its regulatory power to the provincial board and consequently the provincial board was not required to relinquish this power. This interpretation was challenged, quite correctly, by federal spokesmen.[7]

On the question of the procedures followed by the federal government, Premier Johnson was also extremely critical:

I was very much surprised by the haste in which this measure concerning motor vehicle transport was submitted to Parliament.

Your letter dated August 4, 1966, emphasizes the necessity of holding federal-provincial discussions so as to determine how we can best settle the problems that face us in this field. I wonder how such discussions could possibly be useful now that the federal government has already decided beforehand what would be their conclusions. If your government sincerely favours provincial consultation, it should necessarily proceed to such consultation before making its decisions, not after. The presentation of such a measure as the one provided for in Part III of Bill C-231 might eventually be the result of our discussions but it could certainly never be the preliminaries to them. For this is putting the cart before the horse.[8]

Johnson concluded this letter with a request that the federal government delete Part III "as a token of good faith."

When Pearson rejected this request, the Quebec premier announced that no discussions would be held because he had concluded that "under the circumstances, I do not see to what purpose officials of our two governments could meet to discuss co-operation. Your government seems determined to follow the policy it has established in this field as in others, regardless of the provinces' views. What good could there be in holding repeated meetings that would lead to nowhere?"[9]

As a result of this decision by the Quebec government, there was no official contact between the two governments to discuss Part III prior to the 1969 federal-provincial conference. The position of the Quebec government, as subsequently articulated by the Quebec minister of transportation and communicaitons, was that "We have every intention of preserving and fighting for our jurisdiction over trucking which we believe should remain a provincial field, at least in Quebec."[10] But Quebec did not make clear how it intended to fight Part III. Its constitutional argument was clearly dubious and, therefore, not a serious challenge. Its argument that the federal government was not offering meaningful consultation did not appear to be a fundamental obstacle because the other provinces did not seem to object to the federal government's methods. Thus, the Quebec government, while sending an obvious message of its opposition to Part III, was ambiguous in terms of what it proposed to do. Quebec's failure to indicate its intentions was interpreted by federal officials to mean that it was going to fight Part III primarily on principle but with no idea of how it could effectively block federal regulation.

The message received from Ontario as to its stance on Part III was at first equally ambiguous. Federal officials experienced great difficulty in arranging an initial meeting with Ontario officials and when the meeting was finally held, the results were disappointing. To federal officials, Ontario appeared unprepared to recognize that there were any serious problems in the existing system or to discuss the advantages and disadvantages of alternatives. According to one federal participant, all that took place was "a rehash of problems already made known to the federal government by the government of Ontario."[11]

Many students of bargaining behaviour have noted that much negotiation takes place within the context of overlapping issues or "simultaneous games" and that negotiations on one issue sometimes intrude on, and affect, bargaining on the others.[12] Apparently this was the case in the initial discussions with Ontario officials. Seven months later one of the federal participants met informally with several Ontario officials and found them quite willing to discuss the issue, unlike "their rather tight-lipped attitude" at the first meeting. Why the change? The explanation was relatively simple. Prior to the meeting on Part III, the Ontario officials had met with another group of federal officials on another transportation matter and had been disturbed by their attitude. To them, the federal official had seemed arrogant in discussing an issue which was solely within provincial jurisdiction. As a result of this earlier encounter, the Ontario officials were skeptical about federal promises of cooperation and consultation.

After the initial problems in establishing communications had been resolved, the federal government found Ontario much more willing to discuss various proposals concerning regulations and regulatory framework. Despite its willingness to discuss the matter, however, Ontario made it clear that it was opposed to Part III. It did not agree that the problems in the existing system were as great as federal officials suggested. The Ontario position was stated most clearly in late 1968 by Premier John Robarts who made what was described as "a strong pitch . . . for the retention of provincial jurisdiction."[13] Mr. Robarts minimized the existing problems and maintained that there was "excellent interprovincial co-ordination," such that "improvements in the existing system can probably be accomplished within the existing framework, than would be the same case under a centralized system."[14] His conclusion was that "an analysis of all the factors . . . has convinced the government of Ontario that the interests of the people are best served by retaining provincial jurisdiction in the field of motor vehicle transportation."[15] Other than signifying its opposition to Part III, Ontario, like Quebec, gave no indication of how it intended to attempt to prevent the implementation of federal regulation.

This round of preliminary exchanges on respective positions was conducted against a backdrop of the Coughlin challenge in the Supreme

Court to the constitutionality of the MVTA.[16] This challenge threatened the basic federal strategy. As one federal official described the situation, it caused a panic, because there was a strong belief that, if Coughlin won his appeal, the federal government would have to implement Part III immediately in order to have some regulatory system in force. So great was the federal concern that the decision would go against the MVTA, that a Cabinet memorandum was prepared recommending an order-in-council to proclaim Part III into force on the same day as the Supreme Court pronounced its judgement. Federal officials were apprehensive that such an action would be misinterpreted by some of the provinces, especially Quebec, because of its strong opposition to Part III. They considered informing Quebec unofficially, prior to the decision, that this course had been forced on the government, but that provincial cooperation was still wanted. Once again, however, another issue intruded on the negotiations. This time the problem was the "Gabon affair" which so infuriated federal authorities that they did not feel the Quebec government deserved advance informal consultation.[17] Coughlin, however, was unsuccessful and federal action on Part III was not necessary at that time.

In the words of J. W. Pickersgill, the president of the CTC, these discussions were only "preliminary, exploratory discussions." He emphasized that they did not "constitute the federal-provincial consultation which . . . the government promised to have with the provincial governments."[18] That consultation was still in the future. Yet the discussions that had taken place were perceived to be crucial to such consultation. They were a means by which the federal government had been able to communicate not only its intentions to proceed with Part III but its desire to have the provinces cooperate in this process. Apparently, given the fact that only one province had been unwilling to discuss the matter, and that the other provinces had not indicated that they considered that Part III could be stopped, the federal government was satisfied that the necessary groundwork had been successfully completed.

THE 1969 CONFERENCE

Confident in its reading of the provincial positions on Part III, the federal government decided in late 1969 to put its strategy for winning provincial cooperation to the test. The test was to occur at a federal-provincial conference of transport ministers called to honour the federal commitment to consult the provinces prior to the implementation of Part III.

The federal government had been preparing for this conference for much of 1969. The basic objective was a limited one in that the federal aims were more symbolic than substantial. The federal government hoped to emerge from the conference with an acceptance by the provinces of the fact that the federal government would begin directly to regulate extraprovincial motor carriers. The federal government intended to announce the first step towards the implementation of Part III, namely, proclamation into law of that section of the NTA. Central to the federal government's desire for provincial cooperation was a concern that its own motives and intentions should be clearly understood by the provinces.

Federal strategy for the conference was to emphasize the practical aspects of the matter by encouraging a discussion on the first day of common problems faced by federal and provincial regulators, and thus avoid emotional overtones and acrimony. One tactic employed by the federal government to help defuse the situation was to commission a number of independent papers from academic experts to bring the basic issues to light in as objective or non-controversial a way as possible.[19] The general approach, in fact, was to attempt to turn the conference into an "educational" affair as federal officials sought to structure it to avoid confrontation. According to a central federal participant:

> We planned that the conference initially should be problem-oriented
> and that an attempt should be made to reach some understanding
> and consensus of the problems before an attempt was made to agree
> on solutions. In this regard, we believed that the material sent to
> the provinces should be factual and designed to focus on fundamental
> problems which both the federal and provincial authorities were
> seeking to overcome by regulation. We believed that suggested
> solutions should only be introduced when there was a common under-
> standing of the problems we are trying to solve.

It must be appreciated, of course, that federal planning for the meeting was dictated in large part by what one official described as a "lack of understanding . . . of the basic nature of the motor carrier industry, its role in the economy, and its relationship to other modes of transport."

One of the fundamental tactics of the federal government at the conference concerned proclamation of Part III. This was to be the first concrete step towards implementation and, as such, was designed to signify its determination to proceed. Yet the federal government sought to diminish the impact of this act by not setting a specific date for proclamation. It merely asserted that "a firm decision" to do so had been made.[20] The federal government, again concerned that its motives should be clearly understood, left the date open so that the provinces would not think that it had already decided how to implement federal regulation.

Perhaps the single most important federal tactic concerned the scope of federal regulation under Part III. The most important message received from the provinces during the exploratory discussions had been that there was no strong provincial reaction to Part III, provided its scope was limited and the provinces did not lose all their regulatory authority. The federal government cleverly sought to exploit this concern. Just prior to the meeting, it distributed a summary of the federal position on proclamation. It announced only that the government intended to proclaim Part III and that its administration would "be implemented in phases."[21] Nothing was said about the scope of Part III. The federal government had, in fact, decided to announce at the conference that implementation would be limited to the strictly extraprovincial operations and that the intraprovincial operations would continue to be regulated by the provinces. This tactic was predicated on a federal assumption that the provinces would come to Ottawa prepared to fight a holding action. Once that objective had been satisfied, as it would be by the federal announcement on the limited scope, it was thought inconceivable for the provinces to switch to an aggressive stance. The federal government was not required constitutionally to be so accommodating and therefore it was assumed that the provinces would perceive that too aggressive a provincial stance following the federal announcement would be counter-productive. Such a stance might provoke the federal government to dig in its heels and assert its complete jurisdiction. Such, at least, was federal thinking prior to the conference.

After developing such a finely honed conference strategy, the federal government did not want other issues to intrude to frustrate its success. One such issue was the Canada Labour (Safety) Code, which was concerned with safety standards of all companies under federal jurisdiction. The provinces had expressed their opposition to parts of the code and, at a meeting several months earlier, a Quebec official had submitted a memorandum to the federal minister of transport. In this memorandum it was charged that "the controversial aspects of Part III are being sneaked in through the back door via the Labour Safety Code." The federal government did not want to get into discussions of this topic because it was not thought relevant to Part III, despite Quebec's claim. In particular, the Department of Transport, which was responsible for the conference, did not want to get into this topic because it did not want to have to defend the code. To avoid any discussion of this matter, no representative from the Department of Labour was on the official list of federal representatives, but one was to stand by to aid the minister of transport should the need arise.

Federal officials were also concerned about the potential impact of the conference on Part III on the second meeting of the Constitutional

Conference to be held six days later. The federal government wished to avoid a confrontation which might influence debate at the Constitutional Conference. It feared this possibility in view of Quebec's previous reactions to federal initiatives on Part III. Concern over this matter no doubt influenced the federal conciliatory posture at the conference.

In his opening statement, federal Minister of Transport Donald Jamieson sought to establish the conference mood. The federal government, in moving to implement Part III, he asserted, was not motivated by any jurisdictional claims but solely by its responsibilities under the law. In his only hard stand, Jamieson attempted to put to rest Quebec's dubious interpretation of what had taken place under the MVTA. "It is important to recognize that federal jurisdiction was *not* transferred to the provincial governments by the Act. What the Act did was to make provision for the authorization of provincially constituted boards to act as federal agents."[22]

The MVTA while "appropriate to the circumstances of 1954" was no longer appropriate in 1969 because "extraprovincial trucks and bus services represent a powerful competitive force in the transportation market place." It was because of this change that the federal government intended to implement Part III in order to permit "the Canadian Transport Commission to license and regulate . . . [extraprovincial] undertakings or parts of such undertakings in accordance with a national transportation policy attuned to today's needs."[23]

At this point Jamieson announced the major concession concerning the scope of federal regulation:

> The federal government emphatically does not seek to undertake total administration immediately. We would prefer to proceed on a gradual basis which will provide for orderly transition. . . . In fact, the government has decided that insofar as Part III is concerned, for the foreseeable future, the intra-provincial operations of extra-provincial undertakings would continue to be regulated by provincial boards.[24]

The minister concluded by stating that "no firm decision has yet been taken on the stages or the method of implementing direct federal regulation" and that it was on this question of stages and methods that the federal government wanted "advice and suggestions" from the provincial authorities.[25]

Everything after Jamieson's opening statement was anticlimactic. Most provinces had come to the meeting expecting the worst, including a major federal-provincial donnybrook, as they fought a battle to retain at least partial jurisdiction over motor carriers. With the possible exception of Quebec, all the provinces recognized the strength of the federal government's jurisdictional argument. As one provincial official stated: "Too many people were aware of the impact of the Winner decision and accepted that the federal government had the necessary clout if it wanted to bear down." Although Ontario presented a strong front of opposition to Part III, it was as defensive as the other provinces. According to one member of the Ontario delegation, Ontario's "basic approach was that we have got Winner and Part III and how are we going to keep as much of our authority as possible. It was very much a reaction situation on Ontario's part and a defensive type of operation. We were afraid of federal government action." Another central participant in devising Ontario's strategy expressed his government's attitude more dramatically: "We were terrified that the federal government was going to step in and take over the whole thing. They had the jurisdiction and they indicated they were going to act. We were fighting to get the best deal possible." Moreover, it was not simply federal regulation *per se* that bothered Ontario, according to this official, but the method by which it would be implemented: "We could imagine a federal board made up of a member from Quebec, a member from Alberta and a member from Prince Edward Island deciding what firms would get licences in the province of Ontario. That would have been ridiculous!"

Given this widespread defensive provincial attitude, the federal government effectively pre-empted provincial demands with its opening statement. Thus, when it was the provinces' turn to present their positions, it was primarily a question of going through the motions. Most provinces said they wanted federal regulation limited and wanted assurances that there would be close federal-provincial cooperation in the implementation of Part III.[26] Both the Ontario and Quebec representatives were much more forceful in their challenges to the implementation of Part III but did not offer any serious alternative to federal regulation. Their arguments were based primarily on functional grounds, although Quebec put the federal government on notice that it intended to submit the matter to the Continuing Committee of Officials of the Constitutional Conference, thereby shifting its constitutional position on Part III.[27] Another Quebec argument presented was that it did not see any need for a change in the regulatory system because "the Trucking Association of Quebec maintains that its members prefer to come under the jurisdiction of the Province."[28]

All the provincial statements were, in fact, the "set pieces" expected by the federal government and upon which it had constructed its opening statement. The self-imposed limitations on federal regulation, the call for provincial advice on the stages and method for implementation, and Jamieson's subsequent skilful use of candour and his obvious willingness to listen to provincial arguments defused a potentially difficult situation. So successful was the federal performance that the ministers decided to adjourn the conference on the very day it began and to turn what was to have been the second day of the conference over to a meeting of officials who were to constitute a Joint Technical Committee. It would be the responsibility of this committee to study procedures and implications before federal regulations would be implemented.

It appeared that the federal government had been completely success-ful in achieving its goal for the conference. An experienced federal ob-server at the conference described it as "one of the most successful in establishing a spirit of co-operation with the provinces where a difficult federal initiative was being considered." Part III was to be proclaimed and the federal government had taken the first, and potentially most dif-ficult step towards implementing an important section of the NTA. This had been accomplished not with a major federal-provincial confronta-tion, but with a remarkable degree of accord.

On the evening of the adjourned ministerial conference, a proposal was developed that was to have major consequences for the negotiations. As mentioned above, Ontario had not come to the conference expecting the major federal concession on limited scope. Its strategy had been pre-dicated on a struggle for just such a concession, and, consequently, Ontario officials had given no thought to other demands that the prov-ince might present, given its general opposition to Part III. Ontario had come to the conference hoping to win a limited skirmish. Once this battle had been won, or rather, conceded, Ontario officials scrambled to devise additional demands that might limit even further the implementation of Part III. Accordingly, the Ontario delegation latched on to the federal request for provincial advice on the "staging and method of implemen-tation" of Part III. The result was the "Ontario proposal."

The "Ontario proposal," in fact, was two proposals or, at least, pack-aged in two substantially different versions. The first was drafted late that first night. It argued that the major problems facing the extra-pro-vincial motor carrier industry were the "conglomeration of rules and regulations" and the absence of a mechanism for ensuring joint hearings. To overcome the problem of the lack of uniform regulations, the Ontario government proposed that a set of such regulations be created through negotiations between the provinces and the federal government. Those provinces wishing to retain their delegated authority under the Motor Vehicle Transport Act would be required to adopt these regulations. The second aspect of the initial Ontario proposal was that provision would be made in the Motor Vehicle Transport Act for mandatory joint hearings to be held by those provinces who desired to continue to regulate under the aegis of the Motor Vehicle Transport Act.

The significance of this proposal by Ontario was that it was based on its recognition that it had in fact been outmanoeuvred by the federal government. According to the Ontario perspective, the federal government had made a concession that was in reality no concession at all. The federal government had not wanted to do battle on this issue and, therefore, had not really conceded anything of value. If the federal government was to take over what was considered a major provincial function, it was going to cost that government something of value. The Ontario delegation was not immediately certain what demands it should make, but decided to take advantage of the federal request for advice in order to gain time to reassess the "stakes" of the game. The result of this reassessment by Ontario was a fundamental redefinition of the issue.

The first version of the Ontario proposal did not receive an enthusiastic reception when the Joint Technical Committee convened its first meeting. While several of the provinces, including Quebec, agreed in principle with the proposal, the federal officials stated that it was not acceptable because it bore no relationship to the NTA. When Ontario asked for more time to develop the proposal, the federal officials agreed, being cognizant of their promise to permit consultation. Significantly, it was also agreed that the proposal would be sent to the other provinces to give them an opportunity to comment on it and that the Joint Technical Committee would reconvene to complete the discussions.[29]

Ontario was quick to take advantage of the opportunity presented by the Joint Technical Committee. Two weeks after the first meeting of the committee, it submitted its rewritten proposal. Although Ontario somewhat disingenuously suggested that its proposal was simply "a re-write, in more detail,"[30] in fact the submission was basically a new proposal by means of which Ontario was attempting to redefine the nature of the issue. The goal now was not simply a limiting of the scope of Part III, or ensuring that there was close coordination of the two regulatory systems, or respect for the provincial control over highways. The objective now was to "permit the Provincial Boards to participate in the decision-making process in the granting of extra-provincial authorities."[31] This objective had not been expressed either at the conference of ministers or at the first meeting of the Joint Technical Committee. In part it reflected the change in the definition of the issue that had occurred in the Ontario government. The policy concern no longer was that of pro-

41

tecting provincial jurisdiction but was now the use of motor carrier transportation as a tool for regional economic development.³² More significantly, Ontario officials would attempt to place Part III in the context of the existing regulatory framework in which the provinces had no direct participation. In short, Ontario was attempting to redefine the stakes.

The objective of provincial participation in the decision-making process could be met by one of two methods. "Method One" suggested that mandatory joint hearings by the provincial regulatory boards be held by the provinces concerned with an application for an extraprovincial operating licence. There would be provided under this method a right of appeal on a point of law to the Supreme Court of Canada as well as an appeal on the decision of the joint hearing to the Motor Vehicle Transport Committee of the Canadian Transport Commission. Method One was "basically a method designed to retain the status quo through amendment to the Motor Vehicle Transport Act, but under uniform regulaitons."³³

"Method Two" of the Ontario proposal suggested that applications for extraprovincial operating licences would be made directly to the Motor Vehicle Transport Committee of the CTC. The panel that considered such applications would consist, however, of one federal member of the Motor Vehicle Transport Commission plus one member from each provincial regulatory board involved in the application. In other words, the provincial members would be in a majority on the panel. This method was subsequently dubbed "the joint participation proposal."

The Ontario proposal was devised with several objectives in mind. If its submission did nothing else, it would at least delay the implementation of Part III. Ontario, thus, had gained some time in which to reassess its overall strategy and tactics. The revised proposal was the first indication that such a reassessment had taken place. Ontario officials conceded that submitting the two methods for joint hearings was itself a tactical manoeuvre. Method One provided for no direct federal role except by way of appeal and was clearly unacceptable to the federal government. It was included as an attempt to make Method Two more palatable. Even Method Two, with its call for a majority of provincial members on any licensing panel, was not expected to be acceptable to the federal government but it was thought it might be treated more favourably in view of the extreme demand contained in Method One. Moreover, both methods were perceived primarily as devices to persuade the federal government to discuss the principle of provincial participation in the decision-making process. This principle was to be the focus for all ensuing negotiations.

THE 1970 MEETING OF OFFICIALS

In May 1970, the federal government informed the provinces three days before it took such action of its decision to proclaim Part III. The importance of proclamation was clearly stated by the federal minister of transport for, in his telegram, he acknowledged that proclamation "signifies . . . the government's intent to have the principles of regulation embodied in the National Transportation Act apply to the extra-provincial motor carrier industry." This signal to the provinces was carefully timed and had been deliberately delayed until after the Quebec provincial election of April 29.

Quebec thought it necessary to reaffirm its opposition to Part III, but the other provinces let proclamation pass without comment, although they regarded the act as an effort to put pressure on the provinces. Proclamation of Part III was seen by some of the provinces to be more important symbolically than substantively. As one official stated: "proclamation was not the grounds on which we were going to fight." The grounds for the next battle had been set by the Ontario proposal and the scene would be a meeting of the officials who constituted the Joint Technical Committee.

The 1970 meeting could not have been more different from the 1969 meeting. For the 1969 meeting, the federal government had done a great deal of preparatory work and had drafted its position not only to satisfy most provincial demands but also, and equally important, to reassure the provinces of federal motives and intentions. For the 1970 meeting it appeared that the federal delegation had done little work before the conference and that it was intransigent and its motives highly suspect. For the 1969 meeting, the provinces had come prepared to fight a rearguard action only. At the 1970 meeting, the provinces, acting in concert, presented a position to the federal government expecting it to be answered but, instead, encountered a federal delegation with apparently no counterposition to advance. The goodwill that had been built up at the 1969 conference was lost at the 1970 meeting, where there was a bitter confrontation, with the provinces threatening to walk out. Indeed, some provinces left the meeting early, in deep frustration over the turn of events. Where the 1969 conference had been mutually satisfying, the 1970 meeting was regarded by all participants as a failure. This turn of events was to have serious consequences for future federal-provincial negotiations on Part III.

The 1970 meeting of the Joint Technical Committee was a continuation of the December 3, 1969, meeting. Its purpose was to study the regulations needed by the Canadian Transport Commission to implement Part III. In addition, the meeting was to discuss the Ontario proposal.

In preparation for the 1970 meeting, the federal officials had prepared a draft set of regulations. These, with the proposed agenda, were sent in October to the provinces. To the federal delegation, the Ontario proposal was not acceptable. A working group of federal officials had had a series of meetings in June 1970 and had rejected it. It was perceived as a mechanism by which federal regulation under Part III could be stalled indefinitely through a countless round of discussions. It was also rejected because, in the words of one federal official, "the essential thrust of the Ontario proposal is that it reserves to the provinces, in the first instance, the right to make regulatory decisions and herein lies its major difficulty. As has been amply demonstrated . . . the regulatory philosophies of the provinces vary substantially and, in no case, is there an exact parallel to the federal philosophy as set out in the NTA." The problem, therefore, was that "the provincial philosophies and attitudes would prevail at the expense of the federal philosophy." Moreover, the methods and procedures of the Ontario proposal were dismissed on the grounds of being cumbersome, impracticable, and unworkable. Accordingly, it had been agreed by the federal officials that, at the 1970 meeting, they would reaffirm their position taken in 1969, that the Ontario proposal was unacceptable.

The absence of federal concern with strategy and tactics at the 1970 meeting was in sharp contrast to its approach of the previous year. For the 1970 meeting, its position was simply, as one federal delegate stated, "that regulation of extra-provincial motor carriers was to take place under Part III of the NTA and that federal officials had no mandate to go beyond that position." What distinguishes the federal 1970 approach from that of 1969 was its essentially closed nature. It was closed in two ways. In the first place, it rejected the Ontario proposal without making any attempt to come up with a counter-proposal. There is no indication that in planning for the 1970 meeting, the federal delegation looked beyond the Ontario proposal in order to attempt to satisfy the provincial demand for some participation in the decision-making process involved in granting licences.

The federal approach to the 1970 meeting was closed in a second sense. For the 1969 meeting, federal planning had been based on extensive pre-conference discussions with various provincial representatives. This continuing consultative process was thought to be important in allaying provincial suspicions. However, there was no such prior consultation before the 1970 meeting, nor were the provinces informed that the federal delegation considered the Ontario proposal unacceptable.

Indeed, there appears to have been no communication on this issue between the federal and provincial governments between the meeting of December 3, 1969, and the reconvening of the Joint Technical Committee.

This lack of communication caused some concern to the provincial officials and ministers because they did not know how to interpret it. The concern was so great, in fact, that the initiative for the 1970 meeting came from the provinces. In September 1970, at the annual meeting of provincial ministers responsible for Motor Vehicle Administration, the ministers present expressed concern that they had not heard from the federal government about its intention. Subsequently, a provincial spokesman requested that a federal-provincial conference be held as soon as possible before any implementation of Part III took place. It was only then that the federal government reconvened the Joint Technical Committee.

If the federal delegation was not over concerned with planning for the 1970 meeting, the provinces certainly were. Although there was some evidence of informal consultation between Ontario and Quebec prior to the 1969 conference, there was no evidence to suggest that for that conference the provinces had attempted to devise a common strategy or agree on common objectives.[34] However, for the 1970 meeting, the provinces did act in apparent violation of what Richard Simeon maintained was one of the important norms affecting federal-provincial bargaining, namely, that "The provinces should not get together to work out joint positions or strategies with which to pressure Ottawa."[35] The result was that, for the 1970 meeting, the federal government faced a united provincial front, determined that no progress would be made on Part III until the federal government had responded to a number of provincial demands.

On the day prior to the meeting of the Joint Technical Committee, the provincial delegates met in Ottawa to devise a common position.[36] The provincial officials recognized that the federal threat to their regulatory system was in large measure the result of provincial failings. As one provincial regulator stated: "the best efforts of the provincial transport boards during a considerable number of years have failed to result in the acceptance by the provinces of essential uniform practices, procedures and other non-policy matters that would go far to protect the shipping public and alleviate the regulatory burden on the trucking industry." To correct one of the most serious deficiencies of the present system, the provincial regulators agreed that they would support the drafting of uniform regulations provided they had some input.

To provincial representatives, the most important issue was not uniform regulations but their participation in the extraprovincial regulatory process, the issue raised by the Ontario government proposal. Accordingly, the provinces were concerned with the agenda for the meeting the next day which placed the discussion of the proposed regulations distributed by the Canadian Transport Commission before the discussion of the Ontario proposal. As the Quebec representative stated: "It is our fear that if we embark on an in-depth discussion of proposed regulations tomorrow, *before settling the question of composition of a regulatory authority*, we would be giving tacit approval to federal plans to regulate extra-provincial transport through the Canadian Transportation [*sic*] Commission."[37] The other provincial representatives agreed with this assessment and decided to request that the order of the agenda be reversed so that the Ontario proposal would be discussed first.

Although the order of the agenda was important, changing it did not resolve the substantive problem for the provincial officials with respect to the position to be adopted on the regulatory structure. On this question a number of alternatives were put forward. First, there was the Ontario proposal with its two methods for implementing federal regulation.

At the meeting of provincial officials several other proposals to allow for provincial participation were presented. The Quebec delegation, in line with its general opposition to federal regulation, argued that "we wonder if this group would dare wish to recommend to our ministers the establishment of anything but a provincially-controlled nationally licensing body, acting, of course, as federal agents."[38] The structure recommended by the Quebec representatives was even more provincially dominated than that of Ontario's Method One: "we feel that it is imperative that the proposed body be essentially a loose-knit amalgamation of existing provincial boards, meeting in joint sessions to solve extra-provincial transportation problems, under uniform regulations acceptable to all the provinces. Final authority should also rest with the provinces, based on unanimous or majority decisions by joint sessions of provincial boards."[39]

The Saskatchewan representative adopted a somewhat similar approach in recommending uniform regulations drafted by a federal-provincial committee with the regulatory structure to consist of "joint hearings or other provincial representation in such manner as may be agreed by the provinces."[40]

Other provinces, however, argued against taking an extreme position in favour of provincial control of the regulatory process and attempted to play the role of conciliator. Nova Scotia, for example, was more conciliatory than either Quebec or Saskatchewan. The Nova Scotia delegate argued that attempting to obstruct just for the sake of obstructing would accomplish nothing. Moreover, he argued, in opposition to the Quebec, Saskatchewan, and Ontario Method One proposals, that insistence on retaining the MVTA, which the other provincial proposals assumed, would be unacceptable to the federal government. Accordingly, the Nova Scotia delegate argued that any provincial demand for participation in the regulatory structure should be conditional on amendments to the National Transportation Act. What he proposed was something similar to the Ontario Method Two, a panel system with every province affected by an application for an extraprovincial operating licence represented on the federal regulatory panel hearing that application. The Nova Scotia representative's assessment of the various alternatives presented was that "the joint hearings system is impractical, costly, and burdensome, . . . the examiner system is cumbersome and inappropriate and will result in unnecessary delays in dealing with extra-provincial authorities, . . . and the so-called panel system will be practical, economic and expeditious."[41]

One of the major problems faced by the provincial officials, as they grappled with the difficulties of devising a common position, was that they did not know the federal position on the one proposal before them suggesting provincial participation, namely, the Ontario proposal. When the Joint Technical Committee agreed that the Ontario proposal would be rewritten and submitted for comments, it was assumed, by the provinces at least, that the federal government as well as the provinces would make their comments and suggestions on the proposal. No such comments had been forthcoming from the federal government.

Accordingly, the provincial position was drafted without any clear understanding of what might or might not be reasonably acceptable to the federal government on a number of central issues. In planning a common strategy the provincial officials were, as they were to state, "seriously handicapped" by this absence of a federal position.[42] They were denied clear signals on the range of acceptable alternative provincial demands.

The only definite position that they knew the federal delegation would take concerned the National Transportation Act. As the Nova Scotia delegate pointed out, any proposal based on retaining the Motor Vehicle Transport Act would be rejected, in view of the often expressed determination of the federal government to implement regulation of extraprovincial motor carriers under the National Transportation Act. The other provincial officials accepted this assessment and, as a result, proposals such as Ontario's Method One and those of Quebec and Saskatchewan were dismissed.

On the central question of provincial participation in any regulatory structure, the provincial officials had no similar guidance as to what would be acceptable to the federal officials. At the first meeting of the Joint Technical Committee, the federal members had indicated that the Ontario proposal, as presented at the time, was unacceptable but that they had received no reaction on the revised version, which stressed the importance of provincial participation in the regulatory structure. The absence of federal guidelines gave the provincial officials only one alternative: to request what they considered to be the most acceptable option, calling for a majority of provincially designated representatives on any structure regulating extraprovincial motor carriers.

When the Joint Technical Committee met the next day the ingredients for a confrontation had been prepared, albeit rather unwittingly, by the participants. In his opening remarks, the vice-president of the CTC, and chairman of the Joint Technical Committee, Mr. Taschereau, increased the possibility of conflict by stating, contrary to what had been agreed before the meeting by the federal officials, that the Ontario proposal had not been rejected by federal officials who were keeping an open mind on that question. Rather than outlining the agreed-upon reasons for rejecting the Ontario proposal, Taschereau stated that:

The Ontario proposal, in its main principle, may prove workable. On the other hand, our deliberations may lead to the conclusion that is not the case. Furthermore, in regard to certain types of operations, such as international transport, it is possible that the government would require the Canadian Transport Commission to assume direct regulatory responsibility even though the Ontario Proposal, or something akin to it, was adopted as the general method of regulating extra-provincial operations.[43]

The federal representatives, Taschereau continued, had some questions concerning the Ontario proposal and they were anxious to have provincial views in order to report to their government.

Immediately upon completion of the chairman's remarks, the Saskatchewan representative, as provincial spokesman, informed him of the provincial meeting the previous day and requested that the agenda be changed.[44] Insofar as it appeared from Taschereau's remarks that the Ontario proposal was still under active consideration and was deemed to be a viable option, the provinces requested that the federal officials present their views on the regulatory structure. This procedure was requested, according to the provincial statement, because

We believe we have been seriously handicapped because we have been limited to a discussion of the provincial position on this most important aspect of joint regulation of motor transport. The Ontario proposal and provincial comments have been available to your Commission for some months. We would be interested in hearing your comments, response or proposals at this time.[45]

The process to date had been "too one-sided" because, as the Quebec representative pointed out, "the provinces have no idea how the federal government is looking at implementation of Part III. They have no idea how the federal government plans to look at this in terms of the regulatory body." The provinces maintained that once they had the federal views on the nature of the regulatory body, they would present their statement "embodying the philosophy of the provinces on the regulation of extraprovincial transport."[46]

The federal chairman responded by attempting to place the onus on the provinces. The federal government, he countered, wanted the provincial officials to present it with what they considered to be the best options, but to date there did not appear to be any agreement amongst the provinces on the options. The provincial disagreements, according to Taschereau, were reflected in their submitted comments on the Ontario proposal. What was requested was not that the provinces reconcile their views but "whether some provincial officials have new ideas that would be worthwhile exploring." As far as the federal government was concerned, the question was: "Is there now some consensus by the provinces as to whether Method One or Method Two is preferred? The task would be easier if the federal government officials could report to the government as a result of the meeting that either Method One or Method Two, or a new method is favoured generally by the provinces."

The Ontario representative's response to this comment was that the provincial officials knew of no other alternative except the examiner approach which was suggested in the draft regulations. Before the provinces could suggest anything concrete, other than "a general philosophical situation," they needed to know the federal position on the issue. Other provinces expressed similar positions.

The chairman responded to all these demands for a federal view on the regulatory structure by repeating that the "federal government had no alternative but the one implementing Part III as it stands, with the Commission being the sole regulatory body making the decisions and making the regulations." However, he kept repeating that the federal government had an open mind on the questions and asked if the provinces had any refinements on the Ontario proposal that could be discussed.

As the provincial officials could not get the federal officials to comment substantively on the Ontario proposal, they decided to present their prepared statement, which represented the previous day's consensus, in the hope that the federal delegation would respond to it. The central part of the statement was as follows:

> Our statement is very brief. It does not attempt to delineate methodology because we believe that is premature. The philosophy must first meet with the approval of all the provincial Ministers as well as the federal Minister of Transport. We, as provincial representatives, are agreed that whatever tribunals are selected to deal with extra-provincial transport, be composed of a majority of representatives designated by the provinces.[47]

Taschereau was furious with the provincial position, regarding it as outrageous that the provinces could suggest that they should control a federal regulatory agency. He pointed out again that "federal government officials have nothing up their sleeves by way of counter-proposals, by way of a new scheme that would be advanced to any member of the government." The federal government demanded the justification for the provincial proposal and how it would accord with the principles of the National Transportation Act.

The provinces attempted to justify their demand in a lengthy discussion. One reason given was that since 1954 the provinces had been acting as federal agents and did not see why this could not continue although under a different structure. Another reason was that provincial participation in the regulatory structure was necessary to insure that provincial interests would be well represented and not ignored. A third reason given for direct provincial participation in the form suggested was that the alternative of being simply an "intervener" before the CTC was unacceptable. This objection was put forward by the Ontario representative who had previously been involved as an intervener. From his experience, the Ontario delegate stated, "We would prefer not to be placed in that rather degraded position of interveners in talking about motor transport business. It is a hat-in-hand type of procedure they have been forced into."

The federal delegation was not impressed with the provincial arguments in defence of their demand for majority control. After conferring with his fellow federal officials over lunch, the chairman outlined the federal objections to the provincial proposal. First it was argued that the provincial majority would not be consistent with the national transportation policy or with the main provisions of the National Transportation Act. A second objection was that the federal delegation did not see how the provincial proposal would produce a more efficient transportation system across Canada, which was a fundamental objective of the national transportation policy.

Despite the federal objections to the provincial proposal, Taschereau, nevertheless, did not rule out the possibility of provincial participation. Federal officials could see the value of "a useful and strong contribution by the provinces and particularly the provincial boards in the regulatory system that would have to be developed in extra-provincial transport." At issue was the question of method, of how the provinces could best perform this role. According to the chairman, it was felt that Part III was "flexible enough to permit a provincial contribution. If it does not, Part III ought to be amended, and on this point, federal government officials have not closed their mind at all."

Taschereau's statement did not satisfy the provincial officials. They were not convinced by what they regarded as generalities by the federal officials. The Saskatchewan representative wanted to know precisely "how does the federal group of officials see provincial participation in decision-making?" Provincial officials were generally critical of what had been accomplished thus far. Ontario delegates stated, "There has been no co-ordination between the work that had been developed between provincial technicians and federal technical people. . . . Officials have not sat down together and tried to analyse solutions to the problems." In particular, provincial officials pressed for written comments by federal officials on the Ontario proposal. As the federal officials were not prepared to state specifically what they thought the provincial role should be, the provincial officials became more frustrated. The Saskatchewan representative stated the provincial officials "do not know what they are up against and feel like sitting before a wall and beating their heads."

So frustrated were the provincial officials that several of them walked out of the meeting before the chairman could summarize what he thought had been accomplished. As he interpreted the results of the meeting, the federal people were not prepared to recommend acceptance of the provincial request for majority control of the regulatory process, but they would recommend some form of provincial involvement. Finally, federal officials would report the request from the provincial officials that there be future meetings before Part III was implemented. With this summation the meeting ended, without any serious discussion of the draft regulations that had been prepared by the CTC.

In his report to the president of the CTC, Taschereau asserted that "while the meeting was a necessary exercise as a continuation of the earlier one, it actually served little purpose." His assessment was rather mild compared with that of other participants, both federal and provincial. It was "a dismal failure," it was "a fiasco," "it accomplished nothing." Why was the meeting such a disaster and what effect did the 1970 meeting have on subsequent federal-provincial negotiations on Part III?

A simple breakdown in communications had occurred and most federal participants laid the blame for the breakdown on federal shoulders. One federal official stated that the meeting was a "dismal failure because it was not consultation. We had a fixed position and the meeting was almost a farce. We never explained why the Ontario proposals were unacceptable." Another federal official suggested that the meeting was a "fiasco because the Chairman adopted a very rigid position and because we had two camps facing each other and not talking the same language." Another federal participant also commented on the failure of the federal delegation to communicate effectively with the provincial representatives: "The provinces appeared to be convinced that we had a proposal up our sleeve different from Part III. They were convinced that we were playing a game with them. But we could not be more specific as we had no authority to go further."

The federal lack of preparedness and intransigence caused the provincial frustration and confrontation at the meeting. At the 1969 conference the federal government had requested provincial advice on "the stages and method of implementation" of Part III. The federal officials never clearly explained exactly what they meant by "method of implementation." The committee had agreed that the Ontario proposal would be submitted in a revised form for comments. The provinces had clearly expected the federal government to provide written comments, as they were doing. This the federal government did not do. In the provincial submissions on the Ontario proposal, the provinces, while not unanimous in endorsing it, were unanimous in demanding that the provinces must play an active part in the decision-making process of the regulatory system for extraprovincial motor carriers. The provincial submissions were before the federal government by early May 1970. Yet in the period from May to November, the federal government neither communicated to the provinces its rejection of the Ontario proposal nor attempted to formulate a reply to the provincial demand for some form of participation in the regulatory process. While the federal delegation may have been taken aback at the provincial demand for majority control of the system, it could not have been surprised at the general demand. This lack of federal response to the provincial demand caused consternation and resentment on the part of the provincial representatives.

The federal officials had asked for advice on "the stages and method of implementation" of Part III. Yet they refused to comment substantively on the Ontario proposal and at the same time rejected categorically the provincial demand for majority control. What caused considerable provincial concern was that the federal officials would not express themselves in other than vague generalities —"we have an open mind on the question"— on the provincial demand for some form of direct participation. The provinces had repeatedly asked for a federal view on provincial participation in decision-making, to no avail. This absence of a federal opinion, given the failure of the federal delegation to explain how it thought Part III should be implemented, heightened provincial fears and suspicions. After all, the purpose of the committee was to provide advice on the method of implementation. The provinces had done this, and yet they could not get any opinion on their advice or any lead on the federal approach. Consequently, the provinces felt they were "hitting their head against a wall."

The provincial frustration turned increasingly into suspicion of the federal intentions. The provinces were concerned that the federal officials had "something up their sleeve." Otherwise why would they call the meeting? The federal delegation was making no effort to comment on, let alone accommodate, provincial demands and, therefore, the provincial officials concluded that their worst fears were going to be realized. Despite its promises at the 1969 conference, the federal government was thought to be preparing to implement Part III without seriously considering provincial concerns. This suspicion was to have major consequences for the negotiations.

CONCLUSION

This chapter has employed the assumptions of the unitary-actor model in an attempt to derive an explanation for the fate of Part III by analysing the interactions between the governments. These interactions naturally are influenced by the respective actors' definition of their objectives, their development of strategies, and their tactical use of their resources. An important aspect of the negotiating process is the different perceptions the governments have of one another. Consequently, the communications process, whereby the governments articulate their positions, transmit their demands, and seek to reinforce a specific image is crucial to the negotiations. From this perspective governments must not only have resources; they must be perceived by their adversaries as possessing such resources. Perception, rather than actual possession, may be the more important variable. Another conclusion of the unitary-actor analysis is that the period of negotiations from 1966–70 yields a number of conclusions that are crucial to any explanation of the failure of the federal government to implement Part III.

Federal strategy had been predicated on its recognition that provincial actions in the negotiations would be largely dependent on federal behaviour. Accordingly, the federal government had embarked on a series of straightforward, yet intricate, manoeuvres, designed to increase the possibility that Part III would be implemented with provincial cooperation. It had indicated its determination to act and had sought to impress on the provinces that it was bargaining from a position of strength. Thereafter, it sought to reinforce that image in order to construct its approach to the provinces.

The federal government's strategy called for it to condition provincial expectations about federal plans for implementation. The success of this strategy was demonstrated by the generally defensive attitude the provinces adopted at the 1969 conference. The second major component of federal strategy was to pre-empt a battle at the first conference by giving to the provinces the concession that they assumed would have to be wrenched from the federal government. The federal government intended to tie the concession to a request for provincial advice and a promise of continuous consultation.

For the 1970 meeting the federal government apparently abandoned its strategy because there was no evidence that there was a realization that federal actions, or non-actions, would influence the perceptions and behaviour of the provinces.[48] The federal government, so effective as a communicator prior to and at the 1969 conference, had failed to follow through in order to build on its success. As a result of the federal failure to respond to the Ontario proposal, the provinces were thrown into confusion. They did not know how to interpret federal behaviour as they were uncertain as to the meaning of the signal being sent by the federal government. The result was "two camps facing each other and not talking the same language." This breakdown in communications had important consequences for the negotiations.

The motives of the federal government were now suspect. After having sought to establish its good faith, the federal government was now thought to have made false promises. The provinces believed that the federal government had lulled them into a sense of complacency and was not the least bit interested in provincial "advice." Otherwise, why had there been no federal response to the Ontario proposal other than banal generalities?

Another major consequence was that, instead of fragmented, direction-less opposition to Part III, the federal government now was confronted with united provincial opposition. It had created a consensus where one did not exist. The consensus that existed concerning the demand for majority provincial participation was primarily significant not for the substance of the demand but for what it represented. While it was not clear to what lengths all the provinces were prepared to push the demand, it was clear that they all endorsed the demand as a vehicle by means of which they could force a meaningful federal-provincial exchange. What remained to be seen was whether Ontario had successfully broadened and redefined what was at issue in the negotiations.

Finally, the 1970 meeting was important because it resulted in a re-assessment of the resources of the respective negotiators. The provinces had had time to realize that they had been unnecessarily defensive. Increasingly they perceived the federal promise to consult as an admission that, despite federal constitutional authority, provincial assistance was crucial to the implementation of Part III. The manpower situation within the federal government had changed very little in the four years. Even a federal official was critical of the failure to build the necessary staff because this deprived the federal government of "any psychological strength in dealing with the provinces." Thus the provinces began to appreciate the constraints within which the federal government was oper-ating and to recognize that such constraints were provincial resources. Central to this provincial recognition was the awareness that any federal threat to "go it alone" on Part III was scarcely credible.

The 1970 meeting had undone what the previous meeting had accom-plished. The provinces conceded that Part III was constitutionally un-assailable; however, they also realized that implementation would take place only over their objections and definitely without their cooperation. That cooperation was essential, but the provinces began to prepare for further negotiations determined that it would be forthcoming only if the fiasco of 1970 was corrected. They would force the federal government to honour its promise to consult.

Chapter Four

The Federal–Provincial Negotiations: 1971–1972

No one disputes the contention that the 1970 meeting was a failure. However, it is important to determine the extent of this failure. How crucial was it to the eventual failure to implement Part III? This question resolves itself into a number of subsidiary questions. The federal concern was with the impact of this meeting on its strategy for winning provincial cooperation to achieve implementation. Was the provincial animosity engendered by federal behaviour a temporary phenomenon or was it a fundamental roadblock to implementation? The provincial perspective was more complicated. Was the united provincial front merely illusory, created out of mutual, but passing, antagonism, or was it a fundamental resource to be exploited in the negotiations? An additional question is related to the general assessments of the respective resources of the different governments. Some provinces began to suspect that the federal government was somewhat of a paper tiger. Could it be that the federal government had not provided a detailed plan to implement Part III because it did not know how to do so? Perhaps the federal government had solicited provincial cooperation out of need, not generosity? If this assumption was realistic, as some provinces believed, then they were in a much better bargaining position than they had previously assumed.

Some of the answers were not long in coming after the November 1970 meeting. The provinces appeared now to appreciate the fact, long appreciated by the federal government, that they alone had the necessary experience and manpower to regulate motor carriers. If they chose to withhold such resources, federal regulations could not be implemented satisfactorily. This reassessment is crucial to an understanding of the future bargaining. The negotiations had entered a new phase, based on an awareness of the fundamental equality of the participants. No longer perceiving themselves as supplicants, but equals, no longer defensive, but aggressive, the provinces took the offensive. The federal government was to learn that provincial cooperation would be much more expensive because of the fiasco of 1970.

The provinces were divided, however, on the extent to which they should exploit their advantage. For some, the provincial consensus on participation in the regulatory process was a maximum demand, reflecting a legitimate concern for the recognition of provincial interests. Such provinces, however, had conceded that there were major problems in the existing regulatory system, problems that they had in large measure created and had been unable, or unwilling, to resolve. Two of the provinces saw the provincial consensus as a device for frustrating Part III. Yet, having endorsed the provincial consensus, they could not appear to be too uncompromising lest they alienate their allies.

A recognition of the diversity of provincial motives was central to a revision in federal strategy. When its initial attempts to regain provincial support were rebuffed, the federal government was faced with a dilemma. It could refuse to accede to provincial demands and risk total provincial non-cooperation and possibly harassment. Obviously this was an untenable option because there were no plans for implementation without provincial cooperation. The federal stand had always been Part III with provincial cooperation or no implementation. The alternative now becoming available was to exploit the diversity in provincial motives by wooing enough provincial support for a compromise proposal. By forging a coalition with the majority of provinces, the federal government might thereby manoeuvre the more recalcitrant provinces into endorsing the compromise. The analysis of the apparently successful salvaging of Part III following the fiasco of 1970 is the subject of this chapter. Once again the analysis concentrates on the interactions between the governments on the assumption that it is such interactions that explain the fate of Part III.

THE 1971 CONFERENCE

The significance of the 1970 meeting was immediately forthcoming. At its conclusion, it had been agreed that the federal minister of transport would be informed of the provincial request for further consultations. The provinces were not prepared to wait meekly for a federal response. They seized the initiative by arranging the meeting themselves.

Their dissatisfaction with the 1970 meeting was immediately communicated to the federal government when the provinces demanded an urgent meeting of federal and provincial ministers.[1] They argued that they had hoped the creation of the Joint Technical Committee "would have proved effective in clarifying the appropriate roles to be played by the provincial and federal jurisdictions respectively in the implementation of Part III [but that] the November meeting . . . failed to produce such clarification." Ontario volunteered to host a federal-provincial meeting of ministers in Toronto.

This new aggressiveness caused consternation in Ottawa where there was a great deal of concern about losing the initiative. Particularly upsetting to federal officials was the fact that if the provinces called the meeting and Ontario hosted it, the federal government would lose all control of the proceedings.[2] The federal response to the provincial request was to accept the value of such a meeting but to suggest that it be postponed until the federal government could prepare its "posture on how we see Part III being implemented."[3] The Ontario government persisted in its attempt to host a meeting, even if delayed but, when a date was suggested, the federal minister of transport deflected the provincial move by stating that he was "extremely reluctant to be away from Ottawa" on that date and, therefore, that he would host the meeting.[4] The provinces could do little in reply to this gentle rebuff.

Who would host the meeting was, however, not the major concern of the federal government, no matter how important tactically. The central federal objective was to regain the initiative and the good will of the provinces. A number of considerations were crucial. It was not thought to be shrewd, tactically, for the federal government to go into the meeting simply to respond to the provincial position. It was considered wiser to take the initiative by putting a specific federal proposal on the table and forcing the provinces to respond to it. What was needed was a federal proposal with a definite timetable on the "stages and method of implementation." The federal officials knew they must go into the meeting with a specific proposal in hand because they had been warned by a western official that if "Mr. Jamieson should make a proposal to the provinces and give them time to study it, he will wait until hell freezes over before he receives a reply." Federal strategy for the meeting, therefore, assumed that the provinces would do everything possible to postpone action on Part III.

Federal strategists also recognized that the provincial demand for participation in the regulatory process had to be answered. They knew that some of the provinces, at least, would not be satisfied simply with the right to intervene before the CTC. The Ontario member of the Joint Technical Committee had stated such a posture was "degrading," and Ontario was adamant "that a better mechanism must be found for communicating and having account taken of the 'legitimate' views of the province by the CTC." The role of intervener was "degrading" to the province because it seemed to grant it no more status than any individual or interest group. Therefore, federal planners had to devise a proposal for participation that would be acceptable to the provinces. To supplement its preparations, the federal government also engaged in a new tactic, bilateral negotiations with Ontario and Quebec, the provinces most opposed to Part III. Negotiations with Quebec were not very fruitful as Quebec reiterated the joint provincial demand for majority control over any regulatory body. Federal officials left this meeting not very confident that any progress had been made. They were convinced that if the federal government had won provincial acceptance for any proposal, it would have to make a concerted effort to ensure that Quebec did not appear to have given away powers to the federal government.

Preliminary negotiations with the Ontario government were more successful. Ontario officials emphasized again that the current method of appearing before the CTC was inadequate and an unsatisfactory way of ensuring that provincial views received reasonable consideration. They suggested that there was a need for *in camera* meetings between provinces and the CTC. One of the federal participants was convinced after this meeting that there appeared "to be a strong likelihood of obtaining excellent co-operation from Ontario both during and following implementation if a mechanism could be worked out by which the provinces could express their policies and other concerns in a meaningful way and other than in an open forum."

Although the accuracy of this reading of the Ontario position would be challenged subsequently, federal officials incorporated it in their plan to implement Part III, which they submitted to all the provinces prior to the conference.[5] The federal strategy was obvious. Their proposal deliberately attempted to incorporate provincial views to demonstrate that the federal government recognized the legitimacy of these views although, as the plan sought to emphasize, in a manner "consistent with federal responsibility."[6] The federal government reiterated the limited scope of federal implementation "for the foreseeable future." The plan conceded that it was "a large task: to move to federal regulation of even the extra-provincial operations" and, therefore, "a phased transition" would be necessary. Central to the federal plan was the timetable for implementation proposed:

Stage 1 (to begin April 1, 1972)
Canadian undertakings operating in or through five or more provinces[7]
Stage 2 (to begin not later than January 2, 1973)

Canadian undertakings operating in or through four provinces
Stage 3 (to begin not later than September 1, 1973)
Canadian undertakings operating in or through three provinces
Stage 4 (to begin not earlier than April 1, 1974)
All others including international carriers.

The plan also outlined several proposals designed to satisfy the provincial demand for involvement in the regulatory process. The first clearly demonstrated the federal objective to win Ontario's support. A joint federal-provincial committee was proposed in order "to facilitate the flow of information between regulatory bodies, provide a means of ensuring on a continuous basis an exchange of views on policy matters affecting regulation and facilitate consideration of special problems arising during the transition phase."[8] Such a committee would be composed of a representative from each province plus members of the Motor Vehicle Transport Committee of the CTC.

The second proposal was for the appointment of provincially designated officials to act as examiners "to carry out certain functions on behalf of the Canadian Transport Commission."[9] A similar suggestion had been rejected by some provincial officials at the 1970 meeting, but federal officials thought that it might be more palatable in conjunction with the proposed joint committee.

Despite the extensive planning for the forthcoming meeting and the compromises being proposed, federal officials had no doubt that the meeting would be difficult as they sought to regain the provincial cooperation deemed so essential. Quebec was still adamantly opposed. Although Ontario had appeared to be somewhat more conciliatory, federal officials were convinced that some of the provinces were planning to adopt a hard line. One federal official described the new provincial objective to be "to retain the effective power of regulation within the provincial domain." The federal perception, or perhaps fear, of the conference was that the provinces seemed "to sense that if they can get the federal government to back off now, there is a good chance that Part III will not be implemented."

Federal planners prepared a number of fall-back positions in the event that additional "bending," as one official described it, was necessary to sell the immediate implementation of Part III. The nature of these positions indicates the state of apprehension and uncertainty that had developed in the federal government. Among its alternatives was a proposal to limit federal regulation even further than proposed in the implementation plan. If forced, the federal government was prepared to restrict federal regulation to extraprovincial undertakings and those undertakings operating in or through three or more provinces. In other words, in addition to the intraprovincial operations already promised, the provinces would be allowed to continue to regulate operations involving two provinces. According to information supplied with its implementation plan, if this compromise was offered to the provinces, approximately 40 percent of all interprovincial undertakings would be excluded from federal regulation.[10] Perhaps even more significant is the fact that approximately 65 percent of extraprovincial trucking firms domiciled in Ontario and Quebec would have been exempted from Part III. The federal government's only demand of the provinces, if forced to offer this compromise, was federal chairmanship of the compulsory joint boards of two-province operations. The provinces would be in the majority on such joint boards. This fall-back position is interesting in view of subsequent opposition that developed within the federal government to a similar proposal.

The federal government had good reason to be apprehensive. The provinces were still smarting from the 1970 meeting, and their preparation for the forthcoming conference took place on two levels. First, Ontario sought to convene a meeting of all the provinces one day prior to the federal-provincial meeting to develop a common front. This was to be somewhat more difficult the second time, because the provinces were aware of a more conciliatory federal approach. Those provinces not completely opposed to federal regulation were now less prepared to adopt a rigid hard line. One province, in fact, refused to attend the provincial strategy meeting. The Alberta minister's answer to the call for an interprovincial meeting stated:

> With reference to a suggested meeting of the Provincial Ministers alone to consider a provincial position, may I advise that I personally do not think this is wise; I do think it is better for all provinces to speak frankly at the meeting with federal representatives present in order that all sides can be fully explored before any province takes any final position. I frankly do not think there is anything to be gained by having a meeting . . . ahead of the meeting called by Mr. Jamieson.[11]

The Alberta minister was conscious of something other than the "norms" cited earlier; Alberta had become a supporter of federal regulation because of a case then before the courts that was a fundamental challenge to the provincial regulatory system.[12]

Although Alberta chose not to attend, the provincial strategy session was held. It revealed that the provincial consensus was based more on a common demand for a federal response than on a unified provincial position on the specifics of the regulatory system. The provincial representatives present were not able to agree on a joint provincial statement comparable to that of 1970. Nevertheless, they were able to agree on what an Ontario official described as "a broad outline of what we wanted." Essentially, the provinces wanted the federal government to fulfil its commitment to give a response to the Ontario proposal.

The Ontario and Quebec governments were not satisfied with the unified provincial stance and sought to buttress it. Accordingly, they met after the provincial strategy session to coordinate their respective approaches to the conference. This common front was to prove extremely significant because, as one Ontario official described the approach, they were planning a type of "one-two punch" that might deliver a knock-out blow to Part III. Quebec planned to phrase her position in more political, that is, jurisdictional terms, while Ontario would stick to functional arguments against federal proposals. The approach of Ontario and Quebec was to be carefully orchestrated with Ontario to act as the mediator between Ottawa and Quebec.

For all the planning and attempts to devise proposals acceptable to the provinces, the federal government was not prepared for the confrontation that occurred at the 1971 conference. Indeed, it did not even get an opportunity to "bend" and present its fall-back position. The provinces were insistent that they be given a federal response to the Ontario proposal and that the new federal proposal be submitted to the Joint Technical Committee where both the federal and Ontario proposals could be studied in depth.

The provinces were unanimous in their general disagreement with the proposed federal plan. They demanded that, before the federal government attempt to implement Part III, the proposed joint committee be given definite terms of reference. Such terms of reference would prevent another occurrence of what had happened in the Joint Technical Committee because the terms would stipulate that the committee was to study the federal proposal as well as the other proposals for direct provincial involvement in the regulatory process.

The general provincial demand was made more palatable by its contrast to the demands of Ontario and Quebec. Federal officials who had discussed the issue with Ontario prior to the conference had either misread the Ontario position or had been deceived by it. The Ontario attitude was reflected in the following report submitted after the 1970 meeting:

The convening of the meeting elicited no information from the

Federal representatives. . . . The Provincial representatives were faced with a request to discuss, insofar as the Federal representatives present were concerned, a position which might or might not be the Federal position. . . . The Provinces endeavoured to elicit from the Federal representatives concrete proposals which might be rationally discussed and although the Federal people met separately on at least two occasions, no basis for discussion was put forward by them. No discussion was proceeded with on the Ontario proposal or on the various provincial submissions.[13]

Ontario was adamant in its support of the general provincial position that no progress could be made on Part III until this shortcoming had been corrected. It was not enough for the federal government merely to put another proposal on the table. The Ontario government demanded a federal response "on the merits or practicability of the Ontario Government's position."[14]

Ontario wanted the question sent back to the Joint Technical Committee, with the committee having explicit terms of reference, to "complete its assigned responsibilities and report to the federal and provincial ministers on the merits of the Ontario proposal, the submissions of the several provinces relative to the Ontario proposal and any input the federal people may wish to present."[15]

This was "punch-one" from the Ontario-Quebec team. It was based on a fairly dispassionate review of the reasons why the federal government should not proceed with its plan of implementation but instead should send it to a federal-provincial committee for further study. Implicit in the Ontario statement was the implication that, if the federal government should choose to ignore what was an eminently reasonable position, necessary provincial cooperation would not be forthcoming.

The Ontario position was eminently reasonable in view of "punch-two" from the Quebec government. Quebec declared that any partial delegation of federal powers, such as that proposed, was unacceptable.[16] Quebec reminded the federal government that the provincial governments had the right to control those who use provincial highways and the significance of this reminder was subsequently clarified: "Si le gouvernement fédéral décidait d'exercer les pouvoirs directs qu'il se réserve dans le partie III de la Loi nationale des transports, nous serions dans l'obligation de rappeler à ses représentants que le système routier releve directement et uniquement de la juridiction des provinces et que les provinces ont le droit de déterminer les conditions d'utilisation de leurs routes."[17] The Quebec spokesman explained that if the federal government chose to ignore the provincial objections, Quebec would feel compelled to enact 350 safety regulations that would be enforced solely against federally licensed carriers. If Part III was implemented over the opposition of the provinces, Quebec dramatically promised to turn Highway 401 from Windsor to the Quebec border into a "parking lot"[18] by enforcing those regulations at the Ontario-Quebec border.

Non-cooperation was one thing, but the federal government had never anticipated that Quebec or any other province would threaten harassment. Some of the other provinces were taken aback by this extreme position. According to participants, Joe Borowski, Manitoba's representative, was so infuriated by the Quebec position that he and his Quebec counterpart almost came to blows when Borowski attempted to explain what it meant to be in Confederation!

However much some of the provinces may have disagreed with the Quebec tactic, they were unanimous in rejecting the federal proposal. Any attempt by the Quebec government to harass federally regulated trucks by a clearly discriminatory set of regulations would be illegal,[19] but the threat was important because it symbolized an absence of provincial goodwill and cooperation. The federal government was thus forced to respond to the provincial demand that the issue be sent back to the Joint Technical Committee. The outlook was so negative that the federal government did not attempt to win the provinces over with the additional concessions it had prepared. The conference did not get beyond the presentation of the opening statements when the federal government recognized the futility of the exercise. The federal minister of transport instructed one of his officials to take a number of his provincial counterparts to lunch to draft an acceptable agreement to end the impasse.

The success of the provinces' "ganging up" on Ottawa was shown by the results of the luncheon negotiations. The federal government recommended the creation of an Advisory Council on Motor Carrier Regulation, composed of a representative from each of the provinces and the federal government and chaired by the latter.[20] The council was to be given explicit terms of reference as demanded by the provinces:

1. To proceed with drafting of uniform regulations.

2. To examine impact studies put forward by either the provinces or the federal government.

3. To make a joint assessment of proposals made to date including the Ontario proposal.

4. To facilitate a two-way flow of information.[21]

After a perfunctory discussion, the creation of the council was accepted by the conference. The agreement was that the council would have a year to report and implementation would "follow after full federal-provincial Ministerial review of these recommendations . . . but not later than six months after the report is received."[22] This latter stipulation was the only concession gained by the federal government, although it was a limited one in that Quebec "reserved" its position.

There were a number of factors that had made the impasse inevitable. The provinces had come to realize that the federal government's constitutional authority was its only significant bargaining ace. The provinces now viewed their cooperation as a prerequisite for the successful implementation of Part III. They were determined to exercise the enormous leverage that this advantage gave them to force the federal government to make good on its promise to consult with the provinces before proceeding. Satisfaction of the promise now meant that the fiasco of 1970 would be corrected.

Within the federal government there was obvious dissatisfaction with the turn of events. It had won and then lost provincial cooperation and now had to backtrack even further. If anything, they were back to where they had been before the 1969 conference. Some federal officials saw the results of the 1971 conference as the beginning of the end of Part III. They regarded the meeting as a disaster for the federal government. Others were less pessimistic. They saw the creation of the Advisory Council as another chance for the eventual implementation of Part III. If the federal government was to be successful, however, it would have to learn from its mistakes. Officials who adopted this attitude placed the blame for the failure of the 1971 meeting squarely on federal shoulders. Despite intensive preparations and attempts to obtain reliable soundings from Ontario and Quebec, it was realized that the conference had been doomed from the beginning. Although the conference had polarized more than had been predicted, polarization was to have been expected because of the 1970 meeting. According to one federal official, the positions adopted by the provincial ministers "reflected advice based on the 1970 meeting. Had the federal people given a meaningful exchange and dialogue in 1970, the provincial Ministers would have come to the table to make decisions. But the Ministers were strongly advised that Ottawa was not a body that could be talked to." Although the Ontario-Quebec approach was important to the outcome of the 1971 meeting, it was successful because the other provinces were receptive to a hard line, remembering the 1970 federal unwillingness to discuss seriously provincial arguments.

THE ADVISORY COUNCIL, MAY 1971–APRIL 1972

The May 1971 Ministers' Conference had established that the provinces possessed sufficient leverage to frustrate the successful implementation of Part III. This confronted the federal government with a fundamental dilemma. It could decide not to implement Part III, and accept the consequences, or it could attempt to reach an accommodation with the provinces that would be far more expensive than had been previously imagined. It was apparent from the first meeting of the council that the federal government had opted to strive for an accommodation.

The revised federal strategy recognized the mixed motives of the provinces. For the majority of the provinces, the consensus behind the demand for majority representation on the regulatory agency resulted from the federal government's failure to provide an adequate reading, prior to the 1970 meeting, of its position on the Ontario proposal. These provinces had been forced into their position because the federal government had given them little choice. Now they were committed to forcing the federal government to study with the provinces the feasibility of the various options. Thus for these provinces, the provincial demand was the maximum demand they would make.

Ontario and Quebec did not share the other provinces' perceptions of the situation. To them, the provincial position was a minimum demand inasmuch as they were completely opposed to federal regulation. They had been prepared to endorse the provincial statement in order to forge a common front against the federal government. Of the two, Ontario faced the greater dilemma. Unlike Quebec, Ontario had not objected to Part III *per se* but merely to the functional problems involved in implementation. If the federal government endorsed a proposal acceptable to the other provinces, Ontario would be constrained in its options. Too extreme a position might alienate the other provinces.[23]

The Advisory Council had two major tasks: to draft uniform regulations and to assess proposals for the regulatory structure, including the Ontario proposal. The question of uniform regulations occasioned little disagreement. The participants agreed in principle with the objective and, after the council's first meeting, agreed on the areas where uniformity was desirable and necessary. The result was a comprehensive set of regulations and a system of uniform classification of accounts.[24]

The major difficulty was the regulatory structure. At the very first meeting of the council, the federal government immediately responded to the pressing provincial demand for a response to the Ontario proposal. Although the response was negative, the provinces were impressed with the directness of the federal position. They were also impressed with the apparent conciliatory tone being adopted by the federal members of the council.

The Ontario proposal was unacceptable to the federal government for two basic reasons. It was argued that the mechanism for implementing the regulations must "be able to react quickly and flexibly, and . . . the Ontario proposal as currently drafted would not allow this." The second reason was that "the effect of intermodality and the requirements of the National Transportation Policy would not be adequately considered as there was no mechanism in the Ontario proposal for federal policy input."[25]

The important aspect of the federal presentation was that it did not rule out completely provincial participation in the regulatory process. Instead, two basic requirements for the regulatory structure were enunciated: "It must fully reflect national transportation policy and it must allow for a channel of appeal to the Federal Government." If provinces could accept these conditions, then federal acceptance of provincial participation might be forthcoming. To facilitate its work, the council accepted the chairman's suggestion that it establish two sub-groups, one on regulations and the other on regulatory structure, to meet simultaneously in order to meet the council's deadline. The proposal was a shrewd tactical move by the federal government, as the sub-groups were chaired by Alberta (Regulations) and Nova Scotia (Regulatory Structure) on the recommendation of the federal chairman. According to a federal participant, the move was designed to defuse Ontario's power in the council because "Ontario had been 50 percent of the weight of the provinces" against federal regulation. Although considering the move as an attempt to "shaft" the province, Ontario conceded that little was to be gained by opposing the move. An additional advantage to the federal government was that creation of the sub-groups under chairmen not identified with either of the two competing positions freed the federal chairman to participate in the discussions.

Federal strategy was to seek agreement on the fundamental principles that any regulatory structure would have to incorporate. The federal government maintained that the following set of principles derived from the National Transportation Act and its policy statements must be respected:

1. that regulation of the extra-provincial motor carrier industry was primarily a federal concern;

2. that the National Transportation Policy must be the guiding force behind regulation;

3. that the industry must not be considered in isolation but rather as part of the total transportation system of Canada;

4. that a single paramount federal regulatory body would be required to meet these requirements.

The provinces contended that the following two principles must be incorporated in any regulatory proposal:

1. that the motor carrier industry was vital to the economic development of each province and that the means of focusing on this was through regulation;

2. that regardless of the form of regulation to be adopted, a very substantial part of the industry would remain constitutionally within the jurisdiction of each province and an effective means had to be found to bridge the jurisdictional split between extra-provincial and intra-provincial motor carrier regulation.

Once there was agreement on the respective sets of principles at issue, the council turned its attention to the various regulatory alternatives.

When the council began its deliberations, two regulatory proposals had to be assessed in light of the principles enunciated. They were the Ontario proposal, presented at the December 1969 meeting, and subsequently rewritten, and the federal phasing proposal presented at the May 1971 meeting. The members of the council readily agreed that neither of the two proposals on the table was acceptable. The Ontario proposal, Method One, amounted to maintaining the status quo except under conditions of uniform regulations. To federal officials this proposal was unacceptable because of the limited federal role in the regulatory system. The Ontario proposal, Method Two, was somewhat more acceptable but was considered as well to have some major flaws. Although Method Two would allow for more federal involvement in the drafting of regulations and direct participation by the Canadian Transport Commission, the federal officials were concerned with a certain degree of ambiguity in Method Two that might give the provinces too much leeway and flexibility. The federal concern was that there was no guarantee of uniformity in the regulations across the country because the provinces would be permitted individually to negotiate with the federal government. Moreover, the Ontario proposal in either form was unacceptable because it was predicated on the continued operation of the Motor Vehicle Transport Act and not on Part III of the NTA.

The provinces had unanimously, and repeatedly, expressed their position that the federal proposal did not give the provinces sufficient voice in the regulatory process. The suggestions made by the federal government at the May 1971 meeting with respect to an examiner role for the provinces and a provincial advisory committee to the CTC were rejected by the provinces as not fulfilling their demand.

At the second meeting of the Advisory Council, the Nova Scotia member again attempted to play the role of mediator by presenting a proposal that would allow for both federal and provincial participation in the decision-making process. His initial proposal called for a "regional regulatory agency with provincially selected people appointed under a federal Order-in-Council."[26] Although reaction to this proposal was generally favourable, it was agreed that no action would be taken until the members of the council had had an opportunity to discuss it with their respective ministers.

At the next meeting, the Nova Scotia representative presented a more detailed proposal to the council as a compromise. Nova Scotia proposed to amend the National Transportation Act to provide for provincial representation on the Motor Vehicle Transport Committee of the Canadian Transport Commission. The restructured Motor Vehicle Transport Committee would consist, in effect, of a "floating membership." The membership of the committee for any application would depend on the number of provinces affected. The committee would be composed of one provincial nominee from each province involved in the application and one federal nominee who would act as chairman. It was suggested individual provinces would nominate a pool of nominees from whom the federal authority would designate by order-in-council members of the Motor Vehicle Transport Committee.

There was some question raised, however, that the Nova Scotia proposal was beyond the council's terms of reference and, therefore, of its right to discuss it. The Ontario delegate suggested the following motion which was unanimously accepted by the council:

> The Chairman present to the Minister of Transport an outline of
> the Nova Scotia proposal, indicating possible structure and legislative
> changes that might be required and seeking clarification as to
> whether or not the examination of this proposal could be considered
> within the terms of reference of the Council and therefore whether
> or not the Council should pursue in greater depth this proposal.[27]

The importance of receiving the minister's permission to examine the Nova Scotia proposal was underlined by the Ontario delegate's statement that, if the proposal was within the terms of reference of the council, he would recommend to the Ontario minister that the Ontario proposal be withdrawn.

Despite this motion, there is no indication that the federal officials reported their minister's reply or that the issue was raised. Instead, at the next meeting of the Regulatory Structure Sub-Group of the council, discussion continued on the Nova Scotia proposal as if it were within the terms of reference of the council. A consensus was emerging on the merits of this proposal. The accuracy of this assessment is reflected by the minutes taken of the Toronto meeting of the Structure Sub-Group. After reviewing the various proposals under discussion, the committee noted that:

> it was felt that Proposals I (Ontario) and 2 (Federal) were generally not suitable but should be listed as alternatives. The Committee agreed that there is a convergence toward a combination of 3 (Nova Scotia) and 4 (regional boards) and that the objectives of the NTA would be most likely reached under such a scheme. Such a proposal would see significant and meaningful involvement of the provinces in the decision-making process carried out under federal policy.[28]

So positive was the reaction to the Nova Scotia proposal that it was agreed that there would be no need to split the extraprovincial operations from the intraprovincial.

Not all the provinces were satisfied with the council's activities. The Ontario member wrote a rather curious letter to the chairman in which he stated that he was "deeply concerned about the direction in which the Council is going."[29] He reminded the chairman of the council's terms of reference and suggested that:

> What we seem to be doing is developing two additional proposals to which no reference was made at the meeting of Ministers. At the Halifax Meeting, as the Minutes will disclose, I requested that you obtain clearance from your Minister that the procedure we are following meets with his approval. There is nothing in my file to suggest that such clearance has been granted.

The Ontario letter was sent to the other members of the council as well as to the chairman. The Saskatchewan member also began to express some concern that there was no reply to the council motion of the Nova Scotia proposal. He informed the chairman that his minister had directed him not to attend the next meeting of the Advisory Council if there was no decision from the federal government on the competence of the Advisory Council to discuss the Nova Scotia proposal. Several other provinces also indicated some disquiet over the lack of a federal response.

Thus, when the council met again it appeared that the harmony that had initially characterized its work and the consensus that had been emerging on the regulatory structure would be lost. On the agenda for discussion was the first draft of the "Regulatory Structure" chapter which was to form part of the council's final report. This draft is an important document in view of what was to take place.

It recognized that the initial terms of reference of the council "were limited to examination of the Ontario and Federal proposals" but stated that the terms "were later expanded to include two new proposals which came to be known as the Nova Scotia proposal and the Regional Board proposal."[30] The draft reviewed the four proposals and the various "factors" to be taken into consideration in devising the regulatory structure, and concluded that the Ontario, federal, and regional board proposals were unacceptable for a variety of reasons. On the Nova Scotia proposal, the draft concluded that "The one thrust which became obvious in time was the ability through the Nova Scotia proposal to create a workable regulatory environment or structure which resolves most of the problems inherent in the existing structure than the other three proposals considered by the Council."[31] The Nova Scotia proposal had some disadvantages because legislative amendments would be required to either the MVTA or the NTA, to create the new regulatory structure. However, it was suggested that the "objective and results which can be achieved by the Nova Scotia proposal far outweigh the disadvantages of the legislative amendments required." In conclusion, the draft report offered this assessment of the Nova Scotia proposal: "the proposal is the most serious attempt to date to bring together the Federal Government and the provinces under one umbrella for extra-provincial motor carrier regulation and thereby provides the most effective mechanism to deal with the motor carrier industry yet devised."

When the Advisory Council met in Winnipeg to consider the draft report it appeared it might have been presumptuous to have stated that the terms of reference of the council had been extended. The meeting began with the chairman announcing that no reply had been received from the federal minister of transport on the Ontario resolution and, therefore, discussion of the structure issue would have to be postponed until a reply had been received.

On the fourth day of the meeting, after the other items on the agenda had been discussed, the chairman announced that he had received a reply from the minister of transport.[32] It repeated much of the Ontario representative's letter of October 4 and indicated the minister agreed that consideration of the Nova Scotia proposal appeared to be beyond the terms of reference of the Advisory Council. Moreover, the minister argued that as the Quebec member "has been specifically instructed not to participate in the discussions of structures, . . . it will therefore not be possible to reach a consensus on this subject." The minister concluded by suggesting that, since the various opinions and views of the participants were on record, any provincial government or governments could make "representations" on this matter to him and, therefore, the council should cease discussing the new proposals and "concentrate our efforts on the prime objective of Advisory Council which is the working out of recommendations for uniform regulations."

Given this explicit instruction by the minister of transport, the reaction of the council is curious. It did not, as instructed, "adjourn" its discussions on the Nova Scotia proposal but instead proceeded to find a means of circumventing the minister's statement. The council focused on the third item in the terms of reference, namely, that it was "to make a joint assessment of proposals made to date, including the Ontario proposal." Although the federal chairman repeatedly stated that the instructions from the minister clearly prohibited the council from studying any new proposals, the provinces unanimously argued that the Nova Scotia proposal was not a new proposal but in fact, as the Saskatchewan member stated, "on the table prior to May 3, 1971, and by the Terms of Reference given to the Council . . . it cannot be excluded." The chairman asked if what had become known as the Nova Scotia proposal was "just an expansion of what was done earlier"; the Nova Scotia delegate answered that indeed that was the case since the Nova Scotia proposal "was a part of the stand taken earlier by the provinces to allow the provincial regulatory boards to take a part in the process. The consensus of the provinces was that this would have substantial improvement over either the Ontario or the Federal proposals."

When the chairman asked each province to comment on the minister's statement and to indicate what each delegate considered to be the "scope of the Council's deliberations," individually they affirmed the view that the Nova Scotia proposal was not new but only a revision of the various proposals that had been presented prior to the May 3, 1971, meeting of ministers. It was unanimously agreed that the Nova Scotia proposal was merely an "outgrowth of the earlier concept of provincial participation."

Council agreed, however, that it could not consider what had been labelled the "regional board" proposal, as it was a new proposal. The council had managed to follow the letter of the ministers' instructions but it is doubtful if it followed the spirit. It did not confine itself to drawing up a set of uniform regulations but agreed to continue to discuss the matter of a regulatory structure. By excluding the "regional board" proposal, and by interpreting the Nova Scotia proposal in the manner suggested, the council could argue that it had in fact confined its discussions to those proposals that had been presented prior to the last meeting of ministers.

By so interpreting the terms of reference in order to include the Nova Scotia proposal, the chairman had managed to avoid the collapse of the council. This interpretation of the terms of reference was accepted by all the members of the council and not just by the provincial members. This was demonstrated by the telegram from the minister of transport to the Saskatchewan government following the Winnipeg meeting of the Advisory Council. Saskatchewan had advised the federal government that it was not prepared to continue to participate in the discussions of the Advisory Council if the Nova Scotia proposal was excluded. The federal minister's reply, sent after the Winnipeg meeting, registered his view that "excellent progress" had been made and that he hoped the Saskatchewan member of the council could continue to participate. As far as Saskatchewan's concern about the terms of reference of the council being restricted, the federal minister stated:

> I expect all Ministers assessing results of the last meeting and it may
> be that you will conclude points raised in your telegram now overtaken
> by events. I believe this to be consistent with the goals we set for
> Council in May and I would hope in the circumstances that you will
> agree to permit the representative of Saskatchewan to continue to
> participate.[33]

This intriguing reply raises questions as to the purpose of his telegram to the council.

The council's decisions required a complete rewriting of the draft report on the regulatory structure. In fact, "rewriting" is not perhaps as correct a description of what was to take place as "laundering" would be. In the revised version all references to the Nova Scotia proposal were expunged. This expunging required two drafts, one by the Nova Scotia member of the council who had been the chairman of the Council Sub-Group on Structures and one by the federal Secretariat of the Advisory Council.

In his draft report on the proposed regulatory structure, submitted after the Winnipeg meeting, the Nova Scotia member referred to the "consensus" that developed in the council "that came to be known for reference purposes within the Council as the Nova Scotia proposal." The so-called Nova Scotia proposal was an "evolution from and refinement of the Ontario Method 2 and the 8 Province proposal."[34] He was explicit in stating that his proposal was not a new proposal but "in fact, the Joint Participation proposal certified and restated in a manner that provides for acceptable participation of both Federal and Provincial representations in a decision-making process that will implement the objectives of Federal regulations." The draft report then outlined the considerations that had influenced the council in its recommendations in support of its proposed regulatory structure.

The federal secretariat of the Advisory Council was not satisfied with this rewritten draft. It included references to the Nova Scotia proposal *per se*, which were unacceptable. More importantly, the rewritten draft did not clearly establish the continuity in thought behind the Advisory Council's recommendations. The report was rewritten to omit any reference to the Nova Scotia proposal and the recommended structure was now labelled the "joint participation proposal" throughout the report. It was maintained that "the recent discussion of proposals for regulation was a continuation of earlier discussions extending over many years."[35] The revised draft documented the various proposals presented prior to May 1971 in order to establish the legitimacy of the "joint participation proposal."[36]

When the Advisory Council met again in January 1972, this revised chapter was unanimously accepted. Although there was some delay before the final version was prepared, there was little disagreement on the contents of the report which was submitted in April 1972 to the various ministers responsible for motor carrier regulation.

The Advisory Council had thus succeeded in obtaining unanimous federal and provincial agreement on a proposal to implement Part III of the NTA. The proposal called for joint participation by federal and provincial authorities on the regulatory structure. The specifics of the proposal were that the Motor Vehicle Transport Committee of the CTC should be restructured to include provincial representatives when considering an application for an extraprovincial operating licence. The composition of the federal regulatory committee would fluctuate, depending on the number of provinces involved in the application.[37] Thus, while there would be a federal nominee on the committee, who would act as its chairman, the provinces would be in a majority. One of the functions of the regulatory committee, in addition to deciding on applications, would be the making of regulations applicable to an extraprovincial motor carrier.

The Advisory Council made a number of other recommendations that resulted from the agreement on the composition of the regulatory structure. Two such recommendations were particularly important. The first was, that because of the "degree of participation by provincially nominated persons in the regulatory structure as proposed," there would be no need to separate the intraprovincial operations from the extraprovincial operations.[38] The second major subsidiary recommendation was that there would be no need for a phasing in of federal regulation.[39] The general argument provided by the Advisory Council in defence of its report was that the proposals recommended "embody the positive view that the kind of federal regulatory committee required to implement the federal objectives and successfully cope with existing problems is a composite federally appointed board composed of persons nominated by the federal authority and persons nominated by the provinces and territories and appointed by Federal Order-in-Council."[40]

It is not difficult to understand why the provincial members of the Advisory Council would recommend the acceptance of their report. The central proposal endorsed the provincial consensus position: a majority of representatives on the federal regulatory authority. All previous federal proposals had been rejected because of their failure to meet the provincial demand for "meaningful involvement" in the regulatory process. The Advisory Council report, if accepted, would definitely satisfy the provincial demand. It would satisfy it to such an extent that the provinces were prepared to have all parts of extraprovincial undertakings regulated by the proposed authority. The fact that the majority of the provinces favoured the joint participation proposal precluded recalcitrance on the part of any of the provinces.

It is more difficult to understand why the federal members of the council would concur in its recommendations. The argument provided by the federal members was that if the report was accepted, extraprovincial motor carriers would be finally regulated in terms of the policy of the National Transportation Act. As one federal member stated, "the great significance of the Report was that it was the first time that the provinces accepted the exclusive right of the federal government through the CTC and the Minister of Transport to set policy and to have the final say on all regulatory decisions respecting the whole of extraprovincial motor carrier regulation." Although the provinces would have a majority on the proposed structure, it was argued that the federal government would exercise a great deal of control over the regulators because of its power to veto the appointment of any provincial nominee by requiring appointment by federal order-in-council. The whole of the extraprovincial motor carrier industry would be regulated because the provinces had conceded to the federal regulatory authority jurisdiction over both the extra- and intraprovincial aspects. This would mean that finally the philosophy of the NTA could be implemented. Moreover, there was the overriding recognition by federal members of the Advisory Council that federal regulation could be accomplished only with provincial cooperation. Such cooperation could be attained only by conceding the provincial demand on the regulatory structure. The harassment threatened by Quebec would be avoided because it had concurred in the report. On the positive side, acceptance of the Advisory Council report would provide a pool of provincially experienced regulators at the beginning of federal regulation and, therefore, the demands on the CTC would be far less than if the federal government tried to impose regulation on its own. A final argument was that federal-provincial cooperation would mean that provincial enforcement officers would be available to facilitate immediate and effective federal regulation. Although the federal members of the Advisory Council were prepared to accept that the provincial majority on the regulatory structure was a major concession, they maintained that the benefits more than justified the compromise on the structure.

The Advisory Council appeared to have succeeded where the ministers and officials had failed. Agreement had been reached on implementing Part III with the unanimous support of all members of the council. Most remarkable in the council's success was that it had been accomplished without the discord that had characterized the negotiations on Part III. The council had been created as a means of finding a way out of the impasse resulting from the May 1971 meeting, but the polarization that had developed between the federal and provincial positions was not evident in the work of the council. This can be directly traced to the federal strategy to reach an accommodation. Although it appeared at one point that the council might collapse because of a restricted interpretation of the terms of reference of the council by the federal minister of transport, this obstacle was overcome and the result was a unanimous report. The work of the council appeared to be a classic case of the ability of professionals to succeed where politicians fail. There was much more to the resolution of the conflict than functionalism, however, as will become evident in succeeding chapters.

THE FATE OF THE ADVISORY COUNCIL'S REPORT

When the Advisory Council was created in May 1971, its terms of reference stipulated that "the Council would make its recommendations not later than April 30, 1972, with implementation to follow after full federal-provincial Ministerial review of these recommendations and in light of Federal responsibilities which exist under the law but not later than six months after the report is received."[41] The Advisory Council had met its deadline by reporting in April 1972. It remained for the responsible federal and provincial ministers to review the report to decide whether or not to implement its recommendations. In any event, it had been agreed Part III would be implemented not later than six months after the council reported.

No action was taken on the report of the Advisory Council. The deadline of six months passed without the promised federal-provincial meeting being called. There was no communication between the federal and provincial governments on the issue. There was no official rejection by the federal government of the council report. There was no attempt to implement Part III within the six months, as stipulated when the council was created. Part III was apparently in limbo. It ceased to be a cause of contention between the two levels of government because no one mentioned it.

CONCLUSION

This study began with a question: "why has Part III not been implemented?" This and the preceding chapter have sought an explanation in an analysis of the negotiations between the federal and provincial governments, employing the assumption that the governments, as parties to the negotiations, could be conceptualized as single actors. Once such an assumption is made, the analysis focuses on the interactions between the actors, concentrating particularly on their objectives, resources, constraints, strategies, and tactics. On the basis of such analysis, one should be able to assess the effectiveness of the different governments as actors/negotiators and form a conclusion about the outcome of the negotiations.

From the perspective of this explanatory model, there seems to be little mystery in accounting for the fate of Part III. Federal ineptness and provincial skill at the bargaining table account for it. The federal government's objective in the negotiations was to win provincial cooperation to effect the implementation of Part III. Accordingly, it initially pursued a strategy designed to solicit such cooperation. Despite the very successful (from the federal perspective) first bargaining session, the federal government failed to capitalize on this success. What was even more significant than the federal failure to build on its initial success was that, at the 1970 meeting, rather than continuing to garner provincial goodwill, it appeared to go to great lengths to antagonize the provinces.

The 1970 meeting was a crucial turning-point in the negotiations. The federal government's failure to follow through gave the provinces time and reason to reassess the bargaining situation. In particular, the provinces recognized that they had miscalculated the resources of the respective participants and that they were in a much better bargaining position than had been assumed. In addition, federal obduracy led to a provincial consensus on objectives and strategy. The result was that the provinces "ganged up" on the federal government in order to pursue an aggressive strategy designed to force federal concessions. Ottawa had lost the initiative and failed to regain it. The only alternative open to the federal government was to attempt to forge a coalition with the provincial "moderates" in the Advisory Council.

To a certain extent, the proposals of the Advisory Council were predictable. The two sides to the negotiations had become locked into polarized positions. The only means of breaking the deadlock was some form of compromise that recognized minimum demands of both positions. The onus was on the federal government to offer the compromise because the provinces had come to appreciate that the federal government could implement Part III only by carrying the provinces.

What remains inexplicable about the work of the Advisory Council is the successful circumvention of the direct instructions of the federal minister of transport to cease discussing the question of structure. One can only surmise that, in view of the threatened collapse of the council if its terms of reference were unduly restricted, the federal government permitted the council to complete its assignment as it had interpreted it. Yet this explanation is rather fragile considering the pains taken by the council to expunge references to the Nova Scotia proposal from the final report.

In any event, the Advisory Council presented its report only to have the issue of Part III go into limbo, if not die completely. No further consultations were held; no attempt was made by the federal government to go it alone and implement Part III. The explanation for lack of action may be that, while the federal government needed provincial cooperation, their price was too costly. Accordingly, the federal government decided not to implement Part III.

Several questions remain that challenge the strength of the unitary-actor model's explanation for the fate of Part III. First, given the recognition by the federal government of the importance of provincial cooperation, why did Ottawa fail to follow through to exploit the goodwill that had been created? Indeed, why did the federal government alienate the provinces at the 1970 meeting? The proceedings of the Advisory Council create several additional questions. Why did federal negotiators initially suggest that the Nova Scotia proposal might be acceptable when it was to be rejected? Why did the federal minister of transport send his instructions to the council and then permit them to be so transparently circumvented and with the active participation of the federal members of the council? The recognition of these questions and inability of the unitary-actor model to provide answers to them suggest the necessity of supplementing the explanation derived from the use of that model. Accordingly, another "face" of Part III is analysed in the next two chapters.

Chapter Five

The Intragovernmental Bargaining: 1967–1971

"I don't know why you would want to study this matter. It's like picking up a rotten log to see all the slugs underneath." Such was the comment of a central federal participant in the negotiations on Part III. The "slugs" to which he referred were not the difficulties encountered with the provinces. They were the lengthy and acrimonious bargaining that characterized the federal government's efforts to arrive at a policy on the implementation of Part III.

In contrast to the formalistic view we have of the monocratic nature of the Canadian bureaucracy, an alternative view is that of a fragmented power system involving a diversity of goals. An analysis of the events surrounding Part III demonstrates the utility of this conceptualization. Part III represented not a single issue for the different actors within the federal government: it encompassed many issues. In the debate that developed within the federal government on the implementation of Part III, no actor or bureaucratic unit possessed a monopoly of the resources necessary to ensure acceptance of, and compliance with, a preferred policy. The diversity of goals and the fragmentation of power compelled actors and units within the federal government to engage in strategic planning, tactical manoeuvres, and coalition-building remarkably similar to that which occurs between governments. The following analysis documents this process and demonstrates the importance of bureaucratic politics to the outcome of intergovernmental negotiations.

The first step is to identify the participants in the bureaucratic conflict, isolate the different faces of the issues as they perceived them and describe the various resources the participants possessed that were to be influential in shaping and determining the outcome of the internal bargaining. Once this stage is completed, the various manoeuvres can be detailed and analysed.

The most relevant actors were in two organizations, the Canadian Transport Commission and the Department of Transport. Although numerous persons were to play significant roles at various stages of the bargaining, the central actors were the following: J. W. Pickersgill, president of the CTC, Ray Cope, vice-president of the CTC, Laval Fortier, chairman of the CTC's Motor Vehicle Transport Committee, John Magee, a member of that committee, and A. L. Peel, the director of the Highways Branch in the Department of Transport. Despite the extreme diversity in their institutional positions, these actors dominated the internal political struggle over Part III.

There was no consensus within the federal government on the nature of the issue. Actors occupying different positions within the federal government perceived Part III in a variety of ways. Different definitions of what was at stake were influenced by conflicting personal interests as well. This diversity can be traced to the original amalgam of motives that led to the inclusion of a motor carrier section in the NTA.

When the NTA was being drafted, there were two very different interpretations of the need for Part III, interpretations that were dictated by one's functional role within the federal government. On one hand there were the economists and other officials within the transport department. For these, the NTA philosophy, which emphasized intermodal competition, for which they were responsible, required that the motor carrier industry come under federal regulation. "Part III's inclusion," according to one, "was pure logic in view of the principles in the Act which dictated that we could not leave out a major form of transport." Cope and Peel became two of the most vociferous advocates of its functional and logical necessity.

The officials involved, however, quickly realized that philosophical arguments would not convince the politicians, particularly the incumbent minister of transport, J. W. Pickersgill. Accordingly, in their defence of Part III, they emphasized more practical and political grounds. Their first argument was the threatened breakdown of the existing regulatory system, a consequence of the various court decisions and the Coughlin challenge then before the Supreme Court. Pickersgill was particularly receptive to this argument as he had been a member of the St. Laurent Government which had introduced the MVTA. That this was a major argument from Pickersgill's perspective was shown by his subsequent comment that Part III was included because "the federal government did not want, a second time, to face a legal vacuum which would require emergency legislation when, by a little forethought, Parliament could provide for such a situation."[1]

An even more overtly political reason was proffered for the inclusion of Part III. The government of the day was in a minority situation and the officials played on Pickersgill's perception of the need to mobilize as much support as possible for the legislation as a whole. The officials argued that "some of the opposition sides to the Bill could be helped by the motor carrier industry." If a motor carrier section acceptable to the industry was included, the industry in return promised to lobby for the legislation with opposition members. Winning over such a consistent opponent to federal legislation would be a major tactical coup for the government. It was thought that this could be used as an argument in favour of the obvious soundness of the legislation. Pickersgill obviously appreciated the support that the motor carrier industry in fact did give to the NTA during the legislative process, for, in his first speech as president of the CTC, he thanked the trucking industry "for their intelligent and helpful contribution to the consideration of the Bill which is now law."[2]

At the time of the decision to include Part III in the NTA, the disparities in the weighting of the reasons were not entirely understood. As far as officials were concerned, Part III was included (in order of importance) for functional, that is, philosophical, judicial-constitutional, and political reasons. For Pickersgill, as minister of transport, the ranking was the exact reverse. What in particular was not appreciated by the officials was that once the political and the judicial-constitutional arguments were no longer necessary, for Pickersgill there was no longer a pressing rationale to proceed with the implementation of Part III.

The fragility of the coalition behind the original decision to include Part III became manifest when the Supreme Court rendered its decision on the Coughlin challenge to the constitutionality of the MVTA. The Coughlin appeal had caused "panic" within the federal government because it was thought that the case was a serious challenge to the MVTA. If Coughlin were upheld, Part III would have to be immediately implemented. Coughlin was, in fact, not upheld and this decision had serious repercussions for the implementation of Part III.

For two of the orginal advocates of Part III, the Coughlin appeal was important only with respect to the timing of the implementation of Part III. This was the stance of Cope, who was now a vice-president of the CTC, and of Peel. In fact, they welcomed the decision because it gave them more time in which to plan before the federal government approached the provinces with a concrete proposal for implementation. At this point, Cope and Peel had been joined by another member of the

CTC who was to become one of the principal actors in the internal struggle. The new member was John Magee, long-time executive director of the Canadian Trucking Associations (CTA) and the individual largely responsible for persuading the trucking industry to support the NTA. Magee was appointed a commissioner and assigned to the Motor Vehicle Transport Committee four months after the commission was created. Magee had been actively courted to lobby for Part III on behalf of the NTA and naturally enough he interpreted his appointment in the context of the federal commitment to institute federal regulation of his industry. According to one official within the federal government, Magee "felt strongly that his whole purpose in being on the CTC was hooked into Part III or some form of regulation of motor carriers."[3] Thus, Magee's perceived "mission" would complement the interests of Cope and Peel.

For Pickersgill, the other remaining principal actor in the original coalition behind Part III, the decision on the Coughlin appeal produced a totally different reaction. He was now completely opposed to proceeding with the implementation of Part III. His opposition to implementation illustrates the maxim "where you stand depends on where you sit."[4] When he was minister of transport in a minority government, he was naturally concerned with obtaining the necessary support for his legislation. One method of doing so was the mobilization of the various interests affected by it. In addition, as minister, he had been convinced that the Coughlin challenge was indeed a serious one and, therefore, was cognizant of the need for an alternative in the event that Coughlin won.

After the NTA had been passed by Parliament, Pickersgill resigned from the government to become the first president of the Canadian Transport Commission, with the not unusual result that his perspective on Part III changed radically. In the months before the Coughlin appeal was decided, Pickersgill, in his new capacity, was prepared to have the commission work diligently in the event of a negative decision and he considered the early discussions with the provinces were related exclusively to preparing for the possible emergency. Once the MVTA was upheld, however, Pickersgill was not prepared to take any initiative to implement Part III. Indeed, it appeared that he was prepared to frustrate any initiative designed to accomplish this end. According to one federal official, Pickersgill regarded the discussions that followed the Coughlin decision prior to the 1969 conference as being of "a merely technical nature on how to proceed if, as, and when." It became increasingly clear to those federal officials desiring the implementation of Part III that Pickersgill regarded the "if, as, and when" as being extremely remote.

Pickersgill's opposition to Part III's implementation is understandable from the perspective of the arduous workload facing the newly created regulatory agency. Even without motor carrier regulation, the commission had a heavy workload, given its responsibilities for regulating rail and air transportation. According to one commissioner, for the president of the CTC, the overwhelming problem was the railways. Motor carriers were an unnecessary complicating factor, regardless of the philosophy of the NTA.

The reluctance of the CTC president to assume an additional responsibility supports Rourke's argument that bureaucracies are not necessarily imperialistic. Rourke argues that "there are occasions when an agency may increase its power by narrowing, or refusing to expand its scope of legal authority."[5] In support of his argument, Rourke cites the study of New York City by Sayre and Kaufman where they found that agencies "compete to avoid program assignments that are especially difficult and controversial."[6] Rourke then offers the following general explanation for the decision by agencies to opt occasionally to limit their jurisdiction:

> in the quest for power an agency's strategy has to be one of optimizing rather than maximizing its jurisdiction. Activities that have weak political support, are inordinately expensive, or that divert an agency from its essential purposes represent liabilities rather than assets from the point of view of an agency's power balance.[7]

It is the argument of this study that Pickersgill, as president of the CTC, was influenced by such considerations and that from this new perspective came his opposition to the implementation of Part III. The central premise of this analysis is that other actors within the federal government, indeed within the CTC, given their bureaucratic vantage points, did not share this perspective.

In addition to the view from the president's chair, there is a factor that must be considered for its influence on Pickersgill's definition of the problem involved in Part III. That factor was his particular "philosophy" of federalism. It demonstrates the importance of an historical dimension because Pickersgill's position on one of the important aspects of the struggle was influenced by "where he had sat."

One of the principal points of conflict within the federal government was the nature of the commitment that had been given to consult the provinces prior to the implementation of Part III. The different perspectives can be understood in terms of the continuum that Harry Eckstein proposed between negotiations and consultations: "Negotiations take place when a governmental body makes a decision hinge upon the actual approval of organizations interested in it, giving the organizations a veto over the decision; consultations occur when the views of the organizations are solicited and taken into account but not considered to be in any sense decisive."[8]

As far as Pickersgill was concerned, any attempt to permit the provinces any say greater than presenting their views on the question of Part III violated his conception of the nature of Canadian federalism. This became apparent during the parliamentary debate on the NTA when Pickersgill took great exception to a question from an opposition member about provincial consultation prior to the drafting of Part III. He pointed out that Part III was within the exclusive jurisdiction of Parliament and therefore: "If I were the premier of Manitoba or Quebec . . . and if someone in the legislature said to me, 'Did you first consult Ottawa before introducing this legislation that is exclusively within provincial jurisdiction?' I would say, 'Of course not, it is our business; it is not theirs.' I feel the same about legislation exclusively within the jurisdiction of parliament, as this is."[9]

For Pickersgill, the important determinant of the relationship between the two levels of government was the fact that the federal government did have exclusive jurisdiction in the matter. He was offended by any suggestion that the agreement to consult the provinces meant giving the provinces a status they could not possess and was quick to remind the members of Parliament of their constitutional responsibilities:

> We, after all, are the people who must decide what is to be done in
> matters which are exclusively under the jurisdiction of parliament. I
> suggest that if we are to have a country at all it is just as important
> to protect the autonomy of Canada as it is to protect the autonomy
> of any province. . . . I believe that the powers that were given to the
> provincial legislatures were given to them and to them only and
> that we should neither attempt to invade them nor take them away. I
> also believe, however, that provincial legislatures and other people
> should not try to take away from parliament or appear to suggest that
> parliament cannot exercise the jurisdiction which belongs to us
> and to us alone, in this parliament as representatives of the people
> of Canada.[10]

As far as the implementation of Part III was concerned, Pickersgill contended that "so long as jurisdiction belongs to this parliament we are the only ones who have any say how that power shall be exercised."[11] Pickersgill's interpretation of the federal commitment to consult the provinces, therefore, was a promise to solicit and consider provincial views but not, as he was to argue repeatedly and emphatically during the negotiations, to put the federal government "in the posture of asking provincial governments for concurrence in federal action."

The other major actors in the federal government interpreted the federal commitment much more in terms of negotiations as Eckstein defined them. They emphasized the importance of provincial cooperation to the successful implementation of Part III and, thus, were prepared to concede that this meant that provincial authorities would have to concur in any federal action. Their argument was that, given the importance of provincial concurrence, steps must be taken by the federal government to minimize the costs of such concurrence. This awareness of, and emphasis on, the provincial bargaining strength, was a central determinant of the strategy and tactics of the pro-Part III federal actors.

An important influence in the internal struggle was the fact that the interpretation given to the promise of consultation by the pro-Part III actors was in accordance with the prevailing emphasis within other sectors of the federal government on the trend towards "cooperative federalism." As one of the senior members of the transport department pointed out in an interview, Pickersgill appeared unaware of, or unwilling to recognize, the new provincial presence in Canada in the 1960s. It was suggested that his views were more compatible with federal-provincial relationships in the immediate post-war period. Of particular importance to the internal struggle was that the Privy Council Office was a principal advocate for this new approach, a fact that the pro-Part III actors sought to exploit.[12]

What made the opposition of the president of the CTC so important were the powers and responsibilities originally given to the CTC under the National Transportation Act. Although Pickersgill was fond of stating that he could not indicate when Part III would be implemented because it "is a question for the politicians to answer and . . . I gave up being a politician." The day of his appointment as president of the CTC, he was deliberately understating his influence on the fate of Part III.[13] Pickersgill had only ceased to be an *elected* politician.

One of the most significant features of the CTC was its extensive policy advisory role.[14] Following the enactment of the NTA, the Department of Transport saw itself as serving primarily a service or operational role. After examining a list of departmental objectives drawn up by senior officials, one student concluded: "There was clearly little conviction on the part of senior DOT officers that the Department should have a strong policy role. The Department was seen to be primarily concerned with operations and the CTC, through its regulatory and research roles, was viewed as the predominant policy-maker within the national transportation framework."[15]

A principal resource, therefore, in the hands of the president of the CTC was the power that flowed from the CTC's role as the major policy adviser to the minister of transport. The importance of the policy advisory role was recognized by the CTC, as the following comment from one of its first vice-presidents demonstrates:

> The Commission had broad powers and duties which go beyond
> the field of licensing and direct economic regulation of a single mode.
> It is required to perform all its function "with the object of co-
> ordinating and harmonizing the operations of all carriers engaged
> in transport by railways, water, aircraft, extra-provincial motor
> vehicle transport and commodity pipelines." It also has extensive
> advisory functions in support of government transportation policy, as
> well as major responsibilities for research and planning. The Com-
> mission . . . must advise on the relationship between various types
> of transport, the measures required to achieve co-ordination, and the
> financial measures which may be needed for assistance to transport.[16]

The significance of the unprecedented potential power of the CTC was recognized, for it was acknowledged that:

> The Commission has an opportunity, through its extensive powers,
> particularly in the research field, to up-date and define, within
> the limits of the general objectives laid down in the National Trans-
> portation Act, Canadian transportation policy. This contrasts with
> the former concept that regulatory agencies ought to interpret
> and administer the law, without responsibility for initiating or con-
> tributing to change where change is necessary.[17]

It would only subsequently become apparent that the power given to the CTC would permit the frustration as well as the promotion of change.

One of the important consequences of the mandate given to the CTC was the nature of the relationship between the commission and the Department of Transport. The commission, represented by the president, reported directly to the minister and not through the deputy minister. When it was first created, the deputy minister was given no responsibility for the Canadian Transport Commission. It must be emphasized that the link between the commission and the minister was the commission president, for he would be responsible for recommending any federal action on Part III. Pickersgill was correct in his suggestion that ultimate responsibility to implement Part III rested with the government and the minister of transport in particular. Nevertheless, the statutory authority given to the commission meant that it, and particularly the president and the chairman of the Motor Vehicle Transport Committee, would exercise an enormous degree of influence over Part III. That these actors were sensitive to their "territorial imperative" is suggested by the fact that in the early stages of the negotiations they felt it necessary repeatedly to remind members of the Department of Transport that it was the commission's responsibility and not the department's to advise the minister on matters covered by the National Transportation Act.[18]

The institutional power given to Pickersgill by virtue of his role as president of the CTC was not his only resource. He was recognized universally as an extremely skilful politician, well versed in the techniques of politics, in whatever arena. Moreover, he brought to the position of president the stature and personal friendships that had resulted from several decades of public service as official and minister. Because of these institutional and personal resources that Pickersgill could bring to bear in the conflict on Part III, it was readily conceded that he was a formidable opponent.

In sharp contrast to that of Mr. Pickersgill, those who sought the implementation of Part III were not in such a favourable position. Two of the advocates of implementation were Pickersgill's subordinates in the CTC. The other advocate was not in a senior position in the Department of Transport. The influence of the latter actor, A. L. Peel, would be altered when his institutional responsibilities were increased with the reorganization of the federal transport portfolio. At the outset of the internal struggle, their institutional roles were severely limited. The change in Peel's status and the related change in the role of the CTC and, consequently, in that of the president as a result of the reorganization, became evident in the manoeuvring that occurred.

The resources the advocates of Part III possessed were three-fold. There was the fact that the NTA was law and Part III was part of that law. The NTA was predicated on intermodal competition and Part III's defenders could therefore argue that without Part III, the NTA would be incomplete and inadequate as a transportation policy vehicle. The fact that Part III was already on the statute books was important because it resulted in Pickersgill fighting a somewhat defensive battle. Such a stance limited his options. The second resource was to be the demand from the industry affected that Part III be implemented. Just as the federal government was to invoke the support of the industry in its battle with the provinces, so the advocates of Part III sought to strengthen their bargaining position within the federal government by forming a coalition with the trucking industry lobby to press for implementation. The final political resource, one that was not obvious at the beginning of the internal struggle, was the high degree of skill the advocates of Part III would demonstrate in the bargaining. They were to be highly skilful in manipulating their limited resources and in outmanoeuvring, in several instances, their opponents. Of particular importance was their ability to convince other actors not centrally involved to accept their definition of the issue, with the concomitant result that they were successful in winning to their cause allies whose support they could mobilize in their battle. The extent of their skill is demonstrated by the fact that within the federal government the only negative voices came from Pickersgill and his hand-picked chairman of the MVTC. For a period during the negotiations, the advocates of implementation were able to isolate their opposition. Isolation was one thing; however, overcoming the opposition was to prove more difficult. Successful resolution of the issue was to require a complex series of manoeuvres. The same time periods as employed in the chapters on the intergovernmental negotiations will be used in this and the following chapter to facilitate the comparison that is a basic purpose of this study.

THE 1969 CONFERENCE

The president of the CTC obviously could not declare publicly his opposition to the implementation of Part III. The legislation had been premised on intermodal competition and even he was on record that "It does not seem possible to realize these objectives of the National Transportation Policy unless the extra-provincial operations of commercial motor carriers are eventually brought under direct federal jurisdiction."[19] He could attempt to ensure, however, that "eventually" was a very long time. In his efforts to do so, Pickersgill demonstrated that he understood very well the nature of what Richard Neustadt suggested was "the power which consists of sitting still."[20]

Pickersgill's first tactic was to move to defend his flank. He did this by arranging the appointment of Laval Fortier as chairman of the Motor Vehicle Transport Committee. Fortier, who had been Pickersgill's deputy minister at the Citizenship and Immigration Department some years earlier, was close to retirement and consequently it was expected he would demonstrate a lack of enthusiasm equal to Pickersgill's for undertaking what was perceived to be an extremely onerous task.

One method of "sitting still" was to not hire any staff for the Motor Vehicle Transport Committee. According to one CTC commissioner, there was "a battle royal to get the MVTC staffed up." Several times during Prime Minister Trudeau's "war on inflation," Pickersgill proposed that the CTC budget allocation for Part III's implementation, already approved by the Treasury Board, be eliminated as a "volunteer contribution" to the war effort. Although the budget cuts were not made because of the strenuous opposition from the Department of Transport, Pickersgill did win this battle. The first regulatory, as opposed to administrative, support official was not hired until 1971 and when he arrived in Ottawa he was told, according to one source, that he was "the first and last staff."[21] The tactic of non-hiring was felt by advocates of Part III to be extremely detrimental to the federal cause because, according to one participant, it "deprived the Minister of any psychological strength when facing the provinces."

Another tactic employed by Pickersgill to prolong "eventually'" was to suggest a variety of schemes for implementing Part III. No one in the federal government ever assumed that implementation would be anything but a difficult and onerous task.[22] One of Pickersgill's tactics was to emphasize the difficulties and to suggest that Part III be implemented in stages or phases extending over a long period of time. According to one observer, the president of the commission "developed totally spurious plans that were hopeless." Another source commented cryptically that Pickersgill "was a great advocate of phasing in Part III. But he wanted to start with Prince Edward Island." Indeed, at one point it appears that both Pickersgill and Fortier advocated a plan for federally drafted regulations, administered by the existing provincial boards but with the right of appeal to the CTC. This was remarkably similar to the Ontario proposal Method One, which was summarily dismissed by the federal government when proposed by the Ontario government.

It was only after the Coughlin decision, when the CTC president began to manifest his opposition to the implementation of Part III, that its advocates realized the extent of this opposition and his intent not to proceed with implementation if he could avoid it. Those who wanted implementation felt that the first priority was to fulfil the commitment made during the debate on the NTA to consult with the provinces on implementation. The main obstacle, it was now realized, was the fact that, despite the president's public posture, that "if we are to be responsive to the action of Parliament in passing legislation with a motor vehicle part in it, and responsive to the appeals from all sides that the Part be proclaimed, the Commission must move energetically and with some sense of urgency,"[23] within the commission he did not display any sense of energy or urgency. The president maintained that the discussions held during 1967–68, prior to the Coughlin decision, were only of a "preliminary, exploratory" nature. What was most important was that it was the responsibility of the president to recommend to the minister of transport to convene the promised federal-provincial conference and he had indicated no intention of forwarding such a recommendation.

The refusal of the president to recommend a federal-provincial conference resulted in the forging of a covert, informal coalition of those commissioners and DOT officials who hitherto individually had wanted Part III implemented but were now prepared to act in concert to achieve this end. The central problem faced by the coalition was how to overcome the CTC president's refusal to recommend the convening of the conference. Initially, some of the coalition considered challenging Pickersgill at a full meeting of the commission in the hope that they would gain enough votes to overrule him. It was recognized that such a course would be futile because, for many of the other commissioners, Part III was not a central enough concern to warrant a showdown with the president.

The strategy of the coalition was to circumvent the president of the CTC by employing the channels within the Department of Transport to convince the minister, Paul Hellyer, that he should call a federal-provincial conference to discuss the implementation of Part III. To accomplish this objective the actors within the federal government mobilized actors outside the government. They did this by arranging a meeting between members of the executive of the Canadian Trucking Associations with Hellyer. At this meeting the CTA discussed the difficulties that members of the trucking industry were encountering from some provincial regulatory agencies because of their support for federal regulations.[24] They argued that Part III should be immediately implemented to give the industry relief from the provincial agencies.

The tactic was successful and Helllyer was sufficiently convinced that he requested his officials to draft a memorandum to Cabinet recommending that a federal-provincial conference be called. Pickersgill heatedly disapproved of this action, according to one source, because he thought that Hellyer's ambition to be minister of housing prevented him from paying sufficient attention to being minister of transport. Pickersgill felt that Hellyer, because of his preoccupations, was letting his officials tell him what to do and that consequently he was listening "to the blandishments of the trucking industry."[25]

This successful initiative of the coalition was of short duration because Hellyer resigned from the government before the Cabinet memorandum could be proceeded with. Moreover, it initially appeared that the efforts of the coalition were doomed to failure when Don Jamieson, a long-time friend of Pickersgill, was appointed as Hellyer's successor. Pickersgill, having been alerted to the strategy of the coalition, by the meeting arranged for the trucking lobby, immediately sought to convince the new minister to avoid the issue completely. When he did so, the president of the CTC ran into an unanticipated obstacle.

In exploiting his statutory authority to advise the minister of transport directly on matters relating to the NTA, Pickersgill did so by means of "strictly confidential" letters. What he did not realize was that Jamieson was giving these letters to his deputy minister and assistant deputy minister for comment. This action by the minister well illustrates the importance of understanding the diverse interests that influence "men in positions," for one official interpreted this action as "Jamieson's way of telling his DOT people that he had advisers elsewhere but that the DOT people were his senior advisers." The significance of this participation by senior departmental officials lay also in the fact that there was no one in the ministry who was opposed to acting on Part III and, therefore, the minister was receiving advice that differed with that proffered by the president of the CTC.

The coalition was apparently successful in persuading the minister to reject Pickersgill's advice. The officials had been arguing that the federal-provincial conference should be called because failure to do so would constitute a breach of faith with possibly serious repercussions. Pickersgill naturally advised the minister not to call the meeting. Jamieson, however, accepted the advice of his departmental advisers and, particularly important, publicly committed himself to convene a conference before the end of 1969 at a federal-provincial meeting in September 1969.

Winning the public commitment from the minister was a major tactical coup for the coalition. For them, calling the conference was the first hurdle to be overcome before any action could be taken on Part III. The president of the CTC recognized that he had been outmanoeuvred. As there was little he could do now about calling the meeting, he was determined that the position adopted by the federal government reflect his concerns. Accordingly, he called a meeting to discuss the Cabinet memorandum that the minister had requested on a federal position. At this meeting Pickersgill criticized many of the individuals responsible for the minister's actions and argued that there was a conspiracy against him, particularly involving A. L. Peel and John Magee. He maintained that these officials did not understand the difficulties that he had experienced as minister of transport in getting the National Transportation Act through Parliament.

There was great difficulty in establishing the federal position for the conference. The members of the coalition argued that not enough was known about the nature of the motor carrier industry and, therefore, the conference should be problem-oriented. Pickersgill's position was that the conference should be solution-oriented and that, prior to the conference, the provinces should be sent a paper containing several specific regulatory options. In adopting this position, Pickersgill was strongly influenced by his approach to federalism. According to one participant, Pickersgill conceded that the federal government should consult the provinces, but argued very strongly that "since the power to regulate the extra-provincial motor carrier industry is exclusively federal, the federal government should not put itself in the posture of asking provincial governments for concurrence in federal action." It was, Pickersgill argued, "quite a different thing to ask for their views and have their co-operation while reserving clearly, though inoffensively, the ultimate decision as to what will, in fact, be done." In terms of the specific proposal to be presented, Pickersgill argued that the administrative capacity of the CTC should not be overtaxed. This would not have been difficult, as the CTC, because of his actions, had no administrative capacity for regulating the industry. Given such staff limitations, Pickersgill proposed that the federal position should be that it would act only on international traffic and on operations between more than two provinces and then "only when absolutely necessary."

The actors favouring the implementation of Part III were obviously not disposed to endorse Pickersgill's proposal. They did not want what they considered to be "unproven implementation options" presented to the provinces. According to one participant, "attempts to agree on a solution to a problem that was not completely understood by all parties within the federal government naturally led to some disagreement" and it was argued that, if there was no agreement within the federal government, the problem would be even greater if the same approach was made to the provinces. These actors disagreed as well with Pickersgill's justification for federal action at this time. He suggested that, when informing the provinces, it should be argued that federal action was necessitated by the Coughlin case. Advocates for Part III argued that federal action should be justified on the grounds of the NTA because they did not want to give the provinces a strong argument against federal action, in view of the Supreme Court's rejection of the Coughlin appeal. The specific recommendations in Pickersgill's proposal were rejected on two grounds. First, they argued that the proposal to start with international traffic was opposed by the trucking industry which maintained that the key problems were with the provinces, not with the United States. Secondly, they did not want the federal regulation to be as restricted as proposed and they were afraid that if such a proposal was presented it might preclude full implementation of Part III. As the advocates of Part III were not yet decided on the specifics of the federal role in regulation, they did not want to limit their options prematurely.

Once again the coalition's tactics and strategy prevailed. The coalition members considered that the priority issue was to win from the provinces an acceptance of a federal role in regulating interprovincial motor carriers. They agreed with Pickersgill that the constitutional position of the federal government was unassailable but disagreed with him on the importance of carrying them along in support of the federal government. They did not regard an attempt to win provincial support as undermining federal authority; rather they regarded such an exercise as crucial to any long-term successful federal role in this area.

The coalition in favour of Part III was able to persuade the minister of transport to accept its position by emphasizing that the federal government, and the CTC in particular, did not have the necessary capacity for even the restricted role proposed by Pickersgill. In addition, it was argued that such a limited role would result in the loss of trucking industry support without advancing seriously the implementation of the NTA. Moreover, the coalition contended that a specific proposal might provoke an extended battle from some of the provinces at a time when the federal government needed their goodwill, if Part III were to be successfully implemented. A final argument was that Pickersgill's attitude towards the provinces was not in tune with current approaches to intergovernmental relations with the stress on "cooperative federalism." In support of their position, members of the coalition were able to mobilize the Privy Council Office (PCO). In advocating open-ended consultations with the provinces, the coalition actors were able to persuade the PCO that this was the best policy for that office in view of the constitutional conference to take place shortly after the federal-provincial conference on Part III. All these arguments were accepted by the federal minister of transport and the federal position for the 1969 conference was based on the tactics and strategy developed by the coalition members who favoured the implementation of Part III. Once again, the coalition had managed to out-bargain the president of the CTC.

The 1970 Conference

Given the predispositions of the various actors that preceded the 1969 conference, the divergent assessments of that conference were predictable. To members of the CTC-DOT coalition, the conference was a complete success. The federal government had taken the first, and the most difficult, step towards the implementation of Part III. The results of the conference were seen as a complete vindication of the strategy and tactics they had advocated, for the provinces had left the conference apparently predisposed to cooperating with the federal government. For secondary actors in the negotiations, such as the Privy Council Office, the conference was a double success because provincial cooperation had been won without any negative spill-over for the impending second meeting of the constitutional review. The satisfaction with the conference results felt by the PCO was important for the coalition in another important respect. Apparently it convinced the PCO that, of the contending factions within the federal government on the issue, the coalition favouring implementation of Part III seemed to be the more in tune with PCO thinking on federal-provincial relations. The goodwill that was thus engendered was to be important in later stages in the negotiations within the federal government.

The president of the CTC did not share this assessment of the conference. He had been so opposed to the calling of, and the federal strategy for, the conference that he had refused to attend, dispatching one of his vice-presidents as his representative. His constitutional "sensibilities" had been offended by federal behaviour at the conference, for it elevated the provinces to a status to which they were not entitled. As far as Pickersgill was concerned, such an approach to the provinces could only be disastrous to the federal government and, indeed, to good government in general, in Canada.

There was obviously more than offended "sensibilities" in Pickersgill's reaction to the conference. Now that the process of consultation had begun, he was extremely concerned that, with the federal government publicly committed to acting on Part III, and the provinces apparently prepared to cooperate in this endeavour, matters might get out of hand, and he could lose complete control of the situation. He had been out-manoeuvred twice by the pro-Part III coalition and he was now determined that that would not happen again. It was still the responsibility of the CTC to advise the minister with respect to implementation and Pickersgill was the official link between the commission and the minister. Henceforth, he sought to make his approach to implementation dominant within the federal government.

Immediately following the 1969 conference, Pickersgill exercised his prerogative to advise the minister. He recommended that Part III be proclaimed into force immediately and that federal regulation be introduced for international motor carrier operations and only for this segment of the industry for the near future. The third aspect of his recommendation was that the provinces be informed of the federal government's decision regarding implementation. Finally, he recommended that the Joint Technical Committee be reconvened to complete the consultative process that had been promised. As far as Pickersgill was concerned, given federal responsibility, there could be no question of consulting with the provinces. It was enough to inform them in advance of the federal government's decision to satisfy the federal commitment.

Naturally, there was considerable consternation caused by this set of recommendations. The only one that was acceptable was that pertaining to immediate proclamation. But even this act was interpreted differently. For the members of the coalition, proclamation was to be another signal for the provinces of the federal government's firm resolve to act. As for the other recommendations, the pro-Part III actors were convinced that, if followed, they would result in the maximum of confusion and uncertainty for the motor carrier industry and a loss of provincial goodwill that had been so assiduously cultivated.

The coalition members believed that the arguments they had advanced against Pickersgill's pre-1969 conference strategy were still valid, if not more so than before, given the success of the meeting. To start with, the international traffic would only alienate the Canadian Trucking Associations. Moreover, if the industry learned of Pickersgill's proposal to limit federal regulation of this segment, the federal government could conceivably completely lose industry support.[26]

There was also concern about the effect of Pickersgill's recommendations on provincial perceptions of the federal government. It was argued by coalition members that the objective of the federal government at the conference had been to win the active cooperation of the provinces and that this had been satisfied. If the federal government turned around after the conference and simply informed the provinces of the federal intent to implement international regulation, the provinces might interpret this as evidence that the federal government was acting on a plan determined well in advance of the conference.

Advocates of implementation presented, with the support of the deputy minister, a set of counter-proposals to the minister of transport. They argued that it was premature "to make an announcement on the minor part of the regulatory problem and leave the balance up in the air." Although they agreed with the recommended immediate proclamation of Part III, they maintained that the next meeting of the Joint Technical Committee should be held only after the Ontario proposal had been subjected to an intensive analysis within the federal government. It could then be convincingly explained why it was not acceptable. Furthermore, such an explanation should be supplemented by a draft set of regulations and a statement of the regulatory philosophy of NTA, to which the provinces would have to respond. In addition, a federal plan for implementation, setting out a phasing timetable for the regulation of all international and interprovincial operations, should be presented to the provinces for their comments. The central argument of the pro-Part III actors was that there should be no meeting with the provinces before a detailed counter-proposal had been drafted and agreed upon within the federal government.

When Pickersgill realized that the minister had received a set of counter-proposals from senior ministry officials, he sought to make some concessions in his original recommendations which, while not fundamentally distorting his objectives, might appease some of the advocates of Part III. His new recommendations included the right to appeal directly to the minister of transport on decisions of provincial transport boards for those carriers which would continue to be regulated by the provincial agencies. The second concession was that the provinces could be invited to a federal-provincial conference where federal plans would be discussed, although Pickersgill did not suggest a purpose for the discussion, other than to inform the provincial representatives in person, rather than through the mail.

What Pickersgill did not realize at the time of his revised recommendations was that once again he was being outmanoeuvred. On the day that Pickersgill was submitting his revised set of proposals, an order-in-council had been passed proclaiming Part III into force on May 15. That the president of the CTC was unaware of this action is indicative of the extent of the dispute and the strained relations within the federal government. It is also indicative that nominal subordinates can bypass normal hierarchical channels in order to accomplish their objectives.

On April 30, 1970, the minister of transport asked Cabinet to pass the necessary order-in-council proclaiming Part III into force. This was approved and done on May 5, the day that the president of the CTC submitted his revised proposal. According to several participants in this episode, the pro-Part III actors were convinced that Pickersgill was determined to frustrate any attempt to act on the commitment of the federal government given by the minister of transport to the provinces at the 1969 conference. In the words of one participant, "we had an endless series of meetings and it became apparent that we were not going anywhere because of strict rules from Pick." Apparently, his position was that proclamation should not take place until a plan of implementation had been approved. By this, he meant *his* plan of implementation. Until a plan acceptable to him was proposed, he would not recommend proclamation to the minister.

In view of his opposition, the recommendation that the order-in-council be proceeded with was routed through the vice-president of the CTC to the minister of transport, who was not informed of Pickersgill's objections. The order-in-council, according to one of the actors, was "deliberately kept away from Pickersgill." When informed of what had transpired, Pickersgill was indignant and furious and complained bitterly to the minister of transport. Given that proclamation had been announced, there was little that the minister could do but attempt to assuage Pickersgill's feelings. Accordingly, he instructed the deputy minister to write Pickersgill a letter saying that a mistake had been made and that they were sorry that things "had got fouled up." According to one participant, the only thing the deputy minister did not write was "a P. S. saying, 'Sorry Pick, but this was the only way we could do it'."

Not satisfied with the apology, Pickersgill struck back in an attempt to upset the momentum towards implementation. He instructed the vice-president responsible for the legal affairs of the commission to determine whether there were any legal impediments facing the implementation of Part III, so that, if there were any, legislative changes necessary before implementation could be undertaken. That the president of the CTC would wait almost three years after the commission had been created before ordering such a study is indicative of his reluctance to proceed with implementation. Unfortunately for Pickersgill's cause, the vice-president reported that while there were some "serious legal and administrative problems to be resolved . . . Part III does not contain any defect which could be termed fatal."

Proclamation having been accomplished and Part III not open to challenge, Pickersgill acceded to the request from the minister of transport that a task force of CTC, DOT, and PCO officials undertake the necessary analysis of the Ontario proposal. The task force unanimously rejected both methods of the proposal. In addition to assessing the Ontario proposal, the task force was able to agree on a set of draft regulations prepared by officials of the CTC.

Thus, three of the stages of the course of action advocated by pro-Part III coalition had been accomplished. Part III had been proclaimed, the intensive criticism of the Ontario proposal had been completed, and a draft set of regulations produced. It was with respect to the fourth stage, the drafting of a federal counter-proposal setting out the timetable for implementation of Part III, that difficulties developed. Before the different groups and individuals within the federal government could address themselves to this, the most contentious issue, the provinces demanded that the Joint Technical Committee be reconvened.

The decision to accede to the provincial demand was a serious and, ultimately, costly tactical error by the federal government. The provinces, after the 1969 conference, had taken the initial step towards adopting a common position on Part III. The matter had been discussed at the annual Canadian Conference of Motor Transport Authorities, the association of provincial regulators, and at the annual conference of provincial ministers responsible for motor vehicle administration. The demand for the reconvening of the Joint Technical Committee came from the latter body. At these various meetings, the provincial authorities had begun to reassess their respective strategies to discuss the tactical merit of a common front. The basis for such a front was apparent in the responses of seven of the provinces to the Ontario proposal. All the responses supported, at least in principle, the Ontario demand for provincial participation in the federal regulatory process.

Within the federal government no comparable degree of consensus existed. Agreement was possible on what was not acceptable, the Ontario proposal, but not on the much more difficult and important issue of the federal counter-proposal. The federal government had been warned by a trucking industry official that "if nothing definite comes out of the meeting the provinces will be in a stronger position than ever." Yet agreement on a specific proposal for the implementation of Part III was not attained. All the federal actors could agree on was a general "philosophical" position. "It was agreed," according to one participant, "that the federal position at the conference would be, very simply, that regulation of extra-provincial motor carriers was to take place under Part III of the NTA and that federal officials had no mandate to go beyond that position." Other than on this general position, the federal government had, as the chairman of the Joint Technical Committee, the vice-president of the CTC, was to insist at the meeting, "an open mind." Such a posture of openness was the result more of the federal failure to make up the federal mind rather than of a philosophical or strategic preference for a conciliatory attitude.

The results of the November 1970 meeting of the Joint Technical Committee were described in detail in chapter 3. Federal behaviour can only be understood when it is appreciated that the president of the CTC was directly responsible for the strategy and the posture of the federal delegation, particularly of the chairman of the committee who, alone, could speak on its behalf. Unlike the previous conference, this meeting was the responsibility of the Canadian Transport Commission and not of the Department of Transport. Pickersgill was determined that, for this meeting, his perspective and only his perspective would constitute the federal position. Pickersgill was responsible for drafting the statement of the chairman of the committee and, in particular, for the sentence quoted above suggesting that the Ontario proposal was still under active consideration when, in fact, it had been totally rejected by the federal task force several months earlier. Such a statement appeared to offer hope to the provinces but the chairman of the committee was under explicit directions from the president of the CTC not to discuss the merits of the Ontario proposal. DOT officials at the conference were "baffled" by the chairman's behaviour. It was only after the meeting that they appreciated that he was, as one member described it, "under tight rein" and had no authority to go any further than he did.

For everybody but the president of the CTC, the meeting of the Joint Technical Committee had been a clear disaster. Not only had no progress been made but, if anything, the meeting was a major setback because it was apparent that the goodwill of the provinces, so assiduously cultivated in 1969, was no longer assured. As a result of federal actions, and inaction, a degree of polarization had developed between the provinces and the federal government. How to lessen this polarization was now the central issue. How the issue was resolved was to have important repercussions not only on Part III, but also on the coalition of pro-Part III actors within the federal government.

THE 1971 CONFERENCE

The actors within the federal government committed to the implementation of Part III realized after the November 1970 meeting that they would have to act quickly if they were to salvage Part III. Accordingly, two weeks after the meeting of the Joint Technical Committee, a committee of federal officials consisting of five commissioners of the Canadian Transport Commission, including the two vice-presidents, and two officials of the Department of Transport, met to draft a federal position on the implementation of Part III. This meeting was to be highly significant because it was to be the last meeting of the CTC-DOT coalition. Subsequent events were to lead to the collapse of the coalition and to the development of an intense and protracted struggle within the federal government along straight organizational lines.

The general consensus of the CTC-DOT group, as expressed in a draft Cabinet memorandum, was that "the point had been reached where further formal meetings, discussions and consultations with the Provinces, the industry and shipper groups as to the method of implementation would not likely be productive and a specific decision and directive by the Government on the method to be adopted is required." The group then outlined four alternatives for implementing Part III for the consideration of the Cabinet:

A. Implementation of Part III to apply to all of the extra-provincial motor carrier industry as of a specified date, e.g., January 1, 1972.

B. Implementation of Part III to apply progressively to the extra-provincial motor carrier industry, e.g., January 1, 1972

101

to the trucking industry, not later than January 1, 1973 to the household goods moving industry and not later than July 1, 1973 to the motor coach industry. There are several other variations to the phasing technique. . . .

C. Implementation of Part III based on voluntary applications for exemption from the provisions of the Motor Vehicle Transport Act under Section 5 thereof, for an eighteen month period commencing July 1, 1971 with the remaining motor carriers under federal regulation effective January 1, 1973.

D. Amend the Motor Vehicle Transport Act to provide for its better use in conjunction with Part III.

The memorandum made three recommendations. The first was that one of the alternatives be chosen and the second was that the provinces and the industry be informed of the plan adopted and a federal-provincial ministerial conference be convened. Finally, the memorandum recommended that the Canadian Transport Commission immediately begin hiring the staff and creating the administration necessary to implement the plan adopted.

There were two significant features of this draft memorandum and the discussion within the CTC-DOT group that led to it. The first was a call for a show of hands to determine the support for each proposal. Proposal D, which was similar to the Ontario proposal Method One, was supported by the chairman of the Motor Vehicle Transport Committee and one of the commissioners who was a member of that committee. The two DOT officials and Commissioner Magee and Vice-President Cope favoured Proposal A, which advocated the most immediate and comprehensive implementation of Part III. Finally, Vice-President Taschereau endorsed Plan B, the second most immediate plan. Although the draft Cabinet memorandum did not identify the preferred plan the group nevertheless let it be known that the overwhelming majority favoured as complete and immediate an implementation of Part III as was possible.

The second significant feature of this draft memorandum was that it was to be submitted to the minister of transport under the joint signatures of the president of the Canadian Transport Commission and the deputy minister of transport. The significance of this feature relates to the reorganization of the federal transport portfolio that had been under consideration for the better part of two years.[27] Of particular concern for this study is the change that took place in the roles of the CTC within the transport portfolio and in the relationship of the CTC to the deputy minister. This reorganization was to have serious repercussions on Part

III because it accentuated the strained relations that were to develop between the CTC and the Ministry of Transport.

Important to the reorganization of the Department of Transport was the policy-advisory role of the Canadian Transport Commission. As noted, when the CTC had been established, it had been given an extensive policy-advisory role in addition to its regulatory responsibilities. When the task force on the DOT reorganization reported, it recommended that the CTC be stripped of its policy-advisory functions and that these be transferred to the department. According to Langford, the minister of transport appeared to support this recommendation "on the grounds that if the commission chose to exercise the full powers granted to it in this area under the National Transportation Act the intentions of the government could be frustrated."[28] Elsewhere Langford noted that "It appeared to be the view of the minister and his advisers that, to date, the CTC had not exercised its policy research role to the full extent set down in the act."[29] Critics of the CTC would contend that its actions with regard to Part III lend credence to both these criticisms. This recommendation was not completely accepted, however, in that the CTC did not lose its policy-advisory role. What was accepted was that the ministry had both a legitimate policy, and an operational function which lent considerable support to the DOT policy. Henceforth, however, the CTC was to share its policy-advisory role with the DOT. The first indication of this change, as far as Part III was concerned, was the draft Cabinet memorandum, discussed above, which was to be submitted to the minister of transport over the signatures of the president of the CTC and the deputy minister.

A second important aspect of reorganization is the change in the relationship between the Canadian Transport Commission and the deputy minister. Before reorganization, the Canadian Transport Commission had reported directly to the minister of transport. After reorganization, the CTC reported to the ministry executive, which comprised the minister, deputy minister, and senior assistant deputy minister.[30] Of particular importance, as Langford points out, was the fact that the power of the deputy minister was increased "to include the whole of the minister's portfolio. . . . The reorganization was supposed to place the deputy minister in a 'line relationship' with all of the minister's portfolio so that, in practice rather than merely in title, the deputy minister 'deputizes' for the minister in respect of the whole portfolio."[31]

The restricted functions of the Canadian Transport Commission and the enhanced role of the deputy minister are important with respect to the third aspect of the reorganization relevant to this study, the formation of the Canadian Surface Transportation Administration. One of the central characteristics of the "ministry system" is the existence of self-contained administrative units which are to perform the operational roles of the portfolio while the ministry staff concentrates on policy formation and evaluation.[32] The Canadian Surface Transportation Administration, as Langford notes, was "confusingly entitled" because "It has few operational responsibilities."[33] The functions of this administration are "policy formation, long-range planning, and specific program development for all phases of surface transportation."[34]

One of the specific areas of responsibility of the new administration was to develop policy for the regulation of extraprovincial motor carriers. Thus, what had occurred as a result of the reorganization of the transport portfolio was that the roles of the department officials and the Canadian Transport Commission had been somewhat reversed. The officials in the Highways Branch in the Canadian Surface Transportation Administration now had the official responsibility to advise the minister through the deputy minister on the implementation of Part III, and the CTC was now in the subordinate advisory position. Released from the constraints of subordination to the CTC and the need for surreptitious manoeuvring, officials in the Surface Administration responsible for Part III were quick to exercise their newly granted powers.[35]

The results of this exercise in positional policy-making were soon apparent as debate developed within the federal government on the draft Cabinet memorandum prepared by the group of CTC-Transport Department officials.[36] The president of the Canadian Transport Commission refused to send the memorandum to the minister of transport, for he was not prepared to recommend anything but a limited implementation of Part III for the immediate future. His argument was that the proposals favoured by the majority of officials were far beyond the capabilities of the CTC.

In the face of the pressure for some evidence of progress on Part III, Pickersgill submitted a recommendation drafted by himself and Taschereau, the vice-president, to the minister of transport. The basic recommendation was that Part III be implemented in stages because of "the magnitude of the task of substituting direct regulation for the existing administration through provincial boards." Pickersgill estimated that there would be at least 10,000 applications for "grandfather rights"[37] all of which would require careful examination. He outlined the difficulties facing the commission in detail:

This huge task would be necessary in addition to the regular work connected with licensing. Complex questions of fact and law are bound to arise which the Commission has the duty to investigate and determine. Complaints may be made that rates are not compensatory or are against the public interest. Hearings on applications and complaints will have to be held across the country.

Even if the establishment of the Commission was greatly expanded, it is our view that the Commission could not deal efficiently with business of that magnitude and at the same time perform all of its other duties effectively. The recruitment and training of qualified personnel before and during the various stages of implementation will in itself be a major undertaking. We could not assign any worthwhile part of our present staff to do this work without jeopardizing both the quality and quantity of other important work.

These difficulties, according to Pickersgill, dictated that the implementation of Part III must only be undertaken with the greatest of planning and care.

Pickersgill's proposal reflected his "go slow" approach. The recommendation was that Part III be implemented in the following stages to cover:

A. The extraprovincial operators which serve more than seven provinces.
B. The operators which serve more than four provinces and fewer than eight.
C. The operators which serve more than three provinces.
D. The operators which serve more than two provinces.
E. All other operators.

According to Pickersgill's figures, approximately 300 operators would be covered by Stage A, 125 by Stage B, and 150 by Stage C. The bulk of the operators, approximately 1200, according to CTC figures, would be covered by the remaining stages. Particularly significant is that approximately 900 of the remaining operators would not be covered until Stage E had been implemented. To implement Part III even under this plan, Pickersgill advocated extreme flexibility. Accordingly, the proposal submitted suggested that while Stage A could be announced before the end of January 1971, with the administration to begin January 1, 1972, precise dates for the other stages should not be set until experience had been gained by the commission over a two-year period implementing federal regulation under Stage A.

The Pickersgill proposal was clearly unacceptable to the officials in the Highways Branch of the Surface Transportation Administration. While the plan was considered to be "a step in the right direction," it was also felt that there was a long way to go. Specifically, it was considered essential that a definite timetable be drafted, stipulating the dates of implementation for each of the stages. The newly enhanced role of the Ministry of Transport officials was reflected in the minister's reply to the proposal submitted by the president of the CTC. Jamieson indicated that he had accepted the advice of his departmental advisers because he concluded:

> What we require is a detailed proposal outlining the federal position that can be sent to the provinces later this month, preparatory to a meeting to be held early in February. This proposal should include a definitive timetable for each stage of the implementation process plus a clear indication of the exact nature of the firms that would be included in each stage.

It was clear from discussions within the federal government that the Ministry of Transport officials favoured a timetable that stipulated a final date that was within two years of the first stage of implementation of Part III.

Pickersgill sought to meet the demand without placing too great a strain on the commission. Accordingly, he presented the following revised timetable:

Stage 1: (January 3, 1972)
Canadian undertakings operating in or through five or more provinces.
Stage 2: (to begin not later than November 1, 1972)
Canadian undertakings operating in or through four provinces.
Stage 3: (to begin not later than July 1, 1973)
Canadian undertakings operating in or through three provinces.
Stage 4: (to begin not earlier than January 1, 1974)
All others, including international carriers.

This was a substantially changed proposal. Rather than merely setting the starting date for the first stage, as the earlier proposal had done, the new timetable was specific on three of four stages. Moreover, the dates themselves were significant in that three of the four stages would be implemented within eighteen months after the initial stage had been started. What was not a significant change was the number of carriers covered by each of the stages. Implementing three of the four stages within eighteen months meant that approximately eight hundred undertakings would come under federal regulation. The important stage was Stage 4 which covered the remaining 1500 undertakings.

The officials in the Surface Transportation Administration argued that the date for Stage 4 should read "not later than January 1, 1974," rather than "not earlier than." Pickersgill maintained that the capacity of the commission was going to be heavily taxed by the advanced implementation of Stages 2 and 3 and that he was adamantly opposed to setting a specific target date for Stage 4. Pickersgill also was opposed to a suggestion from ministry officials that, because of the George Smith decision, Alberta be included in Stage 1. This proposal was made in an effort to win the support of the Alberta minister of highways and transportation.[38] On both issues, Pickersgill was able to persuade the deputy minister to accept the position advocated by the CTC.

The one issue on which the officials within the Surface Administration were adamant was the need to meet in some form the provincial demand for input into the regulatory process. They were responsible for the bilateral negotiations undertaken with Quebec and Ontario and were the principal advocates of the provincial demand within the federal government.

CTC members were aware of the provincial pressure for input into the commission but were opposed to changing the present situation. This was the first serious sign of the impending break-up of the pro-Part III coalition of DOT-CTC actors. Members of the CTC were concerned that the provinces would demand some form of "national board" to consider applications under Part III, with the CTC excluded from such a board. Some members of the commission also feared that the provinces, especially Ontario, might recommend that "a federal-provincial super-structure" be created that would be concerned not only with motor carriers but all modes of transport. The functions of such an organization apparently would be to consider, advise, and possibly decide the transportation needs for each province. Needless to say, the CTC was completely opposed to any suggestion for provincial participation in any other form on the CTC than through intervention on particular applications.

On the question of provincial involvement in the regulatory process, the officials in the Surface Transportation Administration flexed their new policy-advisory muscle. The apparent division in the CTC on the stages of implementation, and its general opposition, convinced DOT officials to go it alone. Their first step was to win other allies and they persuaded the Privy Council Office that any proposal to implement Part III must include some mechanism for provincial participation. The PCO did not require much persuasion as it was concerned that the meeting must avoid a major federal-provincial confrontation prior to the Victoria meeting of the Constitutional Conference. The DOT officials convinced the PCO that such a confrontation could be avoided only if the provincial demands were satisfied.

Once the officials in Surface Administration had mobilized the support of the PCO, they drafted a paper outlining the federal plan for implementing Part III to be sent to the provinces in advance of the meeting. This draft, including the proposal for a joint federal-provincial committee on motor carrier regulation, was submitted to the deputy minister of transport for his approval. Given that his own officials and the PCO had endorsed the proposal for provincial participation, the deputy minister accepted the plan and forwarded it to the CTC for comment.

The CTC had no choice but to accept the plan. The commission had failed to take any steps to include provincial participation in their implementation plan. Officials in the Ministry of Transport were convinced that some proposal to satisfy the provincial demand was crucial to the success of the conference and had mobilized the necessary support. Thus the ministry officials were able to present the CTC with a *fait accompli*, a plan endorsed by all other significant participants in the process to determine the federal position for the coming conference. Although the commission was absolutely opposed to the proposal for provincial participation, it would have to live with it. Although some attempt was made to water down the proposal slightly by emphasizing that the proposed committee would be strictly advisory and would only operate in a manner "consistent with federal responsibility in this field,"[39] the CTC reluctantly accepted the statement prepared by the Department of Transport as the position of the federal government for the federal-provincial conference.

The CTC, and particularly the president, had been required to accept two of the central aspects of the official federal conference strategy, a definitive timetable and a proposal for a federal-provincial advisory committee on Part III to aid in its implementation. Pickersgill attempted to regain at least partial control when he submitted a paper to the minister of transport suggesting a strategy and alternative tactics for the conference. Pickersgill's suggestions are important as they illustrate again his perception of the "proper" role of the provinces in this area. Moreover, his alternative tactics demonstrate that, although he may have been outmanoeuvred by the ministry officials, he was far from committed to any comprehensive implementation of Part III and would attempt to curtail any such action.

The central assumption of Pickersgill's strategy paper was that the only purpose of the meeting "was to advise the Provincial Ministers of the intention of the Federal Government to exercise a part of the administrative functions in a field in which the Parliament and Government of Canada have *undoubted and exclusive jurisdiction,* namely the regulation of extra-provincial commercial motor transport." The paper outlined some of the background to the meeting and concluded "the purpose of the meeting would appear to be to announce and explain *how* the federal government intends to proceed, not to discuss *whether* it should proceed." After discussing several courses open to the minister and various tactical problems, Pickersgill returned to his concern that the constitutional authority of the federal government must not be blurred: "Whatever strategy is followed, it would surely be very dangerous to say anything which could be construed as an indication that, under the law as it now stands, the provincial governments have any right to veto federal decisions, although the fullest possible consideration will, of course, be given to their views." Pickersgill repeatedly expressed concern with the rights and responsibilities of the federal government, which seemed almost a fundamental creed on his part, was one of the central determinants of his position on Part III. This creed, indeed dogma, had been invoked whenever the issue of Part III was raised.

Although Pickersgill was dogmatic about the exclusive right of the federal government to decide on the fate of Part III, he was far from dogmatic about whether the federal government should exercise its rights in this area. The different strategies outlined in his paper to the minister of transport demonstrated his willingness to equivocate. Four alternative courses were outlined. The first was to indicate clearly that the federal government intended to implement the plan presented. The others involved partial or complete postponement of implementation. One course proposed was that the federal government would proceed "only with stage one and re-examine the need for the other stages." The rationale for this proposal indicates the degree of concern demonstrated by Pickersgill for the philosophy of the NTA, because he suggested that some or all of the other stages might not be necessary, "if the provincial authorities could get together and agree to adopt regulations in conformity with the federal regulations applied to carriers coming under stage one." Proponents of the implementation of Part III within the federal government were convinced that the issue involved more than simply uniform regulations and that it was a question of a degree of uniformity in the implementation of such regulations. For such individuals, Part III would only be meaningful if implemented by one set of regulators, not ten, following one philosophy, that of the National Transportation Act.

The other alternative strategies proposed by Pickersgill included postponing a final decision on Part III until after the Constitutional Conference "in order to give the Provincial Governments a chance to raise the feasibility of a constitutional amendment altering the respective jurisdictions of Parliament and the Provincial legislature." Finally, Pickersgill suggested that Part III might be postponed because of concern raised by the industry about problems that might develop. This course was in part suggested because, as Pickersgill had noted, "Now that the Trucking Association is urging delay, there may not be much public support for direct federal action." Pickersgill, naturally, did not mention what part he might have played in this change in the industry's position. This will be discussed in chapter 7.

Pickersgill, it has been argued, was a determined advocate of as limited an implementation of Part III as possible. In his efforts to persuade the minister of transport, he employed many of the same arguments advanced by the provincial governments. His continued statement of the problems with Part III was successful to a degree because, as a result of his strategy paper and discussions between the vice-president of the CTC and the senior assistant deputy minister of transport, it was decided that "some additional bending may be required" if unanimous agreement could not be reached with the provinces. The "bending" options were discussed in chapter 4.

The federal government never did get the opportunity to do any "additional bending" at the conference. It is not necessary to repeat the discussion of much of what occurred at the conference. However, what must be discussed is the creation of the Advisory Council, for both the decision to agree to the creation of the council and the manner in which it was formed, were to have important ramifications within the government. Such ramifications were to affect very seriously future developments on Part III.

What occurred at the 1971 conference was an excellent illustration of what Allison called a "foul-up."[40] When Transport Minister Jamieson instructed one of his officials to draw up an agreement to resolve the impasse, the official, A. L. Peel and the head of the legal section in the ministry executive sat down over lunch with officials from Quebec, Ontario, and Saskatchewan. The provincial representatives were adamant that nothing less than a federal-provincial committee, with specific terms of reference to complete the work of the Joint Technical Committee, would be acceptable. The provincial officials made one additional demand. While they would accept a federal chairman for the proposed committee, they would not accept a chairman drawn from the Canadian Transport Commission. Provincial officials blamed Vice-President Taschereau of the CTC, the chairman of the Joint Technical Committee, for the fiasco of the 1970 meeting.

When Peel reported to Jamieson on the results of the lunch meeting and showed him the terms of reference for the proposed committee, they included the following statement: "It will be chaired by the Federal Government (strong representation was made to be chaired by the Ministry of Transport and not by CTC)." The negative reference was meant as a comment only for the minister, as part of a briefing note to inform him that some of the provinces were concerned about the CTC's role on the council. The minister, in the confusion, tabled the complete briefing note and distributed it to everyone. As a result, the negative comment on the CTC became part of the official terms of reference of the Advisory Council.[41]

The members of the CTC were furious with what had transpired, or rather what had appeared to have transpired. During the conference, the commissioners present felt slighted because Jamieson did not consult with Taschereau, the senior commissioner present. Throughout the conference, the minister consulted only officials from the DOT, including the deputy minister, the head of the legal section, and A. L. Peel, from the Surface Administration. When the terms of reference for the Advisory Council were tabled by the minister, the CTC commissioners interpreted the negative reference to the CTC as the worst example of "bureaucratic imperialism." They felt that they had been held up to public ridicule and stabbed in the back by the DOT. The ill-feeling that was created was to have serious ramifications for the negotiations on Part III. The developments following the 1971 conference are discussed in chapter 6.

Chapter Six

The Intragovernmental Bargaining: 1971—1973

The creation of the Advisory Council did not end but exacerbated the "pulling and hauling" within the federal government. The Canadian Transport Commission, bitter over what was perceived as a stab in the back by an imperialistic Department of Transport felt seriously threatened by the council, particularly after the council began its deliberations. This conflict differed substantially in two respects from the one within the federal government prior to the creation of the council. First, the informal coalition of the CTC-DOT officials collapsed and the "conspirators," as J. W. Pickersgill had described them, returned to the fold in order that a united commission could fight off what was to be perceived as a threat to its existence. The second important characteristic of this new period of internal conflict was its increasingly public nature. This aspect of the conflict had serious consequences for the fate of Part III because at least one province attempted to turn it to advantage to derail the work of the Advisory Council.

This period of conflict within the federal government is important for a number of reasons. It illustrates the limitations of the effectiveness of hierarchical controls within governments. Officials within the DOT were able to exploit their control of information on the council's activities, in conjunction with the suspect nature of the information emanating from the CTC, to circumvent direct instructions from superiors within their own department. In effect, subordinates, because of their control of information, were able to control their superiors, to a very real extent, rather than be controlled by them. This is a classic illustration of "defective hierarchy" where "the lines of control running . . . downwards are often weak and imperfect."[1]

A second important feature of this period of internal conflict was the forging of a coalition across governmental lines, as officials within the DOT sought allies in their battles with actors within their own government. DOT officials became convinced their policy objectives had more in common with those of provincial officials than with those of actors in the CTC. This intergovernmental coalition was to be an important resource which DOT officials would be able to exploit to undermine further the degree of control exercised over their activities by their superiors.

This coalition-building across governmental lines was important, given the tactical manoeuvres occurring within the federal government, as the conflicting actors pursued their different objectives. An important tactic was employed by the president of the CTC who, once he realized the direction the council was taking, sought to involve the senior members of the DOT in the dispute. As Keohane and Nye argue, this tactic of attempting "to raise the level in the government at which the issue is considered in order to reduce the scope for governmental and transnational political strategies" is not uncommon when other actors forge coalitions across governmental lines.[2]

THE ADVISORY COUNCIL: 1971–1972

Two radically divergent perspectives developed within the federal government following the creation of the Advisory Council. For the CTC, now united, the Advisory Council signified the death of Part III. Although the DOT tried to understate the difference between the council initially proposed to the provinces at the 1971 conference and that which eventually emerged, by suggesting that the "only significant difference" was that the CTC was not to chair the council, the CTC did not accept this assessment. Members of the commission regarded the council as "totally different" and unacceptable. As a result, Part III was considered dead, so much so that commissioners on the Motor Vehicle Transport Committee were assigned to other tasks and the Treasury Board was told not to worry about its staffing.

The CTC could not state publicly, however, that the council was unacceptable, because the minister had been directly responsible for its creation. In order to show commission displeasure, the president fell back on his "statutory responsibilities." In his reply to the minister's request for nominees from the CTC to the council, the president asserted that, in view of the provisions of the National Transportation Act, and especially because the commission was a court of record, "the Commission as such could not appropriately be represented on the Council and no Commissioner could serve on it, without putting us in the false position of under-taking to advise ourselves." Moreover, the president gave notice to the minister that the commission was responsible for making regulations under Part III, and therefore, "the Commission could not commit itself, in advance, to accept recommendations of another body." To indicate his lack of regard for the council, Pickersgill assigned a junior official of the commission as its official observer.[3]

The perspective within the Department of Transport, particularly that of Peel and his officials within the Highways Branch of the Surface Administration, had also changed dramatically. The only point of commonality with the CTC was the view that Part III, as originally conceived, was dead. For these officials, the cause of death was quite different from that determined by the CTC autopsy. The actors from the DOT were in the process of undertaking a fundamental reassessment of the nature of the problem. The central problem all along had been the unsatisfactory nature of the regulation by the ten provincial boards of what was now a nationally significant industry. After the 1971 conference, DOT officials still regarded the regulatory system created by the MVTA as highly inadequate. The question now was whether Part III was the most suitable alternative. For the DOT officials responsible for the Advisory Council, the answer was a definite no. They maintained that, while Part III had conformed to federal thinking at the beginning of the negotiations, it was no longer satisfactory. The major reason for this change was the high degree of dissatisfaction with the CTC. DOT officials blamed the CTC, particularly its president, for the failure to implement Part III. While remaining convinced that federal regulation was vital to the interests of the motor carrier industry, these officials no longer preferred Part III as it existed as the instrument for accomplishing federal regulation.

The DOT perspective, immediately prior to the Advisory Council beginning its deliberations, is evident in the following comment from one official:

After the 1971 meeting, the Ministry was charged with the need to chair the Advisory Council and I do not think by then we had any particular regulatory tools in mind. We had a series of objectives to be met but no particular tool. The thing pushed was not a regulatory proposal but a series of objectives . . . , we did not give a damn about the tools. We had objectives in mind plus the consideration that the regulatory structure must be acceptable to the provinces and to the industry. We have no empire to win or lose in this game as we will not be involved in the regulatory structure. . . . As far as the Ministry goal is concerned, the goal is to provide a regulatory environment to meet the NTA objectives. It does not matter what the tool is.

115

There were, thus, two elements of the position of the DOT officials that were to be important to future developments on Part III. The first was the recognition, now even more reinforced, that provincial agreement on any regulatory framework was necessary for any successful federal regulation. The second aspect, almost a corollary of the first, was that Part III was expendable, and that an alternative to Part III would be acceptable to the federal members of the Advisory Council, provided the regulatory structure reflected the goals and objectives of the National Transportation Act as they interpreted them. The attempt by DOT officials who were responsible for the federal strategy to satisfy these objectives through the Advisory Council provoked violent disagreements with the CTC.

The members of the CTC did not appreciate the fundamental change in DOT thinking until after the council had met several times. At the second, and particularly the third meeting, the Nova Scotia proposal was discussed as a compromise.[4] As far as the CTC was concerned, the compromise decidedly did not serve federal interests as it defined them. For Pickersgill, the Nova Scotia proposal was anathema on two grounds. First, the proposal recommended sharing with the provinces a power that was, as he so often found it necessary to repeat, exclusively federal. Such a proposal offended the constitution, according to Pickersgill. Equally important, if not more so, was the threat implicit in the proposal (to use Downs' terms) to the "heartland" of the "policy space" of the commission.[5]

According to Downs, "When another social agent proposes actions affecting a bureau's interior territory, the bureau usually cannot forecast all the possible ramifications. What looks trivial today may prove to be a major threat tomorrow."[6] To the president of the CTC—and on this issue he was supported by all the commissioners—the Nova Scotia proposal was not trivial but a major threat. It was a threat because its acceptance was perceived to have ramifications for the very "essence" of the commission and not simply for the Motor Vehicle Transport Committee. If the provinces were granted a say in the regulation of motor carriers, what was to prevent them from demanding, and what arguments could be used to refuse granting, participation in other areas of commission regulation? Pickersgill's concern was not entirely unjustified, as the Ontario member had at the very first meeting of the council expressed interest in provincial regulation of rail and air.

It was the CTC observer, not a provincial member of the council, who first raised the issue of the propriety of its discussing the Nova Scotia proposal. He argued that this was beyond the council's terms of reference and, accordingly, it had no right to discuss any proposal other than the two that had been on the table prior to the 1971 conference. For the council to arrogate to itself the right to raise another proposal would be presumptuous, according to the CTC observer. Because of this public disagreement between the CTC observer and the DOT officials, the Ontario member proposed the motion that the chairman obtain the opinion of the minister of transport as to whether or not the Nova Scotia proposal was indeed within the council's terms of reference.[7] This was not the last time that the Ontario members would take advantage of what was to be an increasingly public dispute within the federal ranks.

Recognizing that the federal officials would not accept the arguments advanced by the CTC, Pickersgill sought to tie their hands by going directly to the minister of transport. He argued that the minister should instruct his officials to stop any discussion of the Nova Scotia proposal, and advanced a number of arguments in support of his position. There was the constitutional problem involved, for, by discussing the proposal, "the Council would be arrogating to itself authority to make recommendations for new legislation in a field which is *exclusively federal.*" Secondly, the Nova Scotia proposal "would be unworkable even if it proved to be constitutional and Parliament was willing to enact the necessary legislation." A third objection was that discussion of the proposal "would negate the firm position' the minister had taken at the conference that the federal government intended to implement Part III. What was particularly objectionable to Pickersgill was that the participation of federal officials in such a discussion might suggest federal acceptance in advance of any recommendations. His final objection was probably the most important. He argued that the Nova Scotia proposal was unacceptable not because of what it was but because of what it represented: "a first step towards the avowed Ontario goal of provincial involvement in air and rail regulation." This last argument would take on added significance when the Ontario government sought to play on Pickersgill's fears about Ontario's designs on the CTC.

Within the Department of Transport itself, Peel, the council chairman, was arguing that a decision to restrict the council's discussion of the Nova Scotia proposal would lead to the collapse of the council itself. His position was accepted by his superiors who consequently recommended to the minister that the council be permitted to continue the discussion on the controversial proposal.

When the council next met and the Nova Scotia proposal was discussed, the CTC observer once again registered his objections. From the discussion that took place, it was apparent that a consensus was developing within the council in favour of the Nova Scotia proposal.[8] This consensus may have been illusory because it was immediately after this

117

meeting that the Ontario representative on the council wrote to the chairman stating his concern about the direction the council was taking.[9] He requested that the council restrict itself to consideration of the drafting of uniform regulations until clearance was received from the federal minister of transport to continue the discussion of the Nova Scotia proposal.

Only a few days later the Ontario representative wrote a second letter to the chairman of the council, surprisingly different in tone and content. Rather than being concerned about the council's unauthorized direction, he was now full of praise: "The institutional sub-committee is, in my opinion, making real progress and may well come up with a model that could be used in all modes of both transportation and communication since the absolute necessity of having provincial participation in the decision-making process is becoming more and more apparent."[10] This second letter must be understood in view of the CTC-DOT conflict that was now known to the members of the Advisory Council. The letter was an obvious tactical ploy by the Ontario government for it raised a red flag for the CTC. A copy of this letter also was sent to all members of the council, including the CTC observer. It would appear that both letters were intended as much for the president of the CTC as for the chairman of the council.

The actions of the Ontario representative had their desired effect. Within the CTC, tempers were running high as a result of the council's activities and the federal chairman's role in them. The members of the CTC, including his former allies, blamed Peel for the formation of the council in the first place because they believed that the "representations" about the CTC not chairing the council came not from the provinces but from the DOT. They traced the problem back to the reorganization of the federal transport department and believed, as one commissioner stated, "the total aim of the Ministry was to advise the Minister on policy development." From the CTC perspective, Peel was one of the worst offenders and was, as one of the commissioners sarcastically described him, that "dreadful man who regards himself as a statesman." The CTC was unanimous in viewing the council as a "bloody disaster" and felt that "it was becoming a dog's breakfast."

One of the central causes of the dispute over the council's activities was the different perceptions of the issues raised. To DOT members of the council, the basic problem was how to reach an agreement with the provinces that would lead to successful regulation of the motor carrier industry. The CTC's concern was how to accomplish this objective within the framework of the National Transportation Act, especially given the mandate of the CTC under that legislation. For the CTC, the council's activities flew in the face of the NTA. What concerned members of the commission, according to several of them, was that the DOT officials were apparently ignorant of the law. They did not seem to appreciate the fact that the commission was a court of record and that the law could not be changed as easily as they were suggesting to the provincial officials. As for the Nova Scotia proposal, it was "an utterly ridiculous notion that you could create a body responsible to two levels of government." According to one commissioner, "Peel was trying to erode the federal government's jurisdiction. . . . He wanted to make his thesis come true but it was based on an ignorance of the constitution."[11] The commission believed that Peel was "leading the Minister down the garden path." It is interesting to note that in their comments, CTC commissioners were as much interested in prescribing a particular interpretation of the law, one that coincided with their objectives, as they were in presenting a "neutral" description of the law.

The president of the CTC had been furious when his initial recommendations to the minister had been rejected. When informed by his observer of the Ontario letter requesting clearance from the minister for the discussion of the Nova Scotia proposal, Pickersgill seized the opportunity to attempt again to block the council. In a letter to the deputy minister, he repeated his concern "about the formation of a sub-committee which was concerning itself with the drafting of new legislation which, if enacted, would make fundamental changes in the law." He expanded on his worry that the minister might be embarrassed, stating that "if it became known that federal legislation was being drafted by provincial officials, I can easily see certain members of the Opposition who might raise a wholly phoney issue about the rights of Parliament." His recommendation was that the letter from the Ontario member was a "perfect opportunity for putting an end to the activity of this sub-committee and urging the Council to concentrate on a set of uniform regulations." The emphasis on the drafting of regulations as the "task" of the council underscores the fundamentally divergent perceptions of it within the federal government. It was in the CTC's interests to have the purposes of the council interpreted as narrowly as possible, in order to limit the threat posed by it. Officials within the DOT naturally fought any such attempt to restrict the council.

Given that this was the second time Pickersgill had expressed his concern with the council, the deputy minister ordered a review to be undertaken by senior members of the department. The review process demonstrates the control that subordinates may exercise over their superiors. The review undertaken was dependent on information from Peel and officials within his section in the department because he was the major, if not the sole, source of information within the DOT about the council's activities. The only other source was the CTC observer on the council, but CTC information was suspect because of its repeated failure to act on Part III prior to the creation of the council.

The review undertaken consisted of two parts. The first was done by the senior legal officer of the DOT, based on a report prepared for him by Peel and his officials. The senior legal officer summarily dismissed Pickersgill's objections. He argued that the first two objections, that the council was drafting new legislation and that this was being done by provincial officials, were based on misleading or incomplete information. What was occurring was simply an exercise to determine what, if any, amendments might be necessary. Furthermore, the exercise was being conducted by a consultant retained by the council as a temporary employee of the federal government.

Pickersgill's narrow interpretation of the functions of the council was quite correctly challenged by the legal officer. He pointed out that under the council's terms of reference, as agreed upon by the ministers, it had four explicit purposes: to draft uniform regulations, to examine impact studies by either the provincial or federal governments, to make a joint assessment of the proposals made to date, including the Ontario proposals, and, finally, to facilitate the two-way flow of information. As for the propriety of the council discussing the Nova Scotia proposal, he argued that it was "squarely within the terms of reference." In any event, even if it was beyond the council's terms of reference, the official contended that it should be allowed to study the proposal on the grounds that its function was "not unlike that of an arbitrator . . . , it would seem to be the right and perhaps the duty of the Council as a good and conscientious arbitrator or adviser, to review and analyse the chance of compromise, and to advise the Minister accordingly." The overall conclusion of this review was that: "It is not considered that a good case exists for alleging that the Council has gone beyond its Terms of Reference. A real danger exists that an attempt by the federal authorities to defeat the Nova Scotia proposal through the highly technical mechanism of the Terms of Reference would be interpreted by all provinces as an act of bad faith on the part of Canada."

Three days after the submission of this report, it was assessed by several other members of the senior ministry executive, with Peel once again participating and providing the information for his superiors on the council's activities. He argued, in its defence, that even under the Nova Scotia proposal the regulations would be federal and the regulators would be appointed by the federal government. In addition, it was argued, there were several precedents for federal appointments of provincially recommended officials.[12] It was pointed out that there was a serious threat of the loss of provincial goodwill and the CTC would find "the task of enforcement of federal legislation very difficult without provincial co-operation." With provincial cooperation, the CTC would not have to recruit and train a force of inspectors duplicating those of the provinces.

On the basis of this top level review, the senior assistant deputy minister reported to the minister that: "the pros and cons of allowing the Council to consider and report on the Nova Scotia proposal would appear to be heavily in favour of allowing this initiative. The proposal would seem to have considerable structural merit, has the support of the provinces, retains total federal jurisdiction, and brings to the federal government meaningful control not now practised." The only qualification to this favourable report was that the minister was recommended to permit the council to discuss the proposal on condition that the federal participants would clearly state that the minister was not committed in advance to its acceptance.

Despite the positive recommendation from the senior officials of his department, the minister of transport instructed the council at its Winnipeg meeting to stop the discussion of the Nova Scotia proposal and "to concentrate . . . efforts on the prime objective of the Advisory Council, which is the working out of recommendations for uniform regulations." The minister had clearly accepted Pickersgill's definition of the terms of reference of the council. Why did he decide at the last moment to overrule the recommendations of his senior officials? The initial reaction of the DOT officials in Winnipeg was to maintain that the minister had not even authorized the telegram, but that it had been sent by Pickersgill over the minister's signature. The reality was somewhat more complicated than the DOT officials had imagined, although they were correct in their assumption that Pickersgill's hand was in the instructions.

The process leading to the decision can be understood in terms of Downs's discussion of the concept of "noise" in large organizations:

> fragmentalization of perception inevitably produces an enormous amount of "noise" in an organization's communications networks. The officials at the bottom must be instructed to report all potentially dangerous situations immediately so the organization can have as much advance warning as possible. Their pre-occupation with their specialties and their desire to insure against the worst possible outcomes, plus other biases, all cause them to transmit signals with a degree of urgency that in most cases proves exaggerated after the fact.[13]

121

Pickersgill was no "subordinate" in the sense suggested, but his actions from the outset of the discussion on the Nova Scotia proposal certainly correspond to the concept of generating "noise" and his motives satisfy the assumptions described.

From the moment he was informed of the council's discussion, Pickersgill's objective had been to emphasize how unprecedented and controversial such a proposal was in order to convince the senior officials in the DOT of the serious dangers involved in the council's activities. The direction the council was taking was perceived as a serious challenge to the integrity of the Motor Vehicle Transport Committee and as a threatening precedent to the CTC itself. Pickersgill's objective was to persuade the senior DOT executive that the Nova Scotia proposal was a threat as much or even more to the DOT, and indeed to the federal government, as it was to the CTC.

Prior to the Winnipeg meeting of the council, Pickersgill's remonstrances had been dismissed repeatedly because of the CTC record on the question of implementation of Part III. His demands that the minister order the council to stop discussing the proposal were viewed as "noise" that had to be answered, but "noise" nonetheless. Immediately prior to the Winnipeg meeting, however, the response of the senior officials in the DOT changed dramatically.

Pickersgill's earlier complaints about the council's activities had been in the form of letters which, once received in the ministry, were sent, in the first instance, to his chief antagonist, Peel, for a reply. Thus, by the time the question was studied by his superiors, Peel had had the opportunity to influence the response to the complaints. This time, however, Peel was already in Winnipeg when Pickersgill sought once again to reverse the direction of the council. This time he adopted a much more direct approach to impress upon Peel's superiors his extreme concern. Just before the Winnipeg meeting started, Pickersgill went over to the DOT and, in the words of one of the senior officials in the ministry, "started raising hell with what was going on."

His basic argument was that Peel had not been telling his superiors the complete story about the activities of the council. This argument was a telling one when the senior officials realized that Peel had been their only source of information on the council. What made Pickersgill's argument even more persuasive was the fact that, coincidentally, concern was developing in the DOT about the ability of Peel's immediate supervisor, the administrator of the Surface Administration. Pickersgill suggested that the administrator was not keeping Peel under sufficient control, with the result that his superiors were not being informed completely. The argument was that the administrator had lost control of a "zealot" and that this would lead to serious embarrassment for the minister.[14]

Pickersgill's direct personal intervention succeeded, strengthened as it was by the concern already apparent about the supervisory capacity of Peel's immediate superior. There immediately developed, according to one of the senior officials, "doubt in the DOT about the proposal because we had not really seen it. . . . We got a bit worried as we were in a bit of a quandary. We really did not know what was going on." Having successfully sown the seeds of doubt, Pickersgill volunteered a suggestion for correcting the situation. He drafted a telegram that instructed the council to stick to the task of drafting regulations. The panic was so great in the department that the senior officials permitted him to send it over the minister's signature.

The DOT officials on the council received the minister's telegram with considerable chagrin. Their first reaction was to claim that Pickersgill had sent the telegram without the minister's permission. Confirmation of its legitimacy by the senior assistant deputy minister only compounded the feelings of frustration. The officials were convinced that Pickersgill's objective was to sabotage the council, so much so that they even suggested to their superiors that he was acting in collusion with the Ontario member of the council to this end.[15]

An understanding of the consternation of the DOT officials at the instruction received, and their suspicions about its origin, is central to the explanation of the reception given to the telegram at the Winnipeg meeting of the council. In chapter 3, it was suggested that the reaction of the council to the minister's telegram was, at least, curious. The council followed the letter of the minister's instructions, yet interpreted its terms of reference in such a manner as to conclude that the Nova Scotia proposal was indeed within the terms. Moreover, by making a show of ruling the "regional board" proposal beyond the terms of reference, the minister's directions to the council were apparently being completely respected. As mentioned in chapter 3, the latter proposal had been rejected as unsatisfactory prior to the Winnipeg meeting and was, accordingly, a convenient and willing sacrifice. The explanation for this behaviour on the part of the council is to be found in the behind-the-scenes manoeuvring that ensued after receipt of the telegram, manoeuvring that demonstrates how subordinates can manage to evade explicit directions from superiors.

When the council meeting began on November 15, the official reply to the Ontario resolution on the Nova Scotia proposal had not been received by the chairman and, as a result, the agenda was changed to leave discussion of the structure issue until a reply had been received. When Peel left Ottawa for the meeting he anticipated that, in view of the recommendation that had been forwarded to the minister from his senior officials, a positive response would be forthcoming. On November 16, Peel received the minister's telegram and, not expecting the negative reply, he immediately telephoned Ottawa to confirm that what he had received was in fact from the minister of transport. When this was confirmed and he failed to persuade the senior officials to reverse the position, Peel had no choice but to present it to the council.

When and how the telegram was presented to the council was another matter. Although the telegram had been received on November 16, it was not tabled for discussion until the afternoon of the eighteenth, ostensibly after the rest of the agenda had been dealt with. The real reason for the delay was to permit Peel time to establish a coalition with several provincial officials and, with them, to orchestrate the council's response carefully. The coalition was possible because of the common interests of the participating actors. Except for perhaps Ontario and the CTC, no one wanted to see the council collapse, especially when it appeared that it was on the verge, after months of work, of producing a series of recommendations thought to be highly innovative. It was generally accepted, however, that if the minister's instructions were followed, the council would indeed collapse. Several provincial representatives were under explicit directions from their superiors to walk out of the council should it be denied permission to discuss the Nova Scotia proposal.

A charade developed when the council was informed of the minister's instructions, carefully planned over two days and executed by the members of the intergovernmental coalition. The chairman was adamant that his minister's directions had to be followed.[16] This was done by interpreting the events before the creation of the council, the Nova Scotia proposal, and the terms of reference, in such a way that both the minister's order and the objectives of the officials present could be satisfied. One by one, the provincial members of the coalition conceded that they should not discuss the Nova Scotia proposal but that this need not preclude discussion of a "joint participation" proposal which had been presented long before the council had been created. Since the terms of reference allowed for discussion of proposals that had been on the table prior to the 1971 conference, the "joint participation" proposal therefore could legitimately be discussed by the council. This position was then echoed by the other members of the council who had not been part of the coalition, with the result that the council unanimously agreed to obey the injunction from the minister of transport to restrict their discussion to proposals within the terms of reference of the council. Everybody was satisfied.

Everybody, that is, but the CTC observers. They were, in the words of one of the architects of the charade, "dumbfounded." They apparently could not believe that the federal officials present would permit such an obvious disregard for the minister's explicit instructions. The president of the CTC was outraged when informed by his observers of this action. Previously he had been concerned that the Nova Scotia proposal violated his constitutional tenets. Now Peel had offended the very norms of responsible government. Pickersgill demanded that Peel, "that dreadful man," be fired immediately for obvious disobedience. When Peel was not fired and it became apparent that no action was intended by the senior DOT officials to correct the damage done at the Winnipeg meeting, Pickersgill curtly informed the minister that the CTC observers could no longer take part in the deliberations of the council. They would attend any future meetings but would participate only to answer technical questions that might be directed to them.

The telegram from the minister of transport to Roy Romanow of Saskatchewan immediately after the Winnipeg meeting is evidence that the department did not share Pickersgill's view of Peel's "treachery."[17] When he returned to Ottawa, he and members of the ministry executive, including the senior assistant deputy minister, sat down to examine once again the Nova Scotia proposal and, in the words of one of the participants, "saw that it was within the terms of reference as we read them and not as Pickersgill read them." This comment actually understates the reaction within some sectors of the ministry. Senior officials were clearly impressed by the demonstration of Peel's bargaining skills. "There was," according to one member of the senior ministry executive, "a certain amount of secret glee because Pick had been out-foxed. . . . The Council pulled a Pickersgill right back on him. The Council had been quite clever in getting around Pick's objections." The skill that Peel had demonstrated in circumventing Pickersgill's manoeuvre was simply another example of how valuable personal bargaining skills can be in the game of internal politics.

Although the council was to meet once more and it was to be more than five months before its report was issued, its direction was irreversible. During the next few months, the DOT officials who constituted the secretariat of the council spent their time carefully editing the report to ensure that it was in accord with the minister's instructions as interpreted at the Winnipeg meeting.[18] For the officials in the Highways Branch of the Department of Transport, the Advisory Council was a clear victory. They were committed to implementing some form of direct federal regulation over the extraprovincial motor carrier industry. To them, the significant aspect of the work of the Advisory Council was the emergence of a consensus that provided for "participation of both federal and provincial representation in a decision-making process that will implement the objectives of federal regulation." The most important cost of this consensus was the shelving of Part III of the National Transportation Act as originally conceived. The overriding commitment for the department officials was federal regulation in accordance with the philosophy of the NTA. To achieve their objective, Part III had to be sacrificed because, as it stood, there was no allowance for provincial participation in the regulatory process. To win provincial acceptance for federal regulation, the federal officials agreed to the necessity of restructuring the regulatory tribunal to include majority provincial participation under a federal chairman.

Just as the CTC president in the earlier rounds of negotiations had not considered it necessary to persuade and bargain with the provinces on this matter, the DOT officials during the council's activities thought it futile to solicit CTC support or acceptance for the council's proposals. They acted on the assumption that they were caught between two groups of extremists. In the interests of the motor carrier industry, as they perceived them, they decided to side with the provincial officials in opposition to the Canadian Transport Commission. Where, before 1971, there had been a coalition of DOT-CTC forces arguing for the implementation of Part III, there were now, as a result of the activities of the Advisory Council, two warring factions within the federal government. The DOT officials decisively won the Advisory Council round in this "civil war." But the battle was not yet over. Although the intergovernmental negotiations were to end when the Advisory Council reported, the intragovernmental clashes were to continue as the members of the CTC fought to recover from what they regarded as the "bloody nonsense" of the Advisory Council.

THE DOT-CTC TASK FORCE: 1972–1973

CTC withdrawal from active participation on the council did not signify a concession of defeat. To the contrary, the CTC had decided that there was a greater opportunity to defend its interests within the federal government. The commission recognized that the council would recommend the restructuring of the Motor Vehicle Transport Committee but that recommendation faced a major hurdle before it could be implemented. The council was after all simply an "advisory" body to the ministers responsible for motor carrier regulation and, of the ministers involved, the position of the federal minister was crucial because he would have to recommend that the federal government accept the council's report. On this issue of federal acceptance of the report the CTC decided to concentrate its energies in a renewed battle with the DOT. In this round of conflict it would be the CTC that would be successful in mobilizing the support of powerful allies to its cause. The immediate result of the internal struggle on the acceptability of the council's report was the creation of a task force of federal officials representing the warring factions. The ultimate result would be a stalemate on the implementation of Part III.

Up to this point, the concern of the DOT actors (especially Peel) had been winning provincial acceptance of a compromise proposal, while fighting off CTC efforts to undermine their activities. During the course of the council's deliberations, Peel had given little thought to what steps were necessary to gain ministerial approval for what was obviously a controversial set of recommendations. Once this was necessary, Peel and his officials adopted a three-pronged strategy. Their first objective was to formulate a response to what were expected to be the major CTC arguments against the report. The second objective was to attempt to minimize the resistance of the CTC by proposing concessions by way of amendments to the report designed to reduce its perceived costs to the CTC. An additional function of the changes was to protect the flank of the council's supporters by providing a protective hedge against some of the more dire predictions of the commission about the consequences of the report, if implemented. While decreasing CTC resistance was a necessary condition for the acceptance of the report, it was far from a sufficient condition. Accordingly, DOT officials resorted to one of their favourite, and previously successful ploys—the mobilization of influential actors in support of the report. The most significant of the actors in this regard was the Privy Council Office.

The first step in the DOT officials' strategy was to answer some of the central CTC reservations about the report. The major repeated CTC fear was that the restructuring of the MVTC would set a precedent whereby the provinces would demand participation in the regulatory process for air and rail. The DOT response to this argument was that this fear was unjustified because the motor carrier industry was "unique in many ways among the modes of transportation that come under federal jurisdiction." It was pointed out that there are only two major airlines or railways but approximately 2700 extraprovincial motor carriers, none of which could be considered large in the sense of the major airlines or railways. A second argument in defence of the proposition that the unique nature of the motor carrier industry justified a special form of regulatory tribunal was that "in contrast to the air, rail or water modes of transport, these carriers operate over way facilities (highways) which are almost exclusively provided and maintained by the Provinces and are under provincial jurisdiction." This was particularly important because while

127

"the federal government has the constitutional power to assume direct regulation of the extra-provincial motor carrier industry, the provinces are in a position to frustrate this move due to their control over the highways in Canada." It was pointed out that one province, Quebec, had already threatened harassment if the federal government unilaterally implemented Part III.

In contrast to the air, rail, and water modes, which are almost exclusively regulated by the federal government, a large part of the motor carrier industry, that part engaged exclusively in intraprovincial operations, would remain under provincial jurisdiction. What was important about this unique feature of the industry was that there was competition between the intraprovincial and the extraprovincial operators within the same market. This competition resulted from the fact that most extraprovincial firms had extensive intraprovincial operations. Accordingly, it was argued that it was important from a sound regulatory perspective that the two regulatory systems be coordinated and that the joint tribunal would facilitate this coordination.

The final reason offered in defence of the uniqueness argument was that the motor carrier industry, the only mode now under provincial authority, was an instrument for regional development within the provinces. The DOT position was that "the social and economic objectives of Canada also depend in substantial part upon the achievement of objectives established and designed to meet provincial and regional goals." It was argued that the regulatory structure must be flexible enough "to permit carriers operating locally or within a region to respond to economic, social and geographic differences which may exist in order to provide maximum benefits to the users of the service." This objective could only be satisfied by the participation of people "especially knowledgeable in matters of local and regional importance." Provincial regulators had that knowledge, it was argued, and in addition they could provide "the Federal authorities with continuity of experience not otherwise available."

A second major CTC concern that the DOT officials sought to assuage related to the legislative mechanics necessary for establishing the new tribunal for the motor carrier industry. The central issue was whether amendments to the NTA would be required. This was an issue because, according to one official, there was "a morbid fear in the Ministry of going back to the House of Commons to request amendments to the NTA." The concern in part related specifically to the incumbent president of the commission for, as a member of the senior ministry executive explained the situation, "there was a pathological dread to opening up the NTA as long as Pickersgill was head of the CTC. He had an enormous number of political enemies. We didn't want the CTC to have to appear before the House Committee considering amendments."[19] The issue was broader than the individuals involved, however, as the following comment from a CTC commissioner indicates: "Once the NTA goes into the House, the whole thing goes up. There are M.P.'s willing and waiting for this from the West and from the Maritimes. They have an interest in freight rates and the national transportation system and not trucking. We don't see opening up the NTA right now nor does the DOT. There is too much going on politically; it's the whole Act that is involved."[20] The president of the CTC had continually sought to exploit these fears during the course of the council's activities.

To overcome this objection, the DOT officials proposed a simple solution. The council's recommendations would be implemented by an amendment to the Motor Vehicle Transport Act rather than by an amendment to Part III of the National Transportation Act. This procedure was justified on the grounds that it was consistent with the fact that the specific laws enforced by the CTC pertaining to the air, rail, and water modes are not contained in the NTA, but in various acts for the specific modes such as the Aeronautics Act, the Canada Shipping Act, and the Railway Act. A further advantage of this procedure was that it "would also serve to isolate in a separate act the concept of provincial participation in the regulatory process which is embodied in the unique structure of the proposed regulatory tribunal for extra-provincial motor carriers." Once the necessary amendments to the MVTA had been passed, it was suggested that Part III could be repealed

The second part of the DOT strategy for winning acceptance of the report was to propose several amendments that were designed to lessen its perceived costs to the CTC. The recommended legislative course of action discussed above was partly designed with this objective in mind. In addition, two specific suggestions were put forward in an effort to make the major recommendations more palatable. The first was designed to increase the discretion of the commission. It was suggested that there might be cases where "matters of truly national interest are to be decided" and that such cases necessitated a federal majority on the regulatory panel. When such cases occurred, the DOT officials proposed that the federal chairman of the MVTC "should have the discretionary power to name a panel having a majority federal representation if the nature of the case so warrants."

The second recommended modification of the report was also designed to enhance the role of the CTC. The DOT officials suggested that, given the intermodal responsibilities of the CTC and the consequent need for consistency in the regulations, the commission should retain its exclusive powers to make rules and regulations. It was recommended, however, that the commission, "act on, and be influenced by, the advice given by the newly constituted regulatory tribunal in much the same way as it acts on the advice of its present regulatory committees."

The DOT officials maintained that if the modifications proposed were accepted, the recommendations of the Advisory Council presented "an acceptable means of protecting the national interest from the federal point of view, while at the same time allowing for meaningful participation of provincially nominated persons in the regulatory decision-making process, thereby meeting the prime provincial objectives in this area."

On the basis of their rationale for accepting the recommendations and the modifications proposed, the DOT officials responsible for the Advisory Council won the support of the senior officials within the department. Within a few weeks of the report's submission and the DOT position on acceptance drafted, the minister advised Pickersgill that, with some modifications "not so far reaching or extensive as to preclude provincial acceptance of the modified plan," his officials accepted the Advisory Council's recommendations for the regulatory structure. A statement of the CTC position on the acceptability of the council's proposals, as modified by the department officials, was now required.

This statement was immediately forthcoming. Members of the commission had been studying the council's draft report and preparing a reply well before the council presented its official report. This reply went through several drafts before being submitted to the minister. Although the commission was unanimous in its conclusions, several drafts were necessary before agreement could be reached on the rationale for those conclusions. This drafting process merits comment for it supports once again a central premise of this study that bureaucratic positions affect perceptions of issues.

The first draft of the commission's report was written by members of the Motor Vehicle Transport Committee. The members of the MVTC would be the most affected by implementation of the council's recommendations because they faced a major loss in status. They would become minority members of an intergovernmental regulatory body rather than the sole regulators if Part III as it stood was implemented. Their concern over this threat was reflected in their draft reply. They argued that the recommendation to repeal Part III was outrageous because "Part III is as vital and essential a part of the Act as the creation of the CTC. The NTA without Part III is meaningless."

Members of the MVTC recognized that their case would be far more convincing if, rather than defining the problem posed by the report in parochial terms solely relevant to their committee, they defined the issues in terms of the larger objectives and interests of the CTC and of the federal government as a whole. Thus the attack on the report focused on more "global" concerns as the following extract indicates:

> The Advisory Council proposals are contrary to the letter and spirit of the National Transportation Policy. Implementation of these recommendations would not achieve the object of co-ordinating and harmonizing the operations of all modes of transport (as prescribed by Section 21 of the Act); the proposals give primacy to provincial interests over national goals and negate federal leadership in the decision-making process; the recommendations could become a blue-print for further provincial intrusion in the administration of all areas of transport.

In expanding on this general position, the MVTC maintained that one of the central reasons for the creation of the CTC was to bring together in one body all the agencies regulating the various modes of transport under federal jurisdiction. Commissioners were to be knowledgeable about all the modes of transport and regulation of any mode was to be based on an awareness of intermodal considerations. If provincial officials were appointed to the commission, it was argued that they would necessarily lack this multimodal background and "well-intentioned as they might be they would not possess the overall expertise to arrive at decisions in the context of national interests." In addition, provincial officials would be biased in favour of provincial interests at the expense of the national interests. This claim of bias was the MVTC reply to the DOT argument of the necessity to include people aware of basic provincial and regional interests: "It is the MVTC's deep-rooted conviction that provincial nominees sitting specifically because of their knowledge of regional or local problems could not in practice divorce themselves from the so-called provincial interests they will continue to serve in reaching decisions purportedly based on the objectives of the NTA."

As for the DOT argument concerning the "uniqueness" of the motor carrier industry, the MVTC quoted Pickersgill's earlier argument that restructuring of the committee would not be limited to motor carriers but "could establish a dangerous precedent directly involving every other committee of the CTC, and, possibly, other government agencies." They challenged the very rationale of the DOT position on the "unique" nature of the motor carrier industry:

> What logical arguments could be marshalled to deny the provinces the right to participate in the decision-making process of the Air,

Pipeline, Rail and Water Committees if they are accepted as bona-fide
ad hoc commissioners of the MVTC. Provincial claims in the field
of communications are already well known. Less apparent to the
general public but acutely felt by the CTC are the pressures of at least
one province to participate in the decisions of the Rail Committee.
At least two provinces, Quebec and Ontario, have indicated that
they wish to become involved in regional air policy issues.

The MVTC suggested that the DOT was being a little less than honest,
pointing to the Ontario letter to the chairman of the Advisory Council
in which it was suggested that the council's proposals might constitute
a "model" for other areas of transportation regulation.[21]

The final thrust of the MVTC draft was to emphasize even more the
potential ramifications of acceptance of the council's report. The committee questioned whether the implication of the council's rationale for
its proposals that "the provinces are more qualified than the Federal
Government to regulate matters where local, regional or provincial socio-
economic priorities are at stake" was so far reaching that it might "negate
the very principle of government under a federal system." In this regard,
the committee raised the following very pointed questions:

Is it not a fact that most, if not all federal laws affect directly or
indirectly, the socio-economic development of the provinces? Is it
not a fact the Council's argument, carried to its logical conclusion,
could lead to the balkanization of this country's interests with each
province administering at will the responsibilities and prerogatives now
resting with the federal government?

To the MVTC, the question of "a precedent-setting mechanism of joint
participation . . . is a matter of negotiation by the governments of this
nation." Such a "fundamental policy question" was clearly not a matter
for the lower level officials who had constituted the Advisory Council.
By implication, the committee was suggesting that the issue was also far
too important to be resolved within the Department of Transport but
was one that could only be resolved by Cabinet.

The draft response by the MVTC was received within the commission
with certain reservations because of the obvious parochial concerns that
had motivated some of the arguments. The president, for example,
demonstrated his continuing ambivalence on the issue of Part III by
questioning the statement that "the NTA without Part III is meaningless." He was quite happy to do without Part III and did not believe that
this was any great loss to the NTA. What he could not tolerate was

implementation of the Advisory Council's recommendations. While he agreed with the general thrust of many of the MVTC arguments, he felt that several of them detracted from the report because of their self-serving nature and that the tone of the report should be less strident. As a result, he instructed the two vice-presidents of the commission to draft the final reply in consultation with the chairman of the MVTC.

What emerged was a much less shrill document. The CTC did not argue that the very foundations of the federal government would be undermined by acceptance of the report but simply outlined what the CTC believed would be the major consequence for the federal government. The CTC maintained that implementation of the council's proposals would:

1. Transfer effective *jurisdiction* over a field in which Parliament has *exclusive jurisdiction* to the effective control of the nominees of provincial governments.
2. Confer the power to make regulations having the force of law on a body answerable neither to Parliament nor the Federal Government nor to any other government or legislature.
3. Nullify the authority vested by Parliament in the CTC under the National Transportation Act:
   (a) to co-ordinate and harmonize the operations of all carriers in different modes of transport;
   (b) to ensure that regulations of all modes of transport are not of such a nature as to restrict the ability of any mode of transport to compete freely with any other modes of transport.
4. Recognize by statute a "provincial" capacity to have majority participation in discharging a responsibility which the Courts have repeatedly held belongs constitutionally to the federal authority alone.

The hand of Mr. Pickersgill in this document is obvious.

The final CTC position was no less critical of the Advisory Council proposals than the draft prepared by the MVTC. It was only more restrained and matter-of-fact in pointing out the problems. The final position also differed in the self-restraint exhibited in recommending to the minister a course to be followed. The CTC adopted a "neutral" posture in accordance supposedly with its functions:

> The Commission, being a creature of a Statute of Parliament, did
> not feel it would be within its competence to express a view as to
> whether its functions should be abridged or nullified by new legislation,

in the manner proposed in the Advisory Council's Report, or,
indeed, whether it would be within the competence of Parliament
to implement all the Council's proposals without a prior amendment
to the Constitution, but the Commission does feel it had a duty to
point out to the Minister what the effect would be, on the assumption
that the proposals could be or were implemented.

It is obvious that, despite its modesty, the CTC was sending a clear message to the minister as to what he should do with the report.

The commission was prepared to suggest that the provincial demand
for participation in the regulatory process should be recognized but that
there would be difficulties and delays in trying to meet that demand by
amending the MVTA or the NTA. This recognition by the CTC constituted, on the face of it at least, a significant shift in the CTC position, a
necessary shift, it was conceded within the commission, if an alternative
to the Advisory Council's report was to be generated. The CTC could
not simply reject the council's proposals. Accordingly, its president suggested that the federal government should "try to meet this aspiration
within the four corners of the legislation as it now stands." To this end,
it was recommended that a CTC-DOT task force of "very senior people"
be created and that no further meetings be held with the provinces "until
the federal position has been thoroughly prepared and approved by the
Minister of Transport and an agreed strategy worked out." It was obvious to everyone within the department that one individual was not a
"very senior" official in CTC eyes. That individual was Peel, who, by
now, was persona-non-grata at the commission.

CTC rejection of the DOT position paper on the Advisory Council's
report was not altogether unexpected. Officials in the ministry had not
been optimistic that they would persuade or appease the commission.
They had incorporated this development in their initial strategy and,
when it occurred, resorted to their third tactic for winning acceptance
of the report. Their third tactic was to mobilize the support of other
actors within the federal government in their battle with the CTC. In
this regard, the most influential actor was the Privy Council Office. Peel
and his officials, throughout the negotiations on Part III, both internal
and external, had always sought to carry along the Privy Council Office
in support of their positions. In designing the objectives, strategy, and
tactics for the intergovernmental negotiations, the DOT officials had
satisfied the PCO that they were working from a "shared image" of contemporary Canadian federalism, an image that definitely was not shared
with J. W. Pickersgill. During the course of the work of the Advisory
Council particularly, the DOT officials kept the PCO informed of the

direction the council was taking and received continued indications of support. After the council reported, DOT officials discussed the question of acceptance with PCO officials and were convinced that they had their support.

Despite the fact that the DOT had been able to win the support of the PCO in all their previous battles with the president of the CTC, and were confident of doing so again, this time they miscalculated the extent of Pickersgill's resources within the federal government. The PCO informed the DOT that it was having "second thoughts" about its original, favourable position on acceptance of the report. The principal reason for this reassessment by the PCO was that Pickersgill had written to R. G. Robertson, the clerk of the Privy Council, informing him of the CTC position on acceptance of the council's report. Pickersgill then followed up on this letter with personal telephone calls to Robertson to emphasize how seriously the CTC regarded the proposals. It was as a result of these actions by Pickersgill that Robertson suggested that the Federal-Provincial Relations Section of the PCO review again the DOT paper on the council's recommendations.

When the PCO completed its reassessment, it was no longer disposed to support the acceptance of the report. The PCO challenged the council's recommendations on two grounds. Officials in the PCO echoed the CTC position when they concluded that practically every field of federal regulation affects provincial policies or regulations directly or indirectly. Therefore an acceptance of the idea of participation simply because a province would be affected by federal action would lead to provincial representation on practically all federal regulatory bodies. Such a policy would be unworkable in theory and in practice.

The PCO also appeared to have accepted the CTC argument about "a dangerous precedent" being established. PCO was well aware of provincial demands for participation on other regulatory bodies such as the Canadian Radio-Television Commission and the National Energy Board. PCO had assessed these demands and had already concluded, in the case of the communications field, that joint regulation of the type proposed by the council was "too risky to contemplate." The PCO concluded its review by suggesting that the preferred alternative was the existing system of separate federal and provincial regulation but with ample opportunity for close cooperation in policy development between ministers and regulatory bodies.

The reversal in PCO thinking came as a shock to DOT officials. On the basis of the past record of the PCO and the preliminary discussions on the report, the DOT was confident it would have PCO support and that this would be sufficient to overcome CTC opposition within the federal government. Whether the change of heart on the part of the PCO was due to the fact that Pickersgill's objections were accepted on their merits or because he was a respected official and a personal friend of Robertson is not important. The CTC, and not the DOT, could now claim the support of the PCO as an influential ally. DOT officials were dejected by this turn of events for they realized that the opposition of both organizations constituted a formidable obstacle. They decided that their only course of action was to accept the CTC recommendation that a CTC-DOT task force be created to further study the issue.

The task force created was chaired by the senior assistant deputy minister of the DOT. Despite the fact that the commission had refused to appoint commissioners to be observers on the Advisory Council, it did agree to appoint them to the task force, although it was stipulated that this was only possible because the task force's "subject matter . . . is to be proposed changes in structure and not the proposed changes in regulation." The MOT members were the "very senior officials" that Pickersgill had requested but also included, much to his chagrin, Peel.[22]

The basic position of the CTC was that the task force should attempt to satisfy the provincial demand for participation in the regulatory process but, as Pickersgill had argued earlier, strictly within the "four corners of the legislation as it now stands." The CTC strategy was to define the term "provincial participation" in such a manner as to accommodate the demand. The CTC had assessed the various provincial statements that related to this demand and argued that "provincial participation" involved:

1. The ability to determine public convenience and necessity bearing in mind both national and local conditions;
2. the ability to make known provincial goals and objectives, particularly concerning development and economic growth, within the confines of the regulatory system and not merely as a "party interested" before the tribunal;
3. the ability to partake in the development of new and modification of existing regulations for the extra-provincial motor carrier industry so that these might reflect both national and provincial thinking.

The recognition of the above as legitimate concerns of the provinces by members of the CTC was a significant change. This recognition reflected a substantial shift away from the rigidity of the CTC posture towards the provinces and towards a recognition that the provinces required and deserved a meaningful role in the regulatory process. The CTC position on provincial participation no longer was grounded in the view that "what's federal is federal and the provinces have no right to a say." No doubt one of the reasons for the moderation of the CTC position was the impending retirement of its president, Mr. Pickersgill. He was, as has been suggested throughout, an avowed "strict constructionist" with respect to the division of powers between the two levels of government in Canada. Another reason for the CTC shift was that DOT officials on the task force were adamant that recognition be given to the provincial demands.

The problem was how to reconcile the provincial demands within the framework of Part III. The CTC attempted to do this by presenting a proposal to the task force recommending that five fully staffed regional offices of the Canadian Transport Commission be created to perform much of the work of the Motor Vehicle Transport Committee.[23] Applications for new licences or amendments to existing licences would be filed at the nearest regional office. Such applications would then be forwarded to the applicable provincial regulatory authorities. The provincial authorities in the first instance would advise the regional CTC office on the merits of the application. The provincial agency would advise whether the application should be granted, denied, or modified. If the provincial agency felt that a public hearing should be held on the merits of the application, it could so advise the regional office.[24]

If a public hearing was recommended by the provincial officials, the Motor Vehicle Transport Committee, according to the CTC proposal, would appoint a panel to conduct such a hearing. The panel would be chaired by the regional CTC director and would consist of a representative from each of the provincial regulatory boards affected, if they so wished. The regulatory panel would assess the case for the application and would recommend to the Motor Vehicle Transport Committee how to handle it.

The CTC members of the task force argued that this proposal satisfied both federal and provincial objectives. Federal objectives were satisfied in that Part III would be the statutory authority with the power of the Motor Vehicle Transport Committee unimpaired. The provinces would be participating in the decision-making process, albeit in an advisory capacity. The provincial boards, in the first instance, would recommend whether the application met the conditions of public convenience and necessity. It would be the provincial agencies which would recommend holding a public hearing and, if such an inquiry were held, the provincial representatives would be in a majority on the regulatory panel considering the applications. Although such a panel would act only in an advisory capacity to the MVTC, it was argued that provincial recommendations

137

would have considerable impact on the disposition of the application.

One of the ironies of the CTC proposal was that it was remarkably similar to the proposal developed by Peel in his MBA thesis on the regulation of motor carriers in 1967.[25] Yet, despite the similarity, there was scepticism within the ranks of the DOT officials about its acceptability. Although they felt that it met federal objectives, they were concerned that while it provided a considerable advisory capacity for the provinces, this would not satisfy the provincial demand. The provinces, it was argued, wanted decision-making powers, not merely to act as advisers to the federal regulators.

Although the DOT officials were not convinced that the CTC proposal could be sold to the provinces, the task force spent considerable time over the next few months concentrating on the new proposal and how to proceed with an approach to the provinces. It was agreed that if the CTC regional proposal was to be implemented, the mistrust of the CTC felt by many of the provinces would have to be overcome. Accordingly, discussion concentrated on how the CTC proposal could be sold to the provinces rather than on the intrinsic merits of the proposal. Within the task force during this period there was an implicit acceptance of the regional proposal, despite the DOT reservations. It was recognized that the task force had been created in part because of the PCO suggestion that alternatives should be sought to the proposal of the Advisory Council. The DOT officials did not have any alternatives in mind; thus, in the absence of competition, the focus was on the CTC proposal.

Eight months after the task force had been created, the apparent consensus on the CTC regional proposal was shattered. The officials in the Highways Branch of the DOT came up with a counter-proposal. Once again the CTC members felt betrayed, especially by Peel, the principal draftsman of the new proposal. They were angered both by the manner in which the proposal was made and by its substance. According to one CTC task force member, the DOT proposal was not presented to the CTC members until 4:30 p.m. prior to a 10:00 a.m. meeting. The meeting had been planned to wind up the discussion of the task force in order to present a position paper to the minister. As a result of the DOT initiative, everything was again up in the air.

The apparent bad faith on the part of the DOT was as bad as the nature of the proposal. It recommended that federal regulation of motor carriers be limited to international carriers. Uniform regulations would be enacted under Part III, and intraprovincial operations of extraprovincial undertakings would be implemented by the provincial regulatory agencies. Interprovincial operations would be regulated by compulsory joint boards composed of officials from the provinces affected by an application. There would be a right of appeal to the CTC on any decision of the joint boards. In effect, the DOT officials were now proposing essentially the position that Pickersgill had favoured and the DOT had opposed, prior to the 1971 Federal-Provinical Conference. The earlier positions had now been reversed. The CTC was advocating the comprehensive implementation of Part III while the DOT was now supporting a drastically limited system of direct federal regulation.

There was a simple explanation for the change in DOT thinking. They argued that the provinces would not accept the CTC proposal. Peel had been involved extensively in preparations for the planned Western Economic Opportunities Conference and argued that the new DOT proposal was the direct result of his extensive contact with the western provinces. According to one source, Peel maintained that: "Without exception, the Western provinces strongly expressed the desire to have a greater say on all matters relating to transportation, particularly as these may affect Western economic development. This led us to conclude that there is much less chance of selling the plan we have been working on than we formerly believed." Peel's conclusion was that the four western provinces, as well as Ontario and Quebec, would reject the task force proposal because it assigned "what are essentially examiner powers to the provinces." An unarticulated yet important reason for the change in DOT thinking was that it was concerned that nothing should impair the goodwill the federal government hoped to create at the impending conference with the western provinces. In the federal government's attempt to "win the West," officials were anxious that nothing be done to endanger the conference or the follow-up intergovernmental discussions and activities. DOT officials were concerned not only with the apparent intrinsic defects of the CTC proposal but with the potentially dangerous spillover it might have.

Two additional reasons were advanced by DOT officials to justify their new proposal. The first was that the trucking industry was in the process of withdrawing its support for federal regulation under Part III. The lobby for the industry, the CTA, had been the main supporter of the federal government but had become increasingly disillusioned by what it regarded as callous treatment at the hands of the federal government, particularly the CTC. Shortly after the DOT presented its counter-proposal to the task force, the CTA announced the formal break with its previous position of supporting Part III. Indeed, the CTA was so dissatisfied with the federal government, that it went on record as being opposed to direct federal regulation of any segment of the extraprovincial motor carrier industry.[26] Following the CTA action, there was an amusing episode within the federal government of claim and counter-claim about which position, CTC or DOT, was less likely to antagonize the trucking industry.

DOT's final argument concerned what they regarded as the significant changes in the character of the industry since the NTA had been enacted and the concomitant need to reassess the nature of the required regulatory system. The DOT officials maintained that, at the time of the passing of the NTA, the most pressing problem had been the fragmented nature of the regulatory system involving costly and time-consuming multiple hearings before individual provincial regulatory agencies as extraprovincial firms applied for licences. It was now the DOT view that the development of the industry was not based on new applications but on "a few large carriers (perhaps less than 300 undertakings—1½% of the total) who frequently increase their operations not through the demonstration of Public Convenience and Necessity, but by acquisition and merger." According to this argument, the need no longer existed for direct federal regulation of the interprovincial motor carrier industry. The crucial problem was "the control of acquisitions and mergers, in particular those involving major undertakings that may have conglomerate, multimodal, or multinational characteristics." In this view, the CTC proposal was directed at correcting problems that no longer existed or at least were no longer so significant. The DOT officials justified direct federal regulation of international operations on the grounds that there was a need for "the regulation by a *national* Canadian body of international motor services, which might receive somewhat greater recognition by the U.S.A. counterpart—the Interstate Commerce Commission—than do the provincial bodies."[27]

The task force collapsed when the DOT presented its counter-proposal. Although it continued to operate for several months, little was accomplished. No meetings of the task force were held for two months after the DOT alternative proposal was submitted for consideration. The CTC officially objected to the Ministry of Transport "unilaterally" advancing the new proposal and reaffirmed its support for its original proposal. When the Highways Branch drafted a Cabinet memorandum outlining the alternatives, the CTC rejected it, citing seventeen instances of pro-DOT bias. The CTC rewrote the memorandum but the DOT rejected this draft on similar grounds.

The following excerpts from both drafts represent very well the conflicting perceptions of the two groups as well as provide excellent illustrations of how the protagonists sought through language, nuance, and evidence to structure the memorandum to Cabinet so as to strengthen their case and weaken that of their opposition:

DOT

The British North America Act makes no specific mention of the motor carrier industry although historically the provinces have presumed almost totally the role of providers and maintainers of highways. As these were developed and their use as a way facility for a surface mode became apparent, the provinces began to establish regulatory controls over the motor carrier industry. Every province and territory has an established motor carrier board of some variety which issues authorities to motor carriers, establishes regulations, and generally governs all aspects of the industry and the services it provides.

Taking no action to implement Part III, or to withdraw certain powers under the MVTA would perpetuate the present procedure which has many disadvantages, paramount of which are that there is no opportunity for federal policies to be reflected in the regulatory process and directions.

The new MVTC, in dealing with any particular application would form a sub-committee comprising one provincial nominee from each province and one federal nominee.

CTC

The British North America Act makes no specific mention of the motor carrier industry. Up to 1954, the provinces had presumed jurisdiction. In that year, the British Privy Council's Judicial Committee ruled that motor vehicle transport undertakings connecting a province with any other or others of the provinces, or extending beyond the limits of a province, were subject to the exclusive jurisdiction of the Parliament of Canada.

The status quo would perpetuate the present procedure which has many disadvantages, paramount of which is the impossibility to implement the national transportation policy and to harmonize and coordinate the operations of carriers engaged in different modes of transport.

. . . these provincial nominees would represent their respective provinces on ad hoc committee panels which would be chaired by a federal nominee. Under this proposal, as at least two provinces would be concerned, the federal nominee on such panels would always be in a minority.

The federal task force of officials in reviewing this proposal, recognized a number of areas where modifications would have to be made prior to its implementation: these were changes which would be necessary to protect the legal responsibilities of the Commission as granted by the federal Parliament with respect to the making of regulations; . . .

The federal officials have reviewed this proposal and have identified a number of areas where the Advisory Council's recommendations would be unworkable or would need modification. This proposal would hamper, if not prevent the Commission from discharging its responsibility, i.e. harmonizing and coordinating the operations of carriers of all modes of transport, ascertaining that regulation of one mode does not restrict the ability of another mode to compete freely, etc., at a time when inter-modal activity is developing capital in Europe and North America.

This proposal is felt to have the least disadvantages and a number of favourable aspects to its credit. It should be relatively speedy to establish, not requiring the establishment of regional offices or the recruitment of a large staff; it should have immediate provincial acceptance and it does allow for future expansion of direct federal regulation should this be desired, for example, to include all extraprovincial motor coach services. It also enables federal resources to be concentrated in the first instances on matters of greatest importance. A minor advantage is that it is somewhat closer to the industry position as reflected in a resolution

The disadvantages of proposal "B", as compared to proposal "A", are that it requires new legislation; limits the federal direct control to the licensing of international operations; appeals to the CTC, Minister of Transport and the Federal Court would be restricted to operations to be defined as international or interprovincial. . . . If it is somewhat closer to the highway carrier industry position . . . it is also in conflict with the same resolutions which opposes "direct federal regulation of segments of the interprovincial and international trucking industry, and particularly international trucking. . . ."

passed at the annual conference of the Canadian Trucking
Association in June 1973. . . .

. . . The Task Force Proposal
"B" represents a scheme that
will probably be immediately
acceptable to all the provinces
and which meets the imme-
diate pressing needs for federal
involvement while leaving the
opportunity for expansion of
the direct federal role in the
future as required.

Proposal "B" represents a scheme
which is closer to the status quo
or the Advisory Council proposals, which would make it
more acceptable to the provinces.
However, the participation of the
federal government in the decision-making is for all practical
purposes non-existent. Proposal
"B" could have as an effect to
render the CTC decision in the
international operations worth-
less as the intra-provincial operations would remain regulated by
the provinces and could therefore restrict an efficient and
necessary international operation.

The selection of an alternative
that may be rejected by the
provinces will render more
difficult the proposal of a
secondary plan. The essential
factor to be considered is "is
it the goal which is important
or the method of achieving
that goal?"

The selection of an alternative
must therefore provide for the
implementation of the national
transportation policy and the
CTC function of coordinating
and harmonizing the operations
of all carriers engaged in different
modes of transport.

It would be hard to find better evidence than the preceding to illustrate
the aphorism "where you stand depends on where you sit" or to demonstrate the significance of position to the politics of memorandum drafting.

Indicative of the fundamentally divergent perspectives of the two
groups was the fact that they could not even agree on a title for the
Cabinet memorandum! The CTC titled its draft "The Implementation
of Part III of the National Transportation Act." The DOT drafts, on the
other hand, were titled "The Regulation of Extra-Provincial Motor Carrier Undertakings." The difference obviously was not simply a question
of semantics but reflected the conflicting definitions of the issue.

Although a group of officials in the Department of Transport attempted to mediate the dispute between their colleagues in the Highways Branch and the Canadian Transport Commission, they had little success. A fundamental impasse had been reached. Officials on both sides of the dispute refused to talk to one another. Indeed, the impasse was never resolved. Before the conflicting sides could be reconciled, the minister of transport publicly announced his extreme dissatisfaction with the National Transportation Act and his intention to recommend that it be substantially revised. The revisions to date have shown no sign that Part III is a priority.

CONCLUSION

Although one observer of this struggle to determine the federal position on Part III described what occurred as "a bit of a thing between the DOT and the CTC," to others, this was somewhat of an understatement. According to one, "the relationship between the DOT and the CTC could be compared to the Russians and Chinese over the Yalu River." The geography may be wrong but the comparison is particularly apt. Although parts of the same government, the DOT and CTC decidedly did not act as members of the same team. The actions discussed in this chapter underscore the central argument of this study that the image of a government "pulling together" in intergovernmental negotiations may be highly questionable. At no time during the period under analysis was there a consensus among the major actors involved on what to do about the implementation of Part III. There was no internal homogeneity with respect to the objectives of Part III or on the means of obtaining these objectives. As a result of the diversity in goals and values within the federal government a complex political process developed, as individuals and groups of actors sought to influence the federal position on Part III in the Advisory Council and on the council's final report.

Although officials within both the DOT and CTC charged one another with bad faith, from the perspective employed in this analysis, there were no villains in this struggle. The struggle within the federal government was natural in that it was the result of different interests and values of the individuals and organizations involved in formulating the federal position on this issue. Indeed the question "what is the issue involving Part III" evoked almost as many answers as there were bureaucratic positions involved. The actors concerned disagreed fundamentally on what in fact the issue was. They sought individually and collectively to ensure that any resolution of the question of implementing Part III reflected their concerns. The result was six years of "pulling and hauling" within the federal government.

There are a number of aspects of this "pulling and hauling" that merit particular mention because of their analytical significance. In chapter 5, it was argued that the struggle within the federal government explained the breakdown of communications between the federal and provincial governments. In this chapter we have seen how the intragovernmental struggle superseded the intergovernmental conflict as the major determinant of the fate of Part III. The creation and, consequently, the activities of the Advisory Council resulted in a fundamental schism within the federal government, a schism that could not be bridged. The intensity of the internal conflict was such that one set of actors came to the conclusion that they had more in common with some of their provincial counterparts than they had with their federal colleagues. Once this mutuality of interests was recognized, the actors were prepared to enter an alliance across governmental lines to reach an agreement on implementation. This gave rise to the interesting spectacle of some provincial and some federal actors, although acting independently of one another, working to the same end—the frustration of the transgovernmental alliance. This episode suggests that, while conditions may not be as conducive to such alliances as they were in the period when program specialists dominated the intergovernmental bargaining process, students of intergovernmental negotiations should nevertheless not underestimate the possibilities for such alliances.

Another major finding of analytical consequence emerging from this chapter pertains to the apparent tenuous nature of hierarchical authority. It was apparent that A. L. Peel, despite his relative lack of seniority, was able to exercise enormous leverage within the Department of Transport. There were a number of reasons accounting for his influence, not the least of which was his skill in bureaucratic warfare. The most important, however, insofar as monitoring the activities of the council was concerned, was the fact that Peel alone was the source of information upon which his superiors based their decisions. The Winnipeg incident, from which Peel emerged not only unscathed but with his reputation enhanced, despite the fact that he had virtually ignored an explicit ministerial directive, reinforces a major contention of this study, that power may be much more dispersed than has been assumed in the Canadian parliamentary system.

Finally, the role of the PCO in the period under analysis merits comment. Far from appearing to be the all-powerful, omnicompetent actors that it has been claimed they are, the central agency officials played much more limited roles in this conflict. For the most part they were basically passive spectators in the process. When they did play a more active role, it was in the capacity of supporting actor rather than direct combatant.

Only in the denouement did the PCO become a dominant force, but it is important to emphasize that it was as a vetoer that PCO influence was felt. The dynamics of the process analysed suggests, in fact, that the capabilities of central agencies may be more limited than has been assumed, and that it is in this essentially negative role, derived from their guardian or gate keeper function, rather than in a more positive role, such as initiator, that central agency influence is greatest in the intra-governmental bargaining process. The roles of central agencies will be discussed at greater length in the concluding chapter.

In reviewing the more significant findings of this chapter, the basic purpose, as it was in chapter 5, was to assess their contribution to an understanding of the fate of Part III. It should be evident that the lack of agreement within the federal government on the issue and the internal manoeuvring that resulted as different actors sought to ensure that their interests were respected in any plan for implementation were major factors accounting for the failure to implement Part III. It would not be an exaggeration to state that, from 1971 to 1973, the struggle within the federal government clearly overshadowed the intergovernmental conflict in determining the fate of Part III. That this internal conflict continued unabated, long after the intergovernmental negotiations had ended, is testimony enough of its importance. From the analysis in this, and the preceding, chapter, it is clear that no explanation of the fate of Part III is complete without an understanding of the impact of the bureaucratic politics within the federal government.

Chapter Seven

The Role of Interest Groups: Caught in the Vice of Federalism

No one pretends Bill C-231 is perfect. Nor does anyone contend
that it will never need amending. Yet the Canadian trucking industry
should find much satisfaction in this massive piece of legislation.
In the years to come, it will have, by all indications, a profound and
beneficial effect on this industry. (February 1967)[1]

For his fair, impartial handling of the trucking industry's position
on the new legislation [Mr. Pickersgill] deserves our praise. . . .
The Canadian trucking industry has waited many years for the status
it now enjoys under the provisions of the National Transportation
Act. (February 1967)[2]

It makes one wonder if it would be possible to put in power a more
gullible, ignorant bunch of transportation illiterates than the crowd
we're stuck with now. (October 1973)[3]

The industry journals from which the above statements are extracted are
not official spokesmen for the trucking industry, but the opinions are
accurate reflections of the change in industry attitude toward the federal
government and Part III. After years of strenuous objection to the threat
of federal regulation, the industry dramatically reversed itself in endorsing Part III. This reversal was of relatively short duration. There were
several reasons for the industry withdrawal of support but the primary
reason was the considerable pressure exerted on it. In the manoeuvres
of the federal and provincial governments to "influence, bargain with
and persuade" one another, the trucking industry was a major victim,
caught in the vice of federalism.

In this chapter we analyse the role of interest groups in both the process from which Part III emerged as well as the bargaining surrounding its implementation. The chapter has two objectives. The first is to determine what such an analysis, a case study within a case study, may tell us about group interaction in the Canadian policy-making process. The second objective is much more specific. It is to test two hypotheses on the relationship between interest groups and federal structures and processes.

The first hypothesis is one common to the writings on interest groups and federalism and finds its most popular characterization in Morton Grodzins's work as the "multiple-crack" attribute of federal systems.[4] This contends that federal systems are particularly valued by interest groups because the existence of two levels of government provides them with multiple access points to pursue their policy objectives. The argument is that groups gravitate to that level of government assumed to be more receptive to their demands and the value of the alternatives presented by a federal division of powers is that groups that fail at one level can seek satisfaction from the other level of government. A related feature of group activity is the assumed ability of a group to play one level of government off against the other to group advantage.[5] Grodzins's definition of "crack" in his thesis best suggests the process. He states that in his work "crack" has two meanings: "It means not only many fissures or access points: it also means, less statically, opportunities for wallops or smacks at governments."[6] The basic thrust of this hypothesis is that interest groups value federal systems because of increased opportunities to pursue their objectives. The only qualification concerns the potentially negative impact of federal systems on group cohesion. If the group has a corresponding federal structure, it will "tend to have less cohesion."[7] Diminished cohesion weakens the ability of the group to articulate and defend its objectives.

It could be argued that federalism would be even more valued by interest groups in a parliamentary system, as compared to a presidential system, in that the fusion of executive and legislative branches, with the consequent dominance of the former over the latter, drastically limits the number of significant access points.

The second hypothesis challenges this assumption. It is drawn from Richard Simeon who concludes that the nature of Canadian federalism is such that group access becomes severely restricted when an issue enters the arena of intergovernmental negotiations. Simeon argues that the machinery of intergovernmental negotiations "limits the participation of interest groups in the bargaining process. Affected groups are not invited to participate or make their views known. The relative secrecy of debate means group leaders may be unaware of developments in federal-provincial negotiations which involve them."[8] Contrary to the assumption of the first hypothesis, Simeon concludes that group effectiveness is seriously undermined because they are frozen out of the process. Even when access may not be so severely restricted, the nature of the Canadian intergovernmental bargaining process has a further negative impact on groups because group interests "to the extent that they are less central than status or ideological goals, will be the first to be jettisoned in the conference room."[9] Henceforth, Simeon's conclusion will be described as the "restricted access" hypothesis.

To test both the general multiple-crack hypothesis and the more specific restricted access hypothesis, the role of one interest group, the CTA, in the negotiations on Part III will be analysed. Where appropriate, evidence involving other interest groups, such as the Canadian Manufacturers Association and the Canadian Industrial Traffic League, will be introduced. From the evidence, it will be argued that the multiple-crack thesis needs to be qualified inasmuch as it fails to give sufficient weight to the costs of a federal system. Such costs are of direct consequence for the other hypothesis. It will be argued that the restricted access hypothesis underestimates the important support function that interest groups may perform in intergovernmental negotiations.[10] Group support may be an important resource, with the consequence that interest groups may play a much more extended and influential role in the bargaining process.

BACKGROUND

Prior to 1966 the CTA position on federal regulation of the motor carrier industry was clear: it was fundamentally opposed. This opposition had long roots. In fact, the CTA was formed in 1937 through the actions of five regional trucking associations as a direct response by the trucking industry to a threat of direct federal regulation.[11] The industry opposition to federal regulation stemmed from its view that the federal government was railway-oriented. The industry view, and it was not far from the mark at this time, was that the railways were the "chosen instrument" of national transportation and, therefore, the trucking industry, not unnaturally, feared the federal government would exploit its regulatory powers to destroy the industry's potential for competition with the railways. As one trucking spokesman said in defence of the industry's position, "We do not intend to be lured to the smiling lips of federal control and there receive the icy kiss of death."

In view of its position, the trucking industry's actions were typical of the pattern predicted by the multiple crack thesis. With single-minded purpose, the CTA sought to ensure that regulatory responsibility rested with the provincial governments. From 1937 on, whenever national

149

transportation matters were at issue, the CTA availed itself of any opportunity to express its continued opposition.[12] Indeed, when the Supreme Court in 1951 ruled that the federal government had jurisdiction over the extraprovincial aspects of the industry, the CTA employed the judicial system to further its objectives by strenuously lobbying provincial governments to appeal the decision to the Judicial Committee of the Privy Council.[13] One of the primary purposes of such an appeal, according to an industry spokesman, was to delay the eventual outcome in order to provide the industry time to draft a motor carrier act acceptable to the industry if federal jurisdiction was upheld.

Although the trucking industry was relieved that the federal government opted for continued provincial regulation, albeit for different reasons, opposition to federal regulation continued unabated, following the enactment of the Motor Vehicle Transport Act in 1954. At the first sign of any federal interest, however diluted, with respect to their industry, truckers made certain that the federal government was aware of their position. In 1958, for example, the trucking industry emphasized that it was opposed to federal regulation because the industry feared its "perversion . . . to sustain the economic position of the Canadian National Railways."[14] Federal authorities apparently gave the industry good cause for such fears. One federal Cabinet minister was quoted as stating that "trucks are a great threat for the economic stability of the railways and should be restricted in a radius of 50 miles from cities."[15]

In the post-1954 period, however, two developments caused the industry to reassess its position. In the first place, regulation by ten provincial agencies lacked uniformity and consistency. The CTA came to argue that a "statute which told provincial boards to wear a federal hat and go away and control routes and rates" in like manner "to existing laws was an unworkable system of regulation."[16] Furthermore, the provinces were not prepared to hold joint hearings for interprovincial licence applications and this added considerably to the costs of the industry. The second factor that caused the industry to reassess its position was the fact that CTA support for provincial regulation resulted in the industry being denied access to the federal government. By turning its back on the federal government, the industry had apparently been shut out of any participation in the making of transportation policy at the federal level. The industry had no effective spokesman to present its point of view within the federal government. This exclusion began to irritate the industry for it was thought that trucking was not getting equal treatment compared to its arch-rival, the railways.

The industry responded to the problems in two ways. With respect

150

to the question of access, the industry demanded that it be given "the right to have its needs and interests considered if they are affected, or about to be affected, by a federal action in the field of transportation."[17] Recognizing that it had no hope of influencing federal policy-making if it had no meaningful access to the federal bureaucracy, the industry demanded that at least one individual cognizant of its needs and views be appointed by the Department of Transport. To the industry's satisfaction, the federal government responded and appointed such an official in 1964, the first "highway's economist" in the federal government.

Despite the gaining of access to the federal department, however, the industry persisted in its opposition to direct federal regulation. The appointment was considered absolutely crucial if the presumed historical bias of the federal government was to be corrected but the industry had no illusions that a single appointment could radically alter such an orientation. At best, trucking would now have an ear and a voice in the federal government.

The other industry problem was less easily resolved. The CTA had been attempting to encourage the provinces to remedy the problems through cooperative interprovincial actions. From 1959 to 1965, the CTA annually petitioned the association of provincial regulatory authorities to draft the necessary uniform regulations and establish a system of joint hearings. The industry requests, however, were regularly rebuffed, forcing it to look for an alternative. Having failed in its attempts to persuade one level of government to act, the CTA took advantage of the "cracks" available in the federal system and sought redress from the other level. The CTA petitioned the federal government to amend the original legislation delegating the regulatory responsibility to the provinces to require the provinces to hold automatic joint hearings and to regulate on the basis of uniform regulations.[18] It is important to emphasize, however, that the industry did not request direct federal regulation, for this was still highly suspect.

The lobbying of the trucking industry until 1965 was thus typical of the pattern predicted by the multiple-crack thesis. The CTA had attempted to exploit the federal division of powers to satisfy its policy objectives. The industry had supported that level of government which was assumed to be the more responsive to its own demands and then had sought to maintain what was viewed as a beneficent constitutional status quo. Only when this beneficence became dubious did the industry deviate from its traditional posture and then only to request the federal government to force the provinces to do what they would not do voluntarily.

PART III: COURTSHIP AND HONEYMOON

Eight months after the CTA had made its recommendations to the minister of transport, Bill C-231, the NTA, was introduced in Parliament. The contents of Bill C-231 appeared to underscore the ineffectiveness of the trucking industry lobby in Ottawa. The federal government was proposing that it undertake direct regulation of interprovincial trucking and do so as part of one agency with jurisdiction for all modes of transport that were within federal authority. Yet, despite the obvious conflict between the proposals submitted by the CTA and the content of the new legislation, the industry endorsed Bill C-231. In an appearance before the House of Commons Standing Committee on Transportation and Communications examining the proposed transportation bill, the CTA declared that "the trucking industry supports Bill C-231 in principle. The industry and its associations will cooperate to the best of their ability in the successful achievement of the National Transportation Policy."[19]

There were many reasons for this rather remarkable, not to say abrupt, change in the position of the CTA. One important factor was the philosophy of the NTA which was to be predicated on free competition between the various modes of transport. The promise to end federal discrimination towards the railways as the "chosen instrument" for national transportation policy was a major influence in CTA postures towards C-231.

More important, however, than any commitment to implement a philosophy of equal competition were several other factors. The CTA had been given "a bureaucratic embrace," an embrace at first invigorating, indeed intoxicating, but ultimately suffocating. The industry had been courted and wooed away from supporting provincial regulation by the federal Department of Transport. The change in the CTA position confirms Rourke's argument that "executive agencies can articulate as well as echo" group interests in that "bureaucrats . . . generate as well as mirror the group pressures which play so important a role in the development of public policy today."[20]

To understand why federal authorities would strive to win the trucking industry's support for Bill C-231, one must appreciate the political circumstances under which the new transportation policy was developed and introduced. The most important factor was the minority situation facing the government. The Liberal government had introduced in 1964 legislation to restructure the transportation regulatory system but this had been allowed to die, in large part because it was a trial balloon to gauge the extent and sources of potential opposition. The 1964 legislation did not include a motor carrier section.

In chapter 5, the various factors leading to the inclusion of Part III in the NTA were discussed and it is not necessary to repeat that discussion.[21] What is relevant, for the present purposes, is the role of the CTA in this process. It will be recalled that the major hurdle to the inclusion of a motor carrier section was not with the officials in the government but with the minister of transport. The advocates accordingly emphasized the possible role that the trucking industry could play in marshalling support for the proposed legislation in the House of Commons. The officials argued that if the legislation were to be passed, the minority government needed as many allies as possible. This argument was apparently a persuasive one because, according to one of the participants, the minister of transport was convinced "at the eleventh hour" of the political wisdom of including a motor carrier section on the grounds that "it was felt that some of the opposition sides to the Bill could be helped by the motor carrier industry." This was a complete reversal of the 1938 situation.[22]

Once the decision had been taken, departmental officials began active courtship of the CTA, a process that offers excellent support for Presthus's contention of the close interaction between the federal Department of Transport and its galaxy of affected interest groups.[23] The general manager of the CTA, John Magee, was asked to participate in the drafting of the motor carrier section. This request was completely unexpected and Magee refused to commit himself in advance to support the legislation. He refused also to participate personally in any preliminary discussions but was prepared to nominate an "unofficial" representative, a lawyer who had previously done work for the CTA. The result was that Part III was drafted by this representative and Peel, of the Department of Transport, in the latter's living room!

Although Magee was pleasantly surprised by the legislation proposed, he was in no position to commit the industry. Given the radical departure that was being requested from the CTA's traditional, and only recently reaffirmed, position on federal regulation, such action could only be undertaken by the CTA's board of directors. To win industry support, several meetings were held in Ottawa at which departmental officials and, subsequently the minister of transport himself, outlined the philosophy of the NTA and discussed the mechanics of implementation. The minister and officials emphasized the legislation's commitment to equality of all modes of transport and declared that they would stand by this promise. If philosophy alone was not enough to satisfy the industry, as a measure of good faith it was offered a more tangible expression of the department's commitment to impartiality. The CTA was promised that "one of the seventeen" commissioners on the proposed Canadian Transport Commission would be "someone who will represent recognition of road transport."[24] This promise was fulfilled when Magee was appointed in September 1967, as a commissioner of the CTC and member of the Motor Vehicle Transport Committee. Finally, as further evidence of departmental good faith, many amendments requested by the industry to Bill C-231 were subsequently accepted by the government as the bill was being piloted through the House of Commons.[25]

As a result of these negotiations, the industry reversed itself and the CTA became an enthusiastic supporter of Bill C-231. In addition to announcing their support for the proposed legislation, CTA members, as desired by department officials, actively lobbied members of Parliament, particularly those from western Canada. Evidence that Pickersgill regarded CTA support as crucial to the successful passing of the NTA is suggested by his repeated singling out of the CTA to express his gratitude after Bill C-231 became law.[26]

In the first bloom of its new relationship with the federal government, the trucking industry was obviously extremely satisfied that it had made the best choice in its new partner. Editorials in trucking journals glorified the "coming of age" of the industry; industry spokesmen revelled in "trucking's formal acceptance by government as one of Canada's major modes of national transport."[27] If the industry needed any reassurance of the soundness of its judgement, it was soon available. In March 1969, the minister of transport proposed that the railway rate subsidy program be continued for shipments from the Atlantic region. The CTA made representations to the minister that such a subsidy to the railways alone discriminated against truckers and thereby contravened the philosophy of the NTA. The result was that the initial legislation was withdrawn and replaced by the Atlantic Freight Assistance Act which extended to the trucking industry the subsidy available to the railways.

The industry was also satisfied that by endorsing the NTA, it was gaining a larger foothold within federal circles. It was confident that the CTC and the department would now represent trucking to other federal departments. Evidence that this might in fact be the case came when the president of the CTC and the minister of transport took the industry's side in a dispute with the federal Department of Labour over standards for working hours in the trucking industry. One industry spokesman summed up the prevalent attitude at this time: "In this early period after the passing of the National Transportation Act, we were pleased that the new authority and the Department of Transport were willing to intervene on our behalf with other departments and were willing to hear the trucking industry's point of view."

The CTA appreciated that Part III did not end all the problems faced by the trucking industry. Recognition of the industry was mainly a symbolic victory. How Part III was to be implemented was the more substantive issue and a central concern to the CTA because Part III, like so many legislative instruments, was merely skeletal legislation. The detailed regulations and procedures remained to be drafted. Naturally the CTA was vitally concerned with the method of implementation.

More important than methods was the timing of implementation of Part III. To the CTA the date was the crucial concern for two basic reasons. To continue the analogy of marriage, the CTA was deeply concerned with how members of the trucking family would adapt to the new partner. Problems of organizational cohesiveness and consensus were to plague the CTA until the industry reversed its position and dropped its support for federal regulation in 1973. Moreover, the CTA was worried about how its earlier suitors, the provinces, would react to being so abruptly spurned. The CTA was extremely conscious of both these factors and accordingly advocated implementation as early as possible. It was to come as a shock to the industry that it was being welcomed into the federal family by some of its new "in-laws" with less than open arms.

PROBLEMS OF "LIVING TOGETHER"

"Cohesion," according to David Truman, "is a crucial determinant of the effectiveness with which the group may assert its claim."[28] As stated earlier, a significant factor affecting the level of group cohesiveness is its structure—unitary or federal—because the latter is presumed to have a negative effect. The literature assumes that the problem is primarily an internal one, in that groups, to be effective, must resolve the conflicts between regional and national interests. What the literature appears to have downplayed is the role of government actors in fostering and exacerbating internal conflict for the purpose of exploiting group division in the intergovernmental arena. Furthermore the "smacks" or "wallops" that Grodzins spoke of may be directed at the groups by governments in an attempt to weaken the groups' ties with the other level of government. The purpose of such "cracks" is to undercut the political support claimed by a government in order to diminish its resources. The events following the support given by the CTA to Part III provide evidence in support of this important qualification to the multiple-crack thesis.

The CTA, as its name suggests, is an interest group formed, as stated earlier, by the coming together of the previously separate provincial and regional associations. Indeed, it is more a confederation in the strict sense of that term in that the central body is heavily dependent on strong provincial associations. As an interest group in a federal system, the CTA experienced all the difficulties cited in the literature in maintaining cohesiveness. The most obvious obstacle to group unity was presented by the Quebec Trucking Association (QTA). Although Quebec nationalism had infected the QTA, as it had so many Quebec sections of national bodies, anti-centralization *per se* was not at issue.[29] The simple argument advanced by spokesmen for the QTA was that Quebec truckers were fairly satisfied with the Quebec regulatory system. While accepting the general criticisms of the regulatory system under the MVTA, the QTA needed to be persuaded far more than any other regional association of the value of Part III.

In fact, the CTA was able to endorse Part III only after the pressure group agreed to accept two QTA-demanded conditions. The first was that the CTA would demand that the implementation of Part III be limited to strictly cross-border operations under provincial regulatory control. If accepted, this proposal would exempt much of the traffic under federal jurisdiction from federal control. The second condition demanded by the Quebec section, and accepted by the national body, was that the provincial regulators be employed as federal examiners under Part III. Although there was considerable disagreement within the industry about the level of competence of some of the provincial regulators, the CTA agreed to incorporate this proposal in its official policy statement on Part III.

Although the CTA was able to endorse the NTA once the two conditions were accepted, it quickly became apparent that the unity achieved was more illusory than real. As a result of the deep division within the CTA over federal regulation, subsequent developments were to provide excellent examples of what Truman so aptly described as the "embarrassing non-conformity" which may result from the lack of unity in a federated interest group.[30] The failure of the compromises to satisfy the Quebec section became obvious when the QTA, shortly after the CTA had made its submission to the Commons committee, wrote directly to all Quebec members of Parliament and senators objecting to the inclusion of Part III in the National Transportation Act.

After the NTA had been passed by Parliament, members of the QTA became more public in their criticism of the act. One official argued that the federal government "by adopting Bill C-231, Part III, is trying to take control of the industry. Ottawa, being the owner of one of the largest railways in the world, is now trying to be competitor and legislator at the same time."[31] This official went on to "deplore Ottawa's unilateral action in presenting Bill C-231 without previously consulting the provinces." Whatever doubts there were that this opposition represented official thinking of the association were dispelled at the 1968 annual convention of the QTA. The president of the QTA was quoted as stating "that the

Association will fight implementation of Part III of the NTA."[32] The QTA position was that federal control be limited solely to individual trucks that travel from one province to another.

The conflict between the Quebec Trucking Association and the CTA came to a head at the CTA's 1969 annual meeting. The internal conflict could no longer be ignored because the Quebec association had been supporting and encouraging a member of Parliament from Quebec to propose private members' bills that would amend the NTA in accordance with the QTA's demands.[33] According to one report, the outgoing president of the CTA was critical of what he regarded as "unilateral action by any member association of CTA in matters of national interest." The president, irritated by the criticism of the NTA by the Quebec association and its attempts to subvert Part III,

> was emphatic in his view that there could be only one voice for
> the trucking industry in Canada and the annual meeting proceeded
> on the assumption that if CTA's position as national spokesman was
> not endorsed, the association might just as well disband. CTA
> must not be used by its members when convenient and ignored when
> its policy doesn't suit a specific purpose . . . nor can any part of it
> sit in judgement on its staff, directors and policies.[34]

As a direct result of the Quebec association's activities, the CTA was forced at the 1969 meeting to resort to a "memorandum of agreement" between its members with the purpose of binding association members to CTA's policies and by-laws. This attempt to unite the CTA was far from successful in that it prompted the QTA to let its membership lapse for a year. The conflict between the national and Quebec associations was to plague the industry throughout the negotiations and was used by some provincial governments to attack the federal government's claim that it had industry support for the implementation of Part III.

The internal conflict faced by the CTA became all the more significant for the group and for the federal government as provincial opposition to Part III developed. By reversing its traditional position on federal regulation, the trucking industry incurred the hostility of the provincial governments opposed to Part III. As a result of this intergovernmental conflict, the industry was the object of intense competition as both levels of government vied for industry support. The CTA came to appreciate that considerable costs can be incurred when an interest group exercises its options in a federal system.

The trucking industry had expected a certain degree of negative reaction from provincial regulators. The recommendations regarding the limited scope of Part III and the use of provincial officials as examiners were proposed not only to achieve unity within the industry but also in an attempt to assuage in advance provincial opposition. The industry had not anticipated, however, the degree of hostility that Part III would in fact engender among some provincial regulators or that this hostility would be directed at the industry for reversing its long-time commitment to provincial regulation. One provincial regulator was quoted as exclaiming that Part III would be implemented "over my dead body!" Such a reaction, albeit extreme, was natural in that those provincial officials whose sole or principal responsibility was motor carrier regulation would find, with the implementation of Part III, the federal government assuming the bulk of their responsibility. This would entail considerable loss of prestige and status for such provincial regulators.

The initial provincial reaction of blind hostility soon became tempered by more strategic concerns. In the preliminary discussions with the provinces, federal spokesmen justified Part III by invoking the support given to the legislation by the CTA. It became obvious to the provinces, especially those adamantly opposed to Part III, such as Ontario, that if this support could be undercut—if the industry could be persuaded to withdraw its support—the federal government would lose one of the major underpinnings for its policy. The Ontario government consequently worked to achieve that end. According to one Ontario official, at the conclusion of a departmental meeting to discuss the negotiations on Part III, the minister of transportation and communications instructed the chairman of the Ontario Highway Transport Board (OHTB) to see what he could do about "bringing the industry around" to supporting the Ontario position.

Provinces opposed to Part III employed a variety of tactics in "bringing the industry around." According to several trucking spokesmen, such provinces first attempted to win the industry back by offering a number of "carrots." One official stated that "after the federal government indicated their intent to move with federal regulation, the provincial boards wined and dined the industry to build up a lot more respect and a better relationship." The provinces promised that they would make a far greater effort to promote uniformity in the regulations and to facilitate joint board hearings. One Ontario government official explained the provincial response by stating that "the truckers have some legitimate complaints and we have begun to act on them and correct them."

Perhaps the most significant "carrot" came from Ontario. Industry officials had repeatedly complained of their poor relationship with the Ontario government. To rectify such complaints, the minister conferred a "mandate" on the Ontario Trucking Association (OTA) as the official and sole spokesman for the industry with the Department of Transportation and Communications.[35] It is significant that, at the time this "mandate" was given to the association, its ardour for Part III was cooling considerably.

The provinces did not limit their efforts to "carrots" in their attempts to "bring the industry around." Some provinces were to exert what both truckers and some provincial regulators described as pressure and intimidation. In this context, it is important to recognize one of the important realities of any regulatory system, the power that regulators possess over those subject to their authority. Rourke sums up this situation very well:

> The power that accrues to administrative agencies, because of their discretionary authority is still vast. Regulatory agencies, for example, exercise a great deal of power merely because they have the authority to give or withhold benefits, and to inflict or refrain from imposing sanctions. The fact that regulatory agencies have such power forces a group subject to their jurisdiction to defer to them even in situations in which their authority may not be altogether clear.[36]

The power to invoke various sanctions is one of the more important that regulatory agencies possess. They can decide not to renew licences or can employ less draconian measures, such as prolonged licence hearings, investigations of licencees, and amendments to licences involving prescribed freight and routes. All such measures can have a direct and immediate impact on the profitability and even the survival of regulated firms. Moreover, even the threat to employ sanctions can be an important and effective power.

When the trucking industry "rebelled" and backed Part III, some provincial regulators made determined efforts to remind truckers of the fundamental reality of their relationship. One trucking official, subject to a great deal of pressure because of his outspoken support for Part III, stated that "the provincial boards have your destiny in their hands. They can do a lot of things to interrupt your service and bring your business to an end." A former provincial regulator conceded in an interview that some provincial officials had employed "some intimidation" and according to a number of truckers, this intimidation constituted "terrific pressure." A major practitioner of intimidation, according to these interviews, was the chairman of the Ontario Highway Transport Board who apparently telephoned the employers of some of the elected officers of the Canadian Trucking Association to complain of speeches about the inadequacies of the provincial boards. He strongly recommended that the companies suggest to their employees that they be more "prudent" in their comments. This pressure was undoubtedly significant in explaining the CTA change in policy on Part III, in that a number of truckers, when questioned, cited "fear of provincial regulators" as a main reason for the change. The president of one of the largest trucking firms in Canada summed up the prevailing attitude among truckers: "Truckers are political animals. We are regulated by OHTB and they are fundamentally against Part III and some of the boys thought they would be discriminated against by the Board. They can put quite a bite on you. There was fear of bucking the Ontario Highway Transport Board and this fear was quite important."

This fear assumed added significance when the industry began to realize that there were important obstacles within the federal government to Part III. Consequently, their resolve began to diminish and they began to succumb to the provincial pressures and intimidation.

Initially, however, industry reaction to provincial pressure was twofold. First, the CTA did what other interest groups often do: it sought allies in order to buttress its position.[37] One group the CTA turned to for support was the Canadian Manufacturers' Association (CMA). The CMA had had several meetings with the Canadian Transport Commission and the CTA's executive director implored the CMA to endorse the CTA position on Part III but met with little success.

The industry's second response to provincial pressure was to demand that the federal government implement Part III as soon as possible. The president of the CTA outlined its dilemma at the 1968 annual convention of the Ontario Trucking Association. He acknowledged that "extraprovincial carriers are reluctant to publicly criticize the present system of regulating extra-provincial operations under the MVTA." (Such an acknowledgement was wise given that the chairman of the OHTB was on the same panel.) He went on to argue, however, that Part III would lead to a "vastly improved" system of regulation and concluded by stating that "we want federal control . . . and the sooner the better."[38] During this period, prior to the calling of the first federal-provincial conference in 1969, industry spokesmen pleaded for immediate action on Part III because of the pressure being placed on the industry by the provinces.

The federal government also attempted to strengthen its position by gaining additional group support. During 1968 and 1969, a series of meetings were held with the other associations that would be affected by Part III, such as the Canadian Industrial Traffic League, the Canadian Association of Movers, the Canadian Motor Coach Association, and of course, the Canadian Manufacturers' Association. The meeting of the MVTC with the CMA offers an excellent illustration of the complex relationship that may exist between interest groups and different levels of government in a federal system. When the CMA spokesman informed the members of the MVTC that the CMA would forward their views to the MVTC on Part III, one of the commissioners "suggested that it might be in the nature of a memorandum with which the Federal Minister of Transport can face the Provincial Governments." The truckers were obviously not the only ones facing problems of unity, for the CMA official turned back the commissioner's suggestion by explaining that the CMA would have problems in preparing such a submission because not all of the provincial branches would agree with one position.[39] Despite this problem, the federal government still was able to claim that, in general, Part III had the support of most of the national associations in the transport field.

If the federal government was to hold trucking industry support, the industry informed the minister of transport that it was imperative that he convene the promised federal-provincial conference. In 1969, two years after the NTA had been enacted, the CTA impressed on the minister that because of the delay in commencing the negotiations the industry was being placed in an untenable position. The industry argued that it had solidly backed the federal government on Part III but that the provinces, through their existing control on licensing, were putting pressure on the industry. It was a direct result of this meeting that the minister of transport ordered his officials to make arrangements for a federal-provincial conference.

The decision to convene the first federal-provincial conference on Part III demonstrates one role, that of catalyst, that interest groups may play in federal-provincial relations. Government officials conceded that without the industry demand for implementation, opponents of Part III within the federal government would have been able to withstand internal pressure for action. In contrast to the findings of Simeon, the CTA did more than make its views known.

Once the federal government had fulfilled its commitment to convene the conference, CTA officers volunteered, despite the harassment they had been receiving from some of the provinces, to do a "little missionary work among the unconverted before the Conference." They would make representations to the provincial ministers, urging them to seek a common position with the federal government in order to resolve the difficulties faced by the industry. One reason the CTA opted for this missionary role is that the QTA had let its membership lapse in the national body and, therefore, the CTA felt it could not make a public statement prior to the conference. Although it is not known what reception was given the "missionaries" by other provinces, the Ontario reception is illuminating. According to an Ontario official, the CTA representative was "pawned off" on a junior official who provided little more than a polite hearing.

Immediately following the 1969 conference, the CTA was briefed by federal officials on what had transpired, particularly on the Ontario proposal advanced as an alternative to Part III. This briefing was important because the CTA president immediately and publicly rejected the proposal as "costly, cumbersome and time-consuming."[40] Rather than freezing out interest groups, the federal government was employing the CTA, by means of its public declaration, to dismiss the Ontario proposal by showing that it was unacceptable to the industry and, at the same time, seeking to reinforce the legitimacy of its own position. Indicative of the extent of CTA support for the federal government was the fact that the Ontario counter-proposal was basically the same as the associations' proposal to the provincial regulators before Part III was introduced.

The trucking industry was kept well informed about the debate within the federal government, again basically for the same reason. The advocates of Part III wanted to be able to invoke CTA support and cite industry opposition to any counter-proposal. Thus, when Pickersgill proposed after the 1969 conference that implementation of Part III be limited to international operations, Peel and the other officials were able to argue successfully that the industry was adamantly opposed to such a suggestion, and that the federal government could not afford to lose industry goodwill.

Following the first federal-provincial conference in 1969, the federal government sought to signal to both the industry and the provincial governments its determination to implement Part III. The nature of the signal was to be the proclamation into law of that section of the NTA. The timing of the signal is of importance in that it indicates the significance attached to CTA support. Proclamation was deliberately delayed until after the Quebec provincial election in April 1970, so as not to inject the issue into the campaign. Equally important, however, was that proclamation was deliberately timed to coincide with the CTA's annual meeting.

Despite proclamation, the industry, because of provincial pressures, was becoming increasingly agitated over the slow pace towards implementation. Industry spokesmen became particularly concerned when they learned that Pickersgill had volunteered to save $500,000 by postponing implementation, as part of the CTC's contribution to the "war on inflation" being waged by the government. One measure of the concern developing in the industry was a meeting held in Toronto in September 1970, attended by some of the major carriers and officials of the Ontario and national associations. It was evident at this meeting that the commitment within the industry, particularly the crucial Ontario component, to backing the federal government was being seriously threatened. The carriers were under serious pressure from the OHTB and did not see any relief in sight. Although no decision was taken to drop support for the federal government, the industry officials let it be known to federal officials that the question was being raised. These officials were increasingly aware of the growing dissatisfaction as they received reports from other parts of the country that truckers were losing confidence in the federal government's ability to defend their interests.

This dissatisfaction was a major factor in the decision to convene the second federal-provincial meeting on Part III. Some federal officials were arguing that they were losing their credibility with the CTA; thus, the 1970 conference was designed specifically to demonstrate that progress was indeed being made. The industry, however, had a more realistic view of the negotiations. The government was warned that unless it presented a clear decision, the provinces would be in a much stronger position than ever. The fact that the federal government did not have a clear position to present to the provinces, because of the unresolved internal conflict, but felt compelled to do something to satisfy the industry, is indicative of the importance attached to the industry's support. The move backfired because the conference was a disaster and merely exacerbated provincial opposition to Part III.

A debate during the 1970 conference supports the hypothesis that interest groups may play a significant support role in federal-provincial negotiations.[41] Everyone recognized that the federal government's policy was in large part conditioned by the demands of the CTA for such a policy of federal regulation. What ensued at the conference was claim and counter-claim by the federal and provincial governments as to the extent to which the federal government did indeed have the support of the industry. The discussion of the importance of the CTA support was started when the federal chairman of the meeting stated that "it is common knowledge that there is pressure on Government to establish a better system of regulation. They all know the stand of the Canadian Trucking Association." The following exchange between the Quebec and federal representatives illustrates the "tug-of-war" approach to interest group support that occurred:

> The Quebec representative then raised what he termed a purely
> theoretical and hypothetical matter. Supposing Provinces got together
> today and found a solution acceptable to all Provinces and presented
> it to industry, that would solve their problems as far as extra-
> provincial transport is concerned. What would CTC do in that

163

eventuality? The Chairman gave his personal reaction, that in this way, they might have removed from the federal government the immediate pressure.

Although the chairman indicated that loss of the CTA support for Part III would not necessarily mean that the federal government would not proceed with implementation, it was obvious to all participants, that if this "eventuality" occurred, the federal position would be seriously damaged. Moreover, the Quebec representative was aware that this was not simply a "theoretical and hypothetical matter," for he pointed out that the industry position was not "a solid one" and that the Quebec association had endorsed "complete and total support of control as far as possible by the province, whether intra or inter, and declared opposition to federal control in this area." The lack of unanimity within the industry and the strenuous efforts by some provinces to bring it around to supporting their position underscored the less than hypothetical nature of the provincial inquiry.

Other factors were working to turn a hypothesis into reality. The CTA was clearly disappointed with the 1970 meeting and complained to federal officials of the confusion and dissatisfaction that existed with respect to Part III. Furthermore, they were concerned that the extended delay in implementing Part III was putting the industry in an untenable position because some provincial boards were clearly playing politics with the carriers. Industry apprehension was accentuated when the president of the CTC refused to meet with the representatives of the CTA to discuss Part III. Although the industry had expressed earlier concern with the apparent reluctance of the CTC to move on Part III, this rebuff was never expected.[42]

An additional cause of industry concern was the Quebec government's attempt to exploit once again the division in the industry ranks. The executive vice-president of the Quebec Trucking Association was initially included as an official member of the Quebec delegation to the 1971 Federal-Provincial Conference of Ministers. This action infuriated CTA officials. They immediately protested to the federal government which requested that the Quebec delegation not include the QTA official. The Quebec government acceded to the request in full knowledge that even without the official in their delegation, its point had been forcefully brought home to the federal government.

SEPARATION AND DIVORCE

The results of the 1971 conference gave the CTA the opportunity for which some of its members had been desperately searching. The pressure from some of the provinces and the conflict within the industry, exacerbated by the fact that no progress had been made on the implementation of Part III in four years, proved too much for the CTA. The federal government was warned that the industry would have to reconsider its position if no progress was made at the 1971 conference. When the result of the conference was merely the creation of an Advisory Council to study the issue, the CTA jumped at the opportunity. The CTA reverted to its pre-1966 position and called for the "creation of a uniform set of regulations at the federal level, to be administered by provincial regulatory agencies and enforced on a uniform basis in each province."[43] The CTA had withdrawn support for federal regulation. The significance of this change can be suggested by the fact that at its first meeting of the new council, the revised CTA position was read into the minutes of the meeting by some of the provincial representatives.

If there was any question of where the industry stood on the matter of federal regulation, this was resolved after the Advisory Council had reported. The trucking industry had played a role, albeit a limited one along with other transportation interest groups, in the work of the Advisory Council. The set of draft regulations had been submitted for comments to all the affected parties by the council and a meeting had also been held at which the industry associations were given an opportunity to discuss a proposed accounting system for the industry prior to the council making its final report. The final straw for the industry was the federal government's failure to announce even where it stood on the recommendations of the Advisory Council to include provincial members on the Motor Vehicle Transport Committee of the CTC. When no response was forthcoming, the CTA in anger turned on the federal government and reverted to its earlier position of total and absolute opposition to any federal role in regulating the industry.

The seven-year relationship was thus ended almost as abruptly as it had begun. The trucking industry which had for years been absolutely opposed to direct federal regulation of the industry returned to this position. The truckers at the 1973 convention, according to one industry official, were "adamant in insisting that there be virtually no federal input in developing or administering a new concept of uniform regulations." The "coming of age" of the industry, heralded by the passing of the NTA and Part III, had, like so many similar experiences, been an extremely painful one. Unfortunately, from the industry perspective, all that had been gained from the process was extreme frustration and bitterness.

There can be little doubt that the industry's withdrawal of support for

165

Part III drastically weakened the position of the federal government. This was confirmed in interviews with both federal and provincial officials. The federal bargaining position had already been seriously eroded by the continuing conflict within the federal government. As far as the actors in the intergovernmental negotiations on Part III were concerned, the action by the CTA was the final death blow to Part III. The federal government had, from the beginning of the negotiations, maintained that the industry demand for federal action was the principal rationale for the inclusion of Part III in the NTA. Although the philosophy of the NTA necessitated a motor carrier section, this philosophy by itself was not much of a political factor in the negotiations. Implementation of Part III would have been possible only if the federal government had been able to invoke the support of the interested parties. Loss of that support effectively ended the intergovernmental negotiations.

While it is important to realize that the CTA withdrawal of support resulted primarily from provincial pressures, provincial tactics could only have been successful because of the conflict within the federal government. The trucking industry withstood the pressure from the provinces for the first few years while constantly imploring the federal government to act on Part III. The industry knew that, once Part III was implemented, the scope for provincial retaliation would be severely limited. The federal government did not act to protect the industry because its own internal conflict made action impossible. The provincial governments were able to cut off that limb while members of the federal government fought with one another. In the conflict between the federal and provincial governments, the trucking industry had been caught in the middle, a casualty because one of the combatants did not possess sufficient unity to do battle.

CONCLUSION

The findings of this chapter are generally supportive of most of the relevant conclusions in the literature. We have seen how the CTA exploited the division of powers by pressing for regulation by that level of government perceived as the more sympathetic to its interests. In pursuing its objectives, the CTA utilized the various avenues available to it such as the Cabinet, the bureaucracy, and royal commissions. A particular target of CTA attention was the courts, through which the group sought to further its ends. In the contemporary period, which is germane to the study of Part III, the example of the close relationship between the federal transport bureaucracy and the interest group corroborates the findings of other students, particularly those of Presthus. What was significant in this relationship was the two-way flow of demands as groups and government actors sought to accomplish shared objectives.

The primary objective of this chapter was to employ the evidence concerning interest group involvement in the intergovernmental bargaining on Part III to test two hypotheses that have been advanced pertaining to the relationship between interest groups and federal structures and processes. The findings suggest that one hypothesis needs to be qualified while the other is open to serious challenge.

One hypothesis was that federalism is valued by interest groups because it provides them with multiple access points to decision-makers. The evidence demonstrates that while the CTA did in fact exploit the division of powers that existed to further its policy objectives, the hypothesis as it stands is too one-dimensional. The government actors also directed demands at the interest group such that the latter learned that there are costs as well as benefits of the "multiple cracks" associated with federal structures. When it reversed its traditional position on direct federal regulation, the CTA incurred the wrath of those provincial authorities affected by Part III.

The trucking industry learned to its sorrow that, in choosing sides, particularly in reversing itself, it made enemies as well as friends. "Cracks" were directed at the industry by some of the provincial authorities concerned about the threat posed to the existing regulatory framework, a framework in which they had much at stake. The problem was not simply one of provincial pique at being "tossed over," although this certainly accounted for some of the provincial attempts at retribution. The more serious problem was the intergovernmental struggle that the CTA was inexorably drawn into as the respective governments sought to satisfy their objectives.

The role of the CTA in this struggle seriously challenges the other hypothesis. That hypothesis was that group access to the intergovernmental bargaining process was severely restricted. The evidence argues the contrary. Rather than being frozen out, there existed close and continuous formal and informal contact between the CTA and governmental actors before and especially during the federal-provincial bargaining process. The evidence was that interest group considerations influenced the timing of the negotiations and, in the case of the federal government, shaped its tactics and strategies. The CTA also performed a communications function by assuming the role of "missionaries" in an attempt to convert some of the provinces. In addition, the group attempted to serve an intelligence function by keeping the federal government appraised of provincial positions.

By far the most important role played by the CTA was that of providing a fundamental political resource for the federal government. Without CTA support for Part III, the federal government had a very weak case to present to the provinces. This political support explains in large part the various "multiple cracks in reverse" directed at the CTA by the provinces. It also explains why the interests of a group may not be "jettisoned in the conference room." The interests of the group were the interests of the federal government, that is, at least of those within the federal government who sought the implementation of Part III. The provinces appreciated this fact and sought to undercut the federal position by "bringing the industry around." The significance of, and possible explanations for, these findings will be discussed in the next chapter.

Chapter Eight

Conclusion

We began this study by asking why Part III of the National Transportation Act has not been implemented. Clearly, if we cannot now answer this question with confidence, any other conclusions we might hope to offer will be of questionable value. Fortunately, the evidence documented in the preceding chapters permits us to derive a clear and unequivocal answer. Moreover, despite the rancour and disagreement that surrounded Part III, the answer is one with which the principal actors in the conflict, federal and provincial, are in agreement.

Part III was indeed the victim of intergovernmental conflict, as successive federal ministers have claimed. But Part III was such a victim only because of the internecine conflict which members of the federal government engaged in during most of the negotiations. This conflict occurred within and between organizations and agencies of the federal government. The provinces did win the battle to kill the implementation of Part III; however, they won not because of their effectiveness in intergovernmental bargaining but because the internal conflict crippled the federal government as an effective negotiator. Provincial successes were dependent on the federal internal division and discord. That some of the provincial actors were able to exploit the internal battle was at best incidental to the provincial success. Indeed it was not so much a provincial success, except in the final result, as it was a federal failure. Moreover, this explanation for the fate of Part III is shared not only by provincial participants and this outside observer but by federal participants in the struggle. As one senior DOT official concluded, "there is no doubt that the internal disagreement in the federal government was more important than provincial bargaining. We were never negotiating from strength because of our internal conflict. We never had a good position because of this." This view is shared by senior CTC participants, one of whom concluded, "we, the CTC and DOT, fought off ourselves. We created the opposition and we fanned the flames." Finally, although as we have shown, other federal actors were not as centrally involved as those from the CTC and DOT, nevertheless the preceding judgements are shared. "The CTC-DOT conflict," according to a PCO participant, "was crucial to the failure of the negotiations on Part III. The federal government was never able to present a strong position to the provinces."

Although accounting for the fate of Part III is a significant goal in itself, given the importance ascribed initially to the goal of federal regulation of extraprovincial motor carriers for both the new national transportation policy and regulatory system introduced in 1967, our interest in Part III stemmed from broader concerns. We were interested in what an analysis of the fate of Part III as an example of intergovernmental negotiations could tell us about the factors that influence the outcomes of such negotiations. Our focus in this respect was even more directed in that we wanted to use the negotiations on Part III to test the utility of two possible approaches for analysing intergovernmental negotiations. The fate of Part III was of interest as well as a case study that might throw light upon some of the internal dynamics of the federal bureaucracy and the impact of those dynamics on the policy process. Finally, although not a central concern, the negotiations on Part III were examined from the perspective of interest groups and their relationships with Canadian federal structures and processes.

In this chapter we will advance a number of conclusions, relevant to our broader concerns, that can be derived from the preceding chapters. We recognize that one must be modest in the claims made about the possible contributions of a single case study and that modesty is especially called for with respect to any attempt to derive general conclusions from the findings of such a study. We do not believe that a single study can be the basis for generalizations or even constitute a fundamental challenge to established generalizations. Nevertheless, in line with the arguments advanced by Lijphart, we do believe that a case study such as this can be a useful testing ground for hypotheses and, especially, a means for directing attention at aspects of the political process which may not be given adequate consideration and for suggesting possible fruitful lines of further research and hypotheses that can build on our findings on Part III's fate.[1]

INTEREST GROUPS AND INTERGOVERNMENTAL NEGOTIATIONS

The findings of this study provide a basic challenge to one of the current generalizations about intergovernmental negotiations, specifically that advanced by Simeon, who concluded that interest group participation and effectiveness are limited in such negotiations. We found that, to the contrary, in the negotiations on Part III, interest group participation was extensive and central to the negotiations. While it may be argued that such findings are exceptional and Part III is an atypical issue, there may be more merit in the argument that it is Simeon's findings that are exceptional and not the norm.

Simeon's conclusions may well be dependent on the nature of the issues he studied. In two of the three (pensions being the exception) there were no interest groups involved. Lawrence Pierce's findings in his study of fiscal policy formation in the United States offer a useful comparison for the constitutional and financial issues examined by Simeon:

in the fiscal policy area, in contrast to the other major policy areas, there seems to arise less often the situation in which one agency, as spokesman for its constituency, lines up to do battle with another agency and its clientele. This is true, in part, because there is no readily identifiable interest group in fiscal policy—the clientele is the country, or economy, as a whole. In general, then the bargaining process involved (the calculations and strategies employed) in the fiscal policy area is more substantive and less interest-group oriented than in other policy areas.[2]

Moreover, it is not only the absence of groups but the specific nature of the issues that is important. The constitutional and financial issues were examples *par excellence* of governmental issues, of issues where the primary constituents, at least in terms of the perspectives of the participants, were the participants themselves. Thus, to modify an earlier argument, it is not that there were no interest groups, but that the governments themselves were the interest groups. As Alan Cairns has recently reminded us, Adam Smith's thesis that businessmen seldom meet but for the purpose of conspiring against the public "is no less applicable to the behaviour of governments. The decisions made by governments are no less likely than business decisions to sacrifice public interests for the varied interests of those who make the decisions."[3] What better way to accomplish such an end than to so structure the process and define the issues as to limit the participation of non-governmental interest groups.

But there are issues where there are "readily identifiable" interest groups. Pratt identified such groups in the negotiations on Syncrude, as did Bucovetsky in the conflict over tax reform.[4] In the struggle over Part III there were several groups, of which the most important was the Canadian Trucking Associations. It is, however, not simply a matter of the presence of interest groups but their influence in such negotiations that challenges Simeon's generalization. In contrast to Simeon, Pratt found the groups to be dominant while Bucovetsky found them to be highly influential. From our perspective, the conclusion of restricted access and limited effectiveness neglects an important group function in intergovernmental negotiations. We saw that group support for the federal government in the conflict over Part III was a vital political resource that the federal government sought to exploit. Indeed, group support may be such a central political resource that actors will jettison it only at their peril. Simeon included the concept of support in his analysis but limited his discussion primarily to a consideration of general public, rather than interest group, support.[5] The role of the CTA suggests that articulating and defending a position in terms of group demands may be a significant determinant of the nature and the course of intergovernmental negotiations. Group support may be particularly effective as a resource if an actor can legitimize a course of action on the grounds that such a course is necessitated by a failure or inaction of the other level of government.

Interest group support, from the group's perspective, however, may be a double-edged weapon. This is, in part, suggested by Simeon's discussion of the concept: "political support is a scarce resource; the participants compete for it; and this competition is part of the bargaining process."[6] The conclusion that can be drawn from this study is that group support, as a particular variant of public support, can be the object of intergovernmental competition. The ramifications of such competition suggest that the multiple crack thesis of Grodzins' needs to be qualified.[7]

The pressure exerted on the CTA by some provincial governments suggests that the multiple-crack thesis, as presently formulated, does not recognize the costs or negative aspects of a federal system for interest groups. Groups may not have the degree of liberty assumed by the multiple-crack thesis in choosing governmental partners, for there are potential hazards for the groups arising from the intergovernmental competition for support. An interest group, to paraphrase Rourke, "makes enemies as well as friends when it identifies with [one level of government], since it inherits hostilities directed at the [level of government] with which it enters an alliance."[8] When a group endorses one level of government it may find itself the object of attention as the other level seeks its support. Perhaps even more significant for group fortunes is the fact that the group may find itself subject to abuse from the rejected government. The cost, therefore, of a federal system for interest groups may be that "wallops or smacks" are directed as much at the groups by the competing governments as they are by the groups at governments.

The "cracks" may be more multiple than is normally assumed.

There is another major conclusion that can be drawn from our findings relating to both the multiple-crack and the restricted access hypotheses. Both assume somewhat of a one-dimensional relationship between interest groups and governments, a relationship predicated on demands flowing from group to government. A conclusion to be derived from chapter 7 is that there is need for hypotheses premised on the assumption of at least a two-dimensional relationship between groups and governments in a federal system. Demands may flow from government to group as well as from group to government.[9] This is clearly not a novel proposition, in that the propensity for governmental actors to generate group pressures on themselves or other actors is well known, as is the fact that governments often create interest groups, or at least act as midwife for their birth. This particular feature of interest group life, however, assumes an added, and hitherto relatively ignored, significance in a federal system, particularly one that is characterized by a high degree of policy-making.

The role of interest groups in the struggle over the implementation of Part III challenges some current conceptions, and, as well, suggests several fruitful areas for further research on the scope and nature of their roles in the intergovernmental bargaining process. From our findings and those of other studies, it seems clear that there are alternatives for interest group influence and power that range from group dominance of the process at one end to government dominance at the other. In between, as this study suggests, are variable degrees of influence for both sets of actors. Indeed, it would appear that groups perform many of the same functions and can exercise the same influence in that process as they do in the intergovernmental policy process. Yet, given the significance of intergovernmental negotiations to the policy process, and consequently to the political fortunes of the participants, group participation is clearly not without its costs. Although the federal system does provide multiple access points, groups who seek to exploit them run the risk of being buffeted about and of being caught, as it were, in the vice of federalism. Until we have much more information, it would seem premature to underestimate the activities, influence, and costs of interest group participation in the intergovernmental bargaining process.

REGULATORY AGENCIES AND THE FEDERAL SYSTEM

In chapter 1, it was argued that regulatory agencies provided a useful starting point for examining potential breaches in the strong central control associated with parliamentary systems and consequently a possible introduction into the world of "bureaucratic politics." In this section, a different aspect of regulatory agencies, as exposed by the struggle over Part III, will be discussed. We turn now to the interrelations between regulatory agencies such as the Canadian Transport Commission, the National Energy Board, and the Canadian Radio-Television and Telecommunications Commission, and the contemporary Canadian federal system.[10]

Regulatory agencies, until very recently, have long been ignored in Canada. This has been unfortunate, for these agencies are not at the "fringe" of the public sector in Canada but are primarily instruments of social, economic, and political control. This is particularly the case for those agencies that perform positive, prescriptive functions, such as promoting and planning in major areas of economic and social activity, as well as more traditional negative or remedial functions associated with the policing function of early regulation. The former type of regulation is now central to those federal regulatory agencies which operate in the energy, transportation, and communications sector. The significance of this aspect of regulatory agencies is that, by virtue of their functions, they have become deeply entwined in the political process. Regulation is no longer a narrow, technical matter but involves agencies "in the making of 'political' decisions in the highest sense of that term—choices between competing social and economic values and competing alternatives for government action."[11] Regulatory agencies are major actors in determining the distribution of benefits and burdens in our society as between firms and industries, and individuals and regions. Their decisions can have an enormous impact on the allocation of resources, on the distribution of income, and on the organization of production and consumption across the country. In short, regulatory agencies are now crucial to the effective organization of economic activity in Canada because of the central roles they play in the organization, planning, and development of the transportation, communication, and energy sectors.

Regulatory agencies are obviously of direct and compelling relevance to present-day intergovernmental relations. What makes them particularly relevant is that same characteristic that made them relevant to the study of bureaucratic politics—their independence. Although their independence is relative, not absolute, regulatory agencies have a unique degree of independence in our parliamentary system. Yet their independence can fly in the face of the interdependence which now characterizes the Canadian federal system. What we have is a situation in which independent agencies with major responsibilities can frustrate or inhibit the intergovernmental collaboration necessitated by interdependence.

The conflicts that can develop are sometimes the result of deliberate design. John Langford, in his study on the reorganization of the federal transport department, has informed us that when the CTC was created in 1967, the CTC was to play the primary policy role, while the department was to play a secondary or operational and service role. This role was reflected in the words of one senior official who noted, according to Langford, that "if any agency of government has responsibility for expanding any mode of transportation, it would be the CTC rather than the department."[12] The CTC's primacy rested on several sources of authority. First was its range of adjudicative powers, that is, to grant operating licences and approve tariffs and fares in several areas.[13] It should be noted in this regard that in exercising such powers, the CTC, like so many regulatory agencies, is guided only by vague and general statutory standards. Moreover, aside from appeals on individual decisions, there were no provisions in the NTA to enable the government to issue to the agency authoritative guidance on policy matters. The second source of authority was the CTC's policy advisory role. In section 22 of the NTA, the CTC is assigned a wide range of powers and it was clear that in 1967 the CTC, not the DOT, was the policy adviser to the minister of transport. The third source of authority was the independence granted to the CTC to enact its own regulations without reference to either the minister of transport or to Cabinet. Such regulations are the means by which the commission can develop secondary policy or binding interpretations of the general statutory guidelines found in the NTA.

The struggle over Part III illustrates very well the interrelationships between regulatory agencies and the federal system and between agency independence and governmental interdependence. The president of the CTC made full use of his statutory authority as the link between the commission and the minister of transport to influence the process and content of the intergovernmental relations. As he repeatedly reminded departmental officials, it was the CTC's responsibility, not their's, to recommend methods of implementation for Part III. One measure of this authority, and of its consequences, was the fact that a CTC representative chaired the 1970 meeting of officials. Equally important was the fact that on this occasion it was the CTC president who dictated the stance to be assumed by the federal delegation. It was only as the process of reorganization described by Langford developed that the department began to "usurp" the CTC's policy advisory role.

Even if such a dominant role was diminished, the CTC possessed other resources. As the president reminded the department on occasion, it was the CTC and not the DOT which would ultimately have to implement Part III and, therefore, notwithstanding any federal-provincial agreement, the CTC's agreement on timing and scope was a prerequisite. Under the NTA as it was, the minister did not possess the authority to order implementation. Furthermore, when CTC-DOT relations were most strained, the president reminded participants of that other source of power the CTC possessed. When the Advisory Council distributed draft regulations to interested parties for comment, the CTC followed this up with a letter which pointedly stated that the CTC alone had authority to make any regulations on this matter.

Such actions by the CTC caused a great deal of concern and resentment in provincial circles. They did not believe that an agency such as the CTC should have an independent policy advisory and implementation role. They were frustrated by the fact that in an area that could have tremendous impact on provincial policies and objectives, not to mention provincial highways, the decisions would be made by an independent agency within the federal government. They were astounded by the fact that intergovernmental policy-making could be blocked by such a body. For the provinces, the "watertight compartments" which had so frustrated policy-making in earlier decades had been resurrected only this time within just one level of government.

It must be appreciated that in this respect, Part III was not exceptional. At the same time as negotiations on Part III were being conducted, Ontario was being frustrated by the CTC in its attempt to introduce a provincially subsidized air service to serve northern Ontario.[14] Saskatchewan and Manitoba were to encounter similar problems in establishing an airline to serve unserviced areas of both provinces. Alberta's decision to challenge the CTC's jurisdiction on its purchase of Pacific Western Airlines is another example. Moreover, the problems of policy control were exacerbated, according to provincial perspectives, by the procedures of the CTC. As mentioned earlier, some provincial officials thought it highly inappropriate that the regulatory agency treated provincial governments as if they were "just another pressure group." The fact that on occasion a province might have to justify its participation in a regulatory hearing and not be granted standing automatically was another irritant.

Part III and other transportation issues have often been matched in other areas of federal regulatory responsibility with the same degree of rancour and conflict. In the negotiations on communications issues (to cite but one example) that commenced around the same time as those on Part III, the CRTC played a comparable role, reminding both provincial and federal participants where authority and responsibility rested within the federal government.[15] The CRTC policy on cable television hardware ownership and its actions in this area led to major disputes between the provinces of Saskatchewan and Manitoba and the federal government. Even when an agreement was reached between Manitoba and the federal government, the CRTC frustrated complete implementation of that agreement by its licensing decisions.

It must be emphasized that the preceding discussion should not be interpreted as a blanket condemnation of agency actions. The point is that the statutes creating these agencies and allocating functions to them have resulted in several instances where there has been little basis for effective intergovernmental relations on matters within the jurisdiction of regulatory agencies. Agencies are, on occasion, statutory roadblocks to intergovernmental collaboration and negotiation. The fact that such roadblocks are sometimes compounded by personality and procedural problems is a significant but secondary consideration.

The emphasis in the preceding discussion on the politics of structure related to regulatory agencies, and in particular the case of Part III, challenges a current conception of the nature of regulatory politics. Bruce Doern has argued that "the regulatory politics of the 1980s are likely to be much more difficult not only because the federal government has succeeded in placing ceilings on earlier open-ended spending programs, but also because it is probably more difficult to influence and bargain about regulatory issues, since they are issues which are more of a zero-sum game."[16] Without disputing the comparative degree of difficulty, the assumption that regulatory politics involve a zero-sum game is open to serious dispute. There is no question that one particular variant of regulatory politics can be so interpreted, namely, the outcomes of the adjudication process, the granting of operating licences and certificates. This is but a small sub-set of the issues, however, covered by the rubric "regulatory politics." Regulatory politics, as Part III and many other examples illustrate, involve issues of structures, policies, procedures, and personalities. On such issues there is ample room for bargaining and trade-offs, for non-zero-sum game behaviour. Governmental participants may not even be interested in those issues decided by adjudication by regulatory agencies so long as there is ample opportunity for negotiation on the broader policy matters which will no doubt condition the adjudication process. As one provincial official expressed this position, "the provinces don't care who does 'it'; their concern is with the service."[17] Regulatory issues may, in the recent past, have assumed a zero-sum character primarily because the defects of the institutional structure merged the different issues into one. Provinces were required to intervene on applications because there was no effective alternative for intervening on broader issues. To the extent that the problems arising out of the scope for independent activity by regulatory agencies are addressed and corrected, the non-zero-sum character of regulatory issues will become apparent.

BUREAUCRATIC POLITICS AND INTERGOVERNMENTAL RELATIONS

We have argued that the most popular mode of analysis in the study of Canadian intergovernmental negotiations today is one that concentrates on the interactions between governments. Such a concentration results from the assumption that the individual governments can be conceptualized as single unified actors, hence the designation, "unitary actor" model. Once this assumption is made, then the analysis searches for explanations for the outcomes of negotiations in the interplay of the resources, strategies, and tactics of the governments. Our analysis of the negotiations on the implementation of Part III argues instead that the outcome of those negotiations cannot be accounted for by the analysis of the interactions between the governments. We have argued that a complete explanation of the fate of Part III requires an understanding of the complex political process that occurred within the federal government and that the bureaucratic politics model aids in the development of such an understanding. It attempts to answer questions such as why the negotiators adopted the objectives, strategies, and tactics they did. The unitary actor model is not particularly interested in such questions, but for the bureaucratic politics model, the answers to such questions may be crucial to the development of explanations. In the case of Part III, this was most definitely the case.

Several further observations relating to the potential wider utility of the bureaucratic politics model are in order. In the first place, the argument is not simply that bureaucrats are influential in the policy process; nor is it that there is often conflict within bureaucratic ranks about goals and strategies. Both contentions are commonplace and indeed commonsensical. Other studies of intergovernmental negotiations in particular and policy-making in general have documented cases of bureaucratic influence and internal conflict. The argument underlying the bureaucratic politics model is that bureaucratic politics can have a direct and contributing impact on the outcome of the negotiations between governments. It is the linkage between the complex internal political process and the equally complex intergovernmental negotiating process that we wish to establish. Other studies of intergovernmental negotiations have neither neglected nor ignored the internal politics of governments in their analyses but rather have chosen to underemphasize the impact of such politics on outcomes. Internal politics may be so crucial to such outcomes, however, that they cannot be subsumed under the general rubric of "other constraints."

Interactions between governments may not, therefore, explain, by themselves, the outcomes of intergovernmental negotiations. From the bureaucratic politics perspective, the complex intragovernmental process cannot be separated from the direct relations between governments. This is not to argue that there will always be political infighting or that one set of actors may never dominate others either from the outset of or during the negotiations. The assumptions upon which the unitary actor model is premised may be valid in individual cases, but this must be established, not defined away. The "pulling and hauling" that engulfed Part III within the federal government was the basic determinant of the outcome of the intergovernmental negotiations. The simple fact is that an analysis that limited itself to the interactions between governments would have ignored or underestimated the importance of the internal conflict as a result of the type of questions that would have been asked.

It should be emphasized that notwithstanding the disagreements over the importance of intragovernmental factors, the two analytical frameworks should be seen as complementary rather than competing. Use of the bureaucratic politics model does not rest on the assumption that the intergovernmental process is necessarily secondary in impact on the outcomes. Such an assumption would be most unwarranted. The contention is that the study of intergovernmental negotiations requires an analysis of the impact of the internal process on the intergovernmental process. In some cases it may be negligible, while in others it may be determinant. Furthermore, any differences between the two approaches may be the result of a focus on different levels of analysis. The primary objective of Simeon, for example, would appear to be to explain the nature of the relationships between governments in Canada, the factors influencing these relationships, and to account for long-term developments. The unitary actor model, as Simeon has employed it, is principally concerned with analysing how governments negotiate, with their "direct and explicit relations." In short, although Simeon does devote attention to explaining the outcomes of the issues he studied, it could be argued that he is more concerned with analysing the intergovernmental system than explaining the outcomes of specific negotiations in that system. Similarly, other studies of intergovernmental negotiations may be more interested in the impact of the negotiations on the specific policy or policy area examined than on the outcome *per se*.

It may well be that Part III involves a most atypical example of both bureaucratic politics and intergovernmental negotiations. Only further research that explicitly addresses the concerns of the bureaucratic politics model can decide such an issue. Notwithstanding this caveat, the case of Part III, while it alone cannot provide definitive answers, does raise a number of intriguing questions related not only to the nature of inter-governmental negotiations, but to a number of conventional notions about the impact of features of the parliamentary system on the policy process. It is to the latter that we now turn.

BUREAUCRATIC POLITICS AND THE PARLIAMENTARY SYSTEM

One of the most important aspects of the analysis of the negotiations on Part III was the portrait of the federal government that emerged. During the negotiations it was not marked by unity and single-minded purpose. Far from it. It was, rather, rife with endemic and pervasive conflict on basic values, goals, strategies, and tactics. By no stretch of an analytical imagination could it be conceived of as a single actor. Throughout, it seldom spoke with one voice; when it did, it was muted. On other occasions, it spoke with multiple voices.

What can this tell us about the nature of the policy process within a parliamentary system? While again one must be cautious, it may be that the central assumptions that underlie the unitary actor model are of questionable validity. Basic to this model, it will be recalled, is the assumption that the genius of the parliamentary system is a strong executive. This executive is endowed with the power, by virtue of its hierarchical position, to coordinate the various actors and interests in the process. In the parliamentary system, there is no separation but rather a fusion of power and, notwithstanding constitutional conventions, the history of development of the parliamentary system is the history of the growth of executive dominance.

But we have seen that, at least in the instance of Part III, power was more widely dispersed and diffused than conventional notions of hierarchic coordination within a parliamentary setting would suggest to be possible. In particular, the example of Part III raises questions about two aspects of those assumptions, namely, the power of central agencies vis-à-vis "operating" departments and the power of superiors vis-à-vis subordinates within such departments. Such questions do not challenge the existence, but the assumed effectiveness, of central and hierarchical control.

Turning to the issue of hierarchy and intradepartmental relationships, this study suggests that the hierarchical controls within departments may not be as effective as formal organizational charts with their emphasis on lines of authority would imply. This suggestion is derived from the analysis of the dynamics of the relationships that existed within the

Department of Transport. The internal conflict and manoeuvring by relatively subordinate actors within the department provides an excellent illustration of a situation of "defective hierarchy" where "the lines of control running . . . downwards are often weak and imperfect."[18]

Many factors may account for the defectiveness in formal lines of control. Subordinates may possess important resources to exploit in their relationships with superiors, and consequently, the power of an individual is relative, to an important degree, to the needs others have for the resources he commands. Peel, for example, dominated the Department of Transport because of his expertise on motor carriers and, especially in the work of the Advisory Council, he had a controlling grip on the information they received. This happened because the only alternative source of information was highly suspect. Therefore, when they needed, for example, to reply to Pickersgill's attacks on the council's activities, Peel's superiors could only turn to him for advice on a response rather than to a somewhat more disinterested participant. They thereby became dependent on him for the information and analysis upon which their decisions were based. A lack of information, thus, is a serious impediment to control. By means of adequate and imaginative managing and marshalling of information, subordinates may be able to carry their superiors along, without their knowing where they are going or why.

Peel's bargaining resources, in fact, far outstripped what one would assume to be the limited resources flowing from his hierarchical position. He was an enterprising, skilful, and, consequently, effective bureaucratic infighter. In addition to information control, his track record enhanced his reputation, and hence, his influence. It must be recalled that Peel had been primarily responsible for the highly successful federal strategy pursued at the 1969 meeting and then for resolving the impasse at the 1971 meeting. As a result of these earlier successes, Peel was allowed a much greater degree of independence in the Advisory Council than one would assume to be normal. When his initiatives seemed threatened, Peel also demonstrated the importance of a highly particularistic variable, personal bargaining skills. The Winnipeg meeting of the Advisory Council required Peel to exploit all the resources at his disposal, particularly his own bargaining ability, and by so doing provided an excellent example of the limitations of hierarchical controls. It will be recalled that at that meeting Peel forged an intergovernmental alliance to disobey a specific directive from his minister and did so successfully. Far from being punished, as his chief adversary demanded, Peel's reputation was enhanced. This episode, perhaps unique in degree, demonstrates the fact that subordinates can indeed control and use their superiors in a manner not envisaged by the more formal theories of hierarchical controls.

A further aspect of the notion of defective hierarchy relates to the role of the minister of transport in the internal conflict. In such a situation, given the norms of the parliamentary system, one would assume that it is the duty of the minister to resolve the conflict and that since this did not occur, the respective ministers—there were three in the period 1967 to 1973—were to a certain extent derelict. Yet such a criticism to be valid must establish that the minister was kept fully apprised of the conflict. In the case of Part III, the minister played a distinctly secondary role because the conflict was kept "in-house" as much as possible by members of the bureaucracy. This was a deliberate part of the "pulling and hauling" because it was in the interests of all the participants to do so for much of the conflict. Only when one set of actors faced the threat of defeat did they attempt to broaden the range of actors represented and, in particular, to include the minister. When this occurred, however, for reasons we have advanced, the minister was dependent upon the officials in his department and this dependency reduced his scope for manoeuvre.

The case of Part III raises several important issues as well concerning the hierarchical controls possessed by central agencies. Our findings, if corroborated by other studies, would suggest that conventional notions about the power and influence of central agencies vis-à-vis operating departments are exaggerated and that there is need for more realistic assumptions about such agencies in the policy process. Indeed, it would appear that what is required is a much more subtle analysis of the contemporary roles of central agencies. In this respect, Doern's conclusion related to the caricature of the Treasury Board as "the bogeyman" is equally appropriate for other central agencies.[19]

There is almost universal agreement that the last decade has seen a continuing, and on the whole successful, effort to make the prime minister a more effective "chief executive."[20] But one cannot emphasize enough that the growth of power and effectiveness is a relative question that involves not only a comparison with circumstances prior to the changes introduced under Trudeau but also a consideration of obstacles that still exist. There seems to have been a general acceptance at face value of the claims of some of the critics of such changes as if they represent the reality rather than at best simply the hopes and dreams of the architects. Moreover, the consequences of these changes may have been misinterpreted. Part III demonstrates that departmental actors are not easily excluded or dominated by actors from central agencies. In fact, central agencies may be in a far weaker position than is assumed. There are many reasons why this may be the case.

In the first place, while much has been made of the growth in the size of central agencies, the disproportionate distribution of manpower resources between the central agencies and the operating departments must be recognized. A brief examination of the Government of Canada telephone directory will suffice to demonstrate this fact. Within the Department of Transport's Ottawa headquarters, for example, there are more officials at the director level and above than there are officers in the Federal-Provincial Relations Office. Notwithstanding popular tales of topsy-like growth, staff within central agencies are over-burdened and over-extended with responsibilities. In the Federal-Provincial Relations Office, for example, an officer may be responsible for monitoring not only two or three departments, but several provinces as well. Much the same situation applies in the case of the Privy Council Office and even more so for the Prime Minister's Office. Given what is in fact a situation of limited manpower and the scope of programs and policies that such personnel must monitor, central agencies face serious handicaps such that their capabilities are stretched if they are required to participate intensively in more than a few issue areas at any one time.

The problems central agencies face, however, are not simply those of numbers of either men or issues. The more critical problems relate to the nature of the individuals and issues. The complexity of most issues, the "big problems—little brains" syndrome, requires reliance upon specialists. Such specialists are primarily found in the operating departments and such departmental specialization is an important resource in the intragovernmental policy process. For their part, central agency officials cannot be expected to be familiar in any great detail with the substance of an issue. It must not be forgotten that central agencies are staffed by individuals who, while they may indeed be specialists in the "machinery of government" or in intergovernmental relations, are essentially amateurs and generalists when it comes to specific policy issues. Furthermore, policies usually emerge in response to specific problems rather than from the application of any "grand strategy." In the intergovernmental arena, although some central agency officials may wax enthusiastic over the development of "common policies for all federal-provincial relationships,"[21] thereby strengthening the role of such officials, agreement on such common policies or a "grand strategy" is likely to be either so elusive or else at such a level of generality as to be virtually useless as a guide for a specific issue. The Trudeau government encountered similar problems in both the 1975 "priorities exercise" and the deputy ministerial review of governmental programs, the so-called DM-10 exercise, of 1976.

It is in the interactions between central agencies and operating departments that such variables as manpower resources and expertise become significant. In such interactions, contrary to the assumption of "strong executive authority," we would argue that the process is tilted in favour of the departments and not of the central agencies. Departments are normally the initiators of the policy process. Simply because problem and issue definition are crucial aspects of this process, and because such tasks are initially and principally the responsibility of the departments, the departments gain enormous leverage over the process. Departments are also the primary sources of policy alternatives and because they are the ones who ultimately must implement programs, these functions further ensure that departmental preferences will be accorded due respect. Moreover, some departments, for a number of reasons, such as their prestige, their mandate, their expertise, their minister of the day, may be extremely aggressive in asserting their prerogative to perform their responsibilities with only minimal policy guidance or coordination from central agencies. Indeed, such departments may not fully accept the coordinating role assigned to central agencies, particularly insofar as the PMO is concerned, as this office is looked upon with suspicion and a not insignificant degree of apprehension over its legitimacy. From this perspective, Trudeau's 1978 economic initiative speech, which has been seen as the apogee of central agency power, should perhaps be understood to represent a failure of such power and be viewed as a desperate call for public support against recalcitrant departments.

Another important consideration in the interactive process between central agencies and departments is the question of timing. Departments, while they may concede that at some point in the process central agencies will have to be involved, may work to ensure that at that point their position is favoured. Departments, for example, may attempt to mobilize sufficient support among other actors such that by the time the central agencies are involved they may be faced with a virtual *fait accompli* endorsed by all the other relevant actors. Central agencies, under such circumstances, face severe constraints in choosing among competing options. Another departmental tactic may be to bide one's time and not go to central agencies until the last moment when a decision is imperative and there is little opportunity to canvass seriously alternative proposals.

When central agencies are major participants in the policy process it must be recognized that departments may not necessarily defer to them in cases of conflict and, if forced "to do battle," possess significant resources. One such resource, already mentioned, is information control which, if exploited imaginatively, can influence any outcome. Departments may flood the central agencies with information which they have neither the expertise nor the time to digest. Alternatively, they may provide only the barest minimum of information, frustrating the central agencies' attempts to gain an informed view of an issue. Another tactic, apparently a common one, is to provide biased information, with the result that central agencies again face severe constraints in their ability to assess such information.

In doing battle with central agencies, departments may exploit certain bargaining tactics, such as the mobilization of necessary support, mentioned earlier, and/or dividing the opposition. Departments may attempt to play off actors within central agencies against one another and this may be easiest in terms of the partisan-bureaucratic divide between the PMO and PCO. Within the bureaucratic, "non-partisan" central agencies, this tactic may also be possible with the "hiving off" of the Federal-Provincial Relations Office from the Privy Council Office. Further, if it thinks its Cabinet submission can get a more favourable reception, a department may try to have it referred to the more receptive Cabinet committee, or if it does not succeed in this, may seek to have a joint Cabinet committee meeting to offset potential critics.

Another aspect of the interaction process is that some senior officials may adopt the view that the role of central agencies is not to adopt, and lobby for, a specific course of action, but to ensure that all the relevant actors within the government who should be, are, in fact, consulted. If departments respect this principle, even in the most perfunctory manner, then central agencies may have little alternative but to go along with a department's proposals. On other occasions, such as that exemplified by Part III, central agency actors may have no particular viewpoint on an issue, with the result that their role is primarily that of ally to those who are advocating acceptance of a specific course of action. The efficacy of central agencies may also be affected even when they adopt a less restrictive or passive role. In some circumstances, actors from central agencies may bring to bear a perspective that emphasizes a desire to establish or maintain a harmonious relationship with provincial governments or other important interested parties, a perspective which may well lead to conflict with a department that wants to implement a specific program. In this context, it may be accurate to suggest that, at times, central agencies responsible for federal-provincial relations regard the provinces as their clientele or constituency with the result that, far from being impartial umpires or coordinators, they may act as partisans or advocates in a dispute. This may diminish the legitimacy of any claim to be coordinators in the eyes of the various actors involved.

In this context, mention should be made of the emphasis placed by Simeon in his explanation for central dominance on the importance of status and prestige concerns.[22] While Simeon's argument is no doubt a valid one in that disputes between governments do assume a different dimension when questions of the status and prestige of the governments become embroiled in the debate over issues, it should be recognized that central agencies are not the only actors within governments that can exploit such concerns. Departments are just as capable as central agencies of defining issues in terms of governmental prestige if such a tactic suits their purposes. A department, for example, to undercut an attempt by central agencies to pave the way for an intergovernmental reconciliation, may articulate its opposition to such a proposed reconciliation in terms of the potential impact on the government as a whole. Such a tactic was indeed employed by the Motor Vehicle Transport Committee when it defined the threat posed by the Advisory Council's recommendations to emphasize the potential impact not solely on the committee but on the "essence" of the commission as a whole.

Finally, it should be mentioned that, in terms of the relationship between Cabinet and individual departments, it would not be an exaggeration to suggest that, in some very important respects, this relationship is very similar to that between the House of Commons and the executive. A common refrain in discussions of the functions of the House of Commons and the constraints surrounding such functions is that the House is often required to approve what is essentially skeletal legislation which, once enacted, is "fleshed out" by the bureaucracy. The lack of legislative detail and the authority delegated to the bureaucracy to develop such detail, normally without any further reference to the House, is said to provide the bureaucracy with enormous policy influence.

Cabinet, and consequently central agencies, similarly can be at the mercy of departments. Cabinet is often not asked to approve the detail of legislative proposals or the substance of approaches that departments will be taking in intergovernmental negotiations. Cabinet may be asked only to approve the principles and the thrust of such approaches. It is the responsibility of the minister and his advisers to provide the substantive argument and approaches ostensibly based on the general terms agreed to by Cabinet. A related consideration in the context of negotiations that are prolonged involves the question of the department's need for subsequent Cabinet approval as the negotiations progress. In the case of Part III, for example, the minister of transport secured Cabinet approval for the approach made at the 1969 Federal-Provincial Conference, but in the next three years the question of Part III was not discussed once by Cabinet. If the CTC-DOT dispute had been resolved, a strong argument could be made that Cabinet, which had never been asked to comment on provincial membership on the CTC, would have had its collective hands tied by the department, given the federal-provincial agreement on the resolution of the conflict over Part III.

186

The purpose of the above discussion is not to deny that central agencies can play an influential role but to question some of the more exaggerated claims about such a role. The basic weakness of the argument of strong central control is its extreme generality. There is simply not enough known about the scope of the autonomy of operating departments and other actors or about the role of central agencies in the policy process. Central agencies may indeed dominate other actors within a government but we need to know at what cost, by what means, and for how long. The central questions are: under what conditions do they attempt to dominate, and why and how do they succeed? Furthermore, it is a plausible hypothesis that central agencies have reached the pinnacle of their influence at least in the area of intergovernmental relations and may now be in a decline. During the 1960s, as intergovernmental relations became more and more complex, officials in such agencies as the Privy Council Office gained pre-eminence because, while they were generalists in a policy sense, they became in fact specialists in the process of intergovernmental relations. It was the complexity of intergovernmental relations in the sixties that helped establish the influence of intergovernmental specialists. This influence may be in the process of being attenuated, however, as the operating departments respond by establishing their own specialized intergovernmental relations units within their own structures. Such specialists within departments may eventually challenge the competence of, and compete for influence with, the central agency process specialists.

Rather than assuming that central agencies are automatically the dominant actors, a more sophisticated analysis of the relationship between central agencies and departments in the policy process would see the former as providing but one set of actors among many within the government. According to such a perspective, the focus would be on the various roles played by central agencies, such as coordinator "knocking heads together," "watch-dog," or "gate-keeper," evaluator, goal-setter, monitor, and advocate or partisan. The influence of central agencies in the policy process will, it is argued, vary in part according to which one of these roles, or combination thereof, such agencies play in specific instances.

Our arguments about the influence of subordinates within departments over their superiors and of operating departments over central agencies lead us to the conclusion that power is far more diffused and dispersed in our contemporary parliamentary system than conventional notions of "hierarchical controls" recognize. Indeed, although our study of Part III can only illustrate some aspects of the distribution of power and suggest others, it may be that the concept of hierarchical controls distorts more that it reveals. Consequently, it may be that the debate over the apparent aggrandizement of power by Pierre Trudeau as prime minister has misread fundamental realities. It may be true, as some commentators have contended, that the growth of central agencies and the introduction of the Cabinet committee system contributed to the decline in the influence of Cabinet, to its relegation to the "dignified" part of the constitution.[23] What is more debatable is who assumed Cabinet's "influence/power quotient." Many have assumed that it went to the officials in the agencies surrounding the prime minister, to the so-called super-bureaucrats.[24]

Could it not be that rather than flowing upward, influence/power, or at least a great deal of it, flowed downward, past ministers, past deputy ministers, into the middle echelons of the bureaucracy? There are many reasons for suggesting this to be a more realistic assessment. We have suggested some in our discussion of the concept of "defective hierarchy" and in the resources that operating departments possess vis-à-vis central agencies. Others could be cited, among which the more important would be the tremendous growth in the public sector in the past two decades and the concomitant emphasis on professional and technical expertise of the public service. Associated with this growth has been the high degreee of mobility of senior, and even of middle level, public servants and the "revolving door" approach practised by Trudeau with respect to changing ministers and deputy ministers in a number of departments. Another reason is one that is a direct consequence of the Cabinet committee system, namely the phenomenal growth of "interdepartmentalism," the internal equivalent to the interdependence which is the contagion of our contemporary federal system. More and more public servants are required to negotiate, not just with their counterparts in other governments, but with officials in other departments within their own level. This negotiation process, bureaucratic politics, can only reinforce both the political role of the members of the public service and correspondingly their influence in the system. In the negotiations on Part III, officials most decidedly did not see themselves simply as "progenitors of technical advice and as transmitters of its results and related advice."[25] Moreover, is it unreasonable to suggest that the current concern expressed about the dimunition of accountability in our parliamentary system is but another manifestation of the diffusion of power in that system?[26]

A single case study such as this cannot, of course, answer such questions. At best it can identify and direct attention to them. In this study we have sought to demonstrate the utility of employing the bureaucratic politics model for analysing both intergovernmental negotiations and internal dimensions of the policy process in a parliamentary setting.

Bureaucratic bargaining usually takes place behind the scenes in a parliamentary system rather than in public, as it does to a large extent in a presidential system like that of the United States. In large part, because of the non-public nature of such bargaining, supported as it is by the canons of collective responsibility and the entrenched high regard for secrecy with respect to the internal dynamics, there simply has not been adequate attention paid to the importance of intragovernmental conflict in the policy process. We need to recognize the potential for competition and conflict and consequently need to know much more about how officials cooperate and compete, bargain and battle among themselves. We need to determine what resources bureaucrats possess and to examine how they exploit such resources to influence the outcome of the policy-making process. The need to understand that process, coupled as it is with questions about democratic control and accountability, may well prove to be crucial to students of Canadian politics.

Appendix

Relevant Extracts from NTA

National Transportation Policy

3. It is hereby declared that an economic, efficient and adequate transportation system making the best use of all available modes of transportation at the lowest total cost is essential to protect the interests of the users of transportation and to maintain the economic well-being and growth of Canada, and that these objectives are most likely to be achieved when all modes of transport are able to compete under conditions ensuring that having due regard to national policy and to legal and constitutional requirements

(*a*) regulation of all modes of transport will not be of such a nature as to restrict the ability of any mode of transport to compete freely with any other modes of transport;

(*b*) each mode of transport, so far as practicable, bears a fair proportion of the real cost of the resources, facilities and services provided that mode of transport at public expense;

(*c*) each mode of transport, so far as practicable, receives compensation for the resources, facilities and services that it is required to provide as an imposed public duty; and

(*d*) each mode of transport, so far as practicable, carries traffic to or from any point in Canada under tolls and conditions that do not constitute

(i) an unfair disadvantage in respect of any such traffic beyond that disadvantage inherent in the location or volume of the traffic, the scale

191

of operation connected therewith or the type of traffic or service involved, or

(ii) an undue obstacle to the interchange of commodities between points in Canada or unreasonable discouragement to the development of primary or secondary industries or to export trade in or from any region of Canada or to the movement of commodities through Canadian ports;

and this Act is enacted in accordance with and for the attainment of so much of these objectives as fall within the purview of subject-matters under the jurisdiction of Parliament relating to transportation. 1966–67, c. 69, s. 1.

2 Powers and Duties of Canadian Transport Commission

Interpretation of Functions

21. It is the duty of the Commission to perform the functions vested in the Commission by this Act, the *Railway Act*, the *Aeronautics Act* and the *Transport Act* with the object of coordinating and harmonizing the operations of all carriers engaged in transport by railways, water, aircraft, extraprovincial motor vehicle transport and commodity pipelines; and the Commission shall give to this Act, the *Railway Act*, the *Aeronautics Act* and the *Transport Act* such fair interpretation as will best attain that object. 1966–67, c. 69, s. 14.

Duties of the Commission

22. (1) In addition to its powers, duties and functions under the *Railway Act*, the *Aeronautics Act* and the *Transport Act*, the Commission shall

(*a*) inquire into and report to the Minister upon measures to assist in a sound economic development of the various modes of transport over which Parliament has jurisdiction;

(*b*) undertake studies and research into the economic aspects of all modes of transport within, into or from Canada;

(*c*) inquire into and report to the Minister on the relationship between the various modes of transport within, into and from Canada and upon the measures that should be adopted in order to achieve coordination in development, regulation and control of the various modes of transport;

(*d*) perform, in addition to its duties under this Act, such other duties as may, from time to time, be imposed by law on the Commission in respect of any mode of transport in Canada, including the regulation and licensing of any such modes of transport, control over rates and tariffs and the administration of subsidies voted by Parliament for any such mode of transport;

(*e*) inquire into and report to the Minister upon possible financial measures required for direct assistance to any mode of transport and the method of administration of any measures that may be approved;

(*f*) inquire into and recommend to the Minister from time to time such economic policies and measures as it considers necessary and desirable relating to the operation of the Canadian merchant marine, commensurate with Canadian maritime needs;

(*g*) establish general economic standards and criteria to be used in the determination of federal investment in equipment and facilities as between various modes of transport and within individual modes of transport and in the determination of desirable financial returns therefrom;

(*h*) inquire into and advise the government on the overall balance between expenditure programs of government departments or agencies for the provision of transport facilities and equipment in various modes of transport, and on measures to develop revenue from the use of transport facilities provided or operated by any government department or agency; and

(*i*) participate in the economic aspects of the work of intergovernmental, national or international organizations dealing with any form of transport under the jurisdiction of Parliament, and investigate, examine and report on the economic effects and requirements resulting from participation in or ratification of international agreements.

PART III

EXTRA-PROVINCIAL MOTOR VEHICLE TRANSPORT

Application of Part

36. While the *Motor Vehicle Transport Act* is in force and notwithstanding section 4 of this Act, this Part applies only to such motor vehicle undertaking or such part thereof as is exempted from the provisions of the *Motor Vehicle Transport Act* under section 5 thereof; and in this Part the expression "motor vehicle undertaking to which this Part applies" means, in relation to a part of a motor vehicle undertaking so exempted from the provisions of that Act, the part thereof so exempted. 1966–67, c. 69, s. 29.

Saving

37. Where a motor vehicle undertaking was in operation immediately before this Part became applicable thereto, the person operating the motor vehicle undertaking is entitled to, and the Commission shall issue to him on his application made within six months from the day that this Part became applicable to the undertaking, a licence under this Part in respect thereof on the same conditions respecting schedules, routes, places of call, carriage of passengers and goods, and insurance, herein referred to as the "operative conditions", as were operative in respect of such motor vehicle undertaking immediately before this Part became applicable thereto, but the Commission may insert in the licence such additional conditions, not affecting the operative conditions or relating to the ownership or control of the undertaking, as the Commission deems necessary in the public interest. 1966–67, c. 69, s. 30.

APPENDIX

Licences

38. (1) Subject to this Part, the Commission may issue to any person applying therefor a licence to operate a motor vehicle undertaking to which this Part applies.

Only in Case of Public Convenience and Necessity

(2) The Commission shall not issue any such licence unless it is satisfied that the proposed motor vehicle undertaking is and will be required by the present and future public convenience and necessity.

Exemption

(3) The Commission may exempt from the operation of the whole or any part of subsection (2), any motor vehicle undertaking or any class or group thereof, or the operator thereof, either generally or for a limited period or in respect of a limited area, if in the opinion of the Commission such exemption is in the public interest.

Routes and Conditions

(4) In issuing any licence, the Commission may prescribe the routes that may be followed or the areas to be served and may attach to the licence such conditions as the Commission may consider necessary or desirable in the public interest, and, without limiting the generality of the foregoing, the Commission may impose conditions respecting schedules, places of call, carriage of passengers and freight and insurance.

Suspension, Cancellation or Amendment

(5) The Commission may issue a licence that differs from the licence applied for and may suspend, cancel or amend any licence or any part thereof where, in the opinion of the Commission, the public convenience and necessity so require.

Cancellation or Suspension of Licence

(6) Where in the opinion of the Commission, the operator of a motor vehicle undertaking has violated any of the conditions attached to his licence, the Commission may cancel or suspend the licence. 1966–67, c. 69, s. 31.

No Operation Without Licence

39. (1) Subject to subsection (2), no person shall operate a motor vehicle undertaking to which this Part applies unless he holds a valid and subsisting licence issued under this Part.

Exception

(2) Subsection (1) does not apply to a person who was operating a motor vehicle undertaking immediately before this Part became applicable thereto

unless such person fails to apply to the Commission within six months thereafter for the issuance of a licence under this Part.

Operating Contrary to Conditions of Licence

(3) No person shall operate a motor vehicle undertaking to which this Part applies contrary to any of the conditions of the licence issued in respect thereof under this Part.

Unlawful Rebates or Concessions

(4) No person shall offer, grant or give, or solicit, accept or receive any rebate, concession or discrimination, in respect of the transportation of any traffic by a motor vehicle undertaking to which this Part applies, whereby any such traffic is, by any device whatsoever, transported at a rate less than that named in the tariffs then in force.

Penalty

(5) Every person who violates a provision of this section is guilty of an offence and is liable upon summary conviction to a fine not exceeding five thousand dollars or to imprisonment for a term not exceeding one year or to both. 1966–67, c. 69, s. 32.

Tolls and Tariffs

40. (1) A person operating a motor vehicle undertaking to which this Part applies shall not charge any tolls except tolls specified in a tariff that has been filed with the Commission and is in effect.

Filing through Tariff Bureau

(2) Where the person operating a motor vehicle undertaking to which this Part applies is a member of an association representing persons carrying on like operations, the association may, in accordance with such regulations as the Commission may make in that regard, prepare and file with the Commission a tariff of tolls on behalf of such person.

Tariffs Contrary to National Transportation Policy

(3) The Commission may make orders with respect to all matters relating to traffic, tolls and tariffs of a motor vehicle undertaking to which this Part applies, and may disallow any tariff or tolls, or any portion thereof,

(a) that the Commission considers to be not compensatory and not justified by the public interest; or

(b) where there is no alternative, effective and competitive service by a common carrier other than another motor vehicle carrier or a combination of motor vehicle carriers, that the Commission considers to be a tariff that unduly takes advantage of a monopoly situation favouring motor vehicle carriers;

195

and may require the person operating the motor vehicle undertaking to substitute a tariff of tolls satisfactory to the Commission in lieu thereof, or the Commission may prescribe other tariffs in lieu of the tariff or portion thereof so disallowed. 1966–67, c. 69, s. 33.

Free and Reduced Rate Transportation

41. Notwithstanding any previous contract or commitment or any other general or special Act or provision, no person operating a motor vehicle undertaking to which this Part applies shall issue free or reduced rate transportation except with the approval in writing of the Commission and under such terms, conditions and forms as the Commission may direct. 1966–67, c. 69, s. 34.

Regulations

42. The Commission may make regulations

(*a*) establishing the classification and form of licences to be issued under this Part, the terms upon which and the manner in which they shall be issued and renewed, the conditions and restrictions to which they will be subject and the issue of duplicate licences;

(*b*) prescribing the terms and conditions to which licences issued under this Part shall be subject;

(*c*) respecting the safety, protection, comfort and convenience of the persons availing themselves of the services of a motor vehicle undertaking;

(*d*) respecting temporary permits authorizing seasonal, emergency or occasional operation of motor vehicles of a motor vehicle undertaking;

(*e*) prescribing forms of accounts and records to be kept by operators of motor vehicle undertakings, and providing for access by the Commission to such records;

(*f*) requiring the operators of motor vehicle undertakings to file with the Commission returns with respect to their assets, liabilities, capitalization, revenues, expenditures, equipment, traffic and employees and any other matters relating to the operation of the undertaking;

(*g*) requiring any person to furnish information respecting control, ownership, transfer, consolidation, merger or lease or any proposed control, transfer, consolidation, merger or lease of a motor vehicle undertaking;

(*h*) requiring copies of agreements respecting any such transfer, consolidation, merger or lease, copies of contracts and proposed contracts and copies of agreements affecting services to be filed with the Commission;

(*i*) excluding from the operation of the whole or any portion of this Part or any regulation, order or direction made or issued pursuant thereto, any motor vehicle undertaking or class or group of motor vehicle undertakings;

(*j*) prescribing fees for licences issued under this Part and requiring applicants for such licences to furnish information respecting their finan-

196

cial position, their relation to other common carriers, the nature of the proposed routes, the proposed tariffs or tolls and such other matters as the Commission may consider advisable;

(*k*) providing for uniform bills of lading and other documentation;

(*l*) governing the filing of bonds and certificates of insurance;

(*m*) establishing classifications or groups of motor vehicle undertakings;

(*n*) prohibiting the transfer, consolidation, merger or lease of motor vehicle undertakings except subject to such conditions as may be prescribed by such regulations;

(*o*) prescribing penalties, enforceable on summary conviction, for

(i) contravention of or failure to comply with any regulations or any direction or order made by the Commission pursuant to this Act or such regulations,

(ii) making any false statement or furnishing false information to, or for the use or information of, the Commission, or

(iii) making any false statement or furnishing false information when required to make a statement or furnish information pursuant to any regulation, direction or order of the Commission,

but such penalties shall not exceed a fine of one thousand dollars or imprisonment for a term of twelve months, or both;

(*p*) respecting safety and the prevention of injury in the operations of any motor vehicle undertaking and prescribing standards of safety therefor;

(*q*) designating persons as examiners to carry out investigations on behalf of the Commission in respect of matters related to the operations of motor vehicle undertakings and providing for the making of reports thereon and for other matters deemed necessary in connection with such investigations; and

(*r*) respecting any matter necessary or advisable to carry out effectively the intent and purpose of this Part. 1966–67, c. 69, s. 35.

Notes

Notes to Chapter One

1. National Transportation Act, Revised Statutes of Canada 1970, c. N–17.
2. The term "extraprovincial" includes both the interprovincial and international sectors of the industry.
3. Hon. E. J. Benson, president of the CTC, speech to senior management training course, October 26, 1973, p. 5.
4. For representative statements of successive ministers of transport in the House of Commons, see *HC Debates*, March 14, 1972, p. 810, and March 7, 1974, p. 268.
5. This is, of course, Professor K. C. Wheare's concept of federal government as developed in his *Federal Government,* 4th ed. (New York: Oxford University Press, 1963), p. 10.
6. M. J. C. Vile, *The Structure of American Federalism* (London: Oxford University Press, 1961), p. 199.
7. Ibid.
8. Richard Simeon, *Federal-Provincial Diplomacy: The Making of Recent Policy in Canada* (Toronto: University of Toronto Press, 1972), p. 13. Other studies that implicitly employ the unitary actor model include Anthony G. S. Careless, *Initiative and Response: The Adaptation of Canadian Federalism to Regional Economic Development* (Montreal: McGill-Queen's University Press and the Institute of Public Administration of Canada, 1977); J. Stefan Dupré et al., *Federalism and Policy Development: The Case of Adult Occupational Training in Ontario* (Toronto: University of Toronto Press, 1973); and Martin W. Westmacott, "The National Transportation Act and Western Canada: A Case Study in Cooperative Federalism," Ph.D. thesis, University of Alberta, Edmonton, 1972. It must be emphasized that to suggest these studies employ such a model is not to argue that they do not recognize internal conflict but rather that they do not attempt to relate such conflict to the outcomes of the negotiations they analyse. Two studies that do explicitly focus on internal dynamics are Laurence J. Close and Ronald M. Burns,

The Municipal Winter Works Incentive Program (Toronto: Canadian Tax Foundation, 1971), and Christopher Armstrong, "Federalism and Government Regulations: The Case of the Canadian Insurance Industry 1927–34," *Canadian Public Administration* 19 (1976): 88–101. Another study which suggests on several occasions that intragovernmental differences impacted on intergovernmental negotiations is Claude Morin's *Quebec versus Ottawa: The Struggle for Self-Government 1960–72* (Toronto: University of Toronto Press, 1976).

9. Simeon, *Federal-Provincial Diplomacy*, p. 38.
10. Ibid., p. 36.
11. Ibid., p. 38.
12. See Donald V. Smiley, *Conditional Grants and Canadian Federalism* (Toronto: Canadian Tax Foundation, 1963).
13. Simeon, *Federal-Provincial Diplomacy*, p. 39.
14. Ibid., p. 38.
15. Ibid.
16. Ibid., p. 282.
17. Graham T. Allison and Morton Halperin, "Bureaucratic Politics: A Paradigm and Some Policy Implications," *World Politics*, Supplement, 24 (Spring 1972): 42.
18. Ibid., p. 43.
19. Graham T. Allison, *Essence of Decision: Explaining the Cuban Missile Crisis* (Boston: Little Brown, 1971), p. 146.
20. Gary L. Wamsley and Mayer N. Zald, *The Political Economy of Public Organizations* (Toronto: D. C. Heath, 1973), p. 64.
21. Anthony Downs, *Inside Bureaucracy* (Boston: Little Brown, 1967), pp. 224–26, as summarized in Wamsley and Zald, *Political Economy of Public Organizations*, p. 64. See also Francis Rourke, *Bureaucracy, Politics and Public Policy* (Boston: Little Brown, 1969), pp. 89–103.
22. Downs, *Inside Bureaucracy*, p. 216.
23. Ibid., p. 212 ff.
24. Allison and Halperin, "Bureaucratic Politics," p. 164.
25. Downs, *Inside Bureaucracy*, pp. 2, 84–87.
26. Peter Self, *Administrative Theories and Politics: An Inquiry into the Structures and Processes of Modern Government* (Toronto: University of Toronto Press, 1973), pp. 234–37.
27. Allison, *Essence of Decision*, p. 144.
28. R. O. Keohane and J. S. Nye, "Transgovernmental Relations and International Organizations," *World Politics* 27 (1974): 43.
29. Wamsley and Zald, *Political Economy of Public Organizations*, p. 66.
30. Allison, *Essence of Decision*, p. 169.
31. Ibid., p. 162.
32. Ibid., pp. 145–46.
33. Ibid., p. 146.
34. I. M. Destler, *Presidents, Bureaucrats, and Foreign Policy: The Politics of Organizational Reform* (Princeton: Princeton University Press, 1972), p. 74.

35. Allison, *Essence of Decision*, p. 16.

36. Destler, *Presidents, Bureaucrats, and Foreign Policy*, p. 75.

37. Ibid., p. 52.

38. J. E. Hodgetts, *The Canadian Public Service: A Physiology of Government 1867–1970* (Toronto: University of Toronto Press, 1973), p. 138.

39. Ibid., p. 141.

40. Arend Lijphart, "Comparative Politics and the Comparative Method," *American Political Science Review* 65 (1971) : 691–93.

41. The decision to treat the provinces, in effect, as unitary actors is based on several considerations. The first is the question of time. Investigating the internal dynamics of governments is time-consuming and to have applied the model to all or most of the eleven participants would have been impractical. Perhaps even more important is the fact that early on in the research, the author surmised that, notwithstanding the existence of a few instances of disagreement within two provinces, such disagreements were very quickly resolved. There are any number of competing explanations that might account for this. One is that in this particular instance it was easier to get unity within provincial governments on an issue that involved a defensive response to thwart perceived "aggression." A second, and more general hypothesis is that it is easier to reconcile conflict at the provincial level than it is at the federal level. In part this may result from the less complex range of interests involved as well as the less developed bureaucratic nature of provincial governments. In any event, a subject of future research should be to test the conditions under which bureaucratic politics ensue within provincial governments.

Notes to Chapter Two

1. Charles Aikin, "The Structure of Power in Federal Nations," in *Public Policy*, 1965, pp. 323–24. For the view of one of the foremost exponents of the study of the federal process, see C. J. Friedrich, *Trends of Federalism in Theory and Practice* (New York: Praeger, 1968), Introduction and Conclusion.

2. A similar argument, although from a different perspective, has been advanced in W. R. Lederman, "The Limitations of Co-operative Federalism," in F. Vaughan et al. (eds.), *Contemporary Issues in Canadian Politics* (Toronto: Prentice-Hall, 1970), pp. 22–38.

3. Senate, *Debates*, February 2, 1937, p. 43.

4. *HC Debates*, March 1, 1938, p. 911. In lieu of bringing trucks under federal regulation as a means of meeting truck-rail competition, the federal government in its 1938 legislation permitted railways to negotiate "agreed charges" with shippers, with such charges being subject to approval by the Board of Transport Commissioners.

5. Royal Commission on Dominion-Provincial Relations (Rowell-Sirois), *Report*, II: 200–203.

6. Royal Commission on Transportation (Turgeon), *Report*, pp. 266, 279.

7. As the case was before the courts prior to the abolition of appeals to the Judicial Committee of the Privy Council, Winner was able to appeal to this body.

8. Section 92 (10) (A) of the BNA Act reads as follows: "Local Works and Undertakings other than such as are of the following Classes: (a) Lines of Steam and Other Ships, Railways, Canals, Telegraphs, and other or others of the Provinces, or extending beyond the limits of the Province."

9. Richard A. Olmstead, ed., *Canadian Constitutional Decisions of the Judicial Committee* (Ottawa: Queen's Printer, 1954), III: 775–820. For commentary see Colin H. McNairn, "Transportation, Communication and the Constitution: The Scope of Federal Jurisdiction," *Canadian Bar Review* 47 (1969): 355–94 and McNairn, "Aeronautics and the Canadian Constitution," *Canadian Bar Review* 49 (1971): 411–45.

10. Motor Vehicle Transport Act R.S.C. 1970, c.M-14, Section Three. Delegation to administrative agencies had been approved in *P.E.I. Potato Marketing Board* v. *Willis* (1962) 2 S.C.R. 392.

11. *HC. Debates*, June 7, 1954, pp. 5947–48.

12. A. F. Hailey, in *Transportation in Canada*, by J. C. Lessard, Appendix A, p. 149, a study for the Royal Commission on Canada's Economic Prospects (Gordon Commission).

13. Royal Commission on Transportation (MacPherson Commission) *Report*, Vols. I and II (1961). For instructive commentaries on the report and its effects on national transportation policy see the articles by Darling and Anderson in K. W. Studnicki-Gizbert, ed., *Issues in Canadian Transport Policy* (Toronto: Macmillan, 1974).

14. D. W. Carr, "Truck-Rail Competition in Canada," in MacPherson Royal Commission on Transportation, *Report*, III: 6.

15. Ibid., II: 102.

16. Carr, "Truck-Rail Competition," p. 90.

17. Ibid., p. 91.

18. *Regina* vs. *Northern Quebec Transport Ltd.*, High Court of Justice, Province of Ontario, July 10, 1964.

19. *Re Kleyson's Cartage Co. Ltd. and Motor Carrier Board of Manitoba* [1965] 48. D.L.R. [wd] 716, Manitoba Court of Appeal, January 5, 1965.

20. The case was initially heard in the Ontario Supreme Court in 1965. The Supreme Court of Canada heard the appeal on May 11 and 12, 1967, and, although it dismissed the appeal, it did not pronounce its judgement until April 29, 1968. See *John D. Coughlin* vs. *the Ontario Highway Transport Board* et al., [1968] S.C.R. 569, 68 D.L.R. [2d] 384.

21. Canadian Trucking Associations, Inc., "The Need for New Federal Legislation to Control Extra-Provincial Highway Transport," December 1965, p. 14.

22. Ibid., p. 2.

23. See, for example, Hailey, *Transportation in Canada*, pp. 147–48, and Carr, "Truck-Rail Competition," pp. 88–91.

24. CTA, "The Need for New Federal Legislation," p. 4. Other more dis-

interested commentators were also extremely critical of the lack of uniformity and fragmentation of the regulatory system. See Paul Pross, "Dominion-Provincial Relations in the Field of Highway Regulations," M.A. thesis, Queen's University, 1963; John M. Munro, "The History of the Motor Carrier Transportation and its Regulation in Canada," M.B.A. thesis, Indiana University, 1963; Robert Ian Logan, "Public Policy and Extra-Provincial Trucking in Canada," M.A. thesis, University of New Brunswick, 1968; and John M. Munro, *Trade Liberalization and Transportation in International Trade* (Toronto: University of Toronto Press, 1969).

25. This is discussed in ch. 7.

26. The Darling and Anderson articles in Studnicki-Gizbert, ed., *Issues in Canadian Transport Policy*, offer some illumination on these questions.

27. See, for example, J. W. Pickersgill, Address to the ATAO, Tuesday, November 26, 1968, Toronto, p. 7.

28. NTA, R.S.C. 1970, c.N–17, s.1a.

29. Ibid., s.21.

30. J. R. Baldwin, "Transportation Policy in Canada: The National Transportation Act of 1967," *Transportation Journal*, Fall 1967, p. 10.

31. Pickersgill, Address to the ATAO, p. 19.

32. Ibid., p. 21.

33. The figures for the size of the Ontario component of the extraprovincial motor carrier industry can be found in Logan, "Public Policy," and Munro, *Trade Liberalization*, p. 56.

34. M. W. Menzies Group, "An Appraisal of the Potential Impact to Ontario from the Implementation of Part III of the National Transportation Act" (hereafter, "Ontario Impact Study"), VII–14.

35. See, for example, "Design for Development," statement by the prime minister of Ontario on regional development policy, April 5, 1966.

36. "Ontario Impact Study," V–13.

37. Ibid., VII–15.

38. This is discussed in Donald V. Smiley, *Canada in Question: Federalism in the 70s* (Toronto: McGraw-Hill, 1976), and in Martin V. Westmacott, "The N.T.A. and Western Canada: A Study in Co-operative Federalism," *Canadian Public Administration* 16 (1973): 447–48.

Notes to Chapter Three

1. Thomas Schelling, *The Strategy of Conflict* (New York: Oxford University Press, 1963), p. 3, fn. 1.

2. On the concept of signals and their importance, see Graham T. Allison, *Essence of Decision* (Boston: Little Brown, 1971), pp. 15–16, 175; and Allison and Halperin, "Bureaucratic Politics: A Paradigm and Some Policy Implications," *World Politics*, Supplement, 24 (Spring 1972): 60–64.

3. The role of pressure groups in the negotiations is the subject of ch. 7. Industry comment is mentioned here as an illustration of the additional poli-

tical resource possessed by the federal government in the form of support from an "attentive audience."

4. Prime Minister Pearson to provincial premiers, August 4, 1966, tabled in House of Commons, January 27, 1967.

5. A. L. Peel, "A Regulatory Structure for Canadian Motor Carriers," M.B.A. thesis, University of California, 1967, pp. 17–27.

6. Daniel Johnson to Lester Pearson, October 13, 1966, tabled in House of Commons, January 27, 1967.

7. The federal government's view of what the MVTA did was expressed by J. W. Pickersgill in the House of Commons on January 26, 1967 (Hansard, p. 12284), and at the 1968 meeting of the Automotive Transport Association of Ontario. See "The Place of Motor Vehicle Transportation in the National Transportation Policy," Address of the Hon. J. W. Pickersgill to the ATAO, Tuesday, November 26, 1968, Toronto, p. 6.

8. Johnson to Pearson, October 13, 1966.

9. Daniel Johnson to Lester Pearson, December 7, 1966, tabled in the House of Commons, January 27, 1967.

10. Quoted in *Bus and Truck Transport*, June 1967, p. 15.

11. The reader is reminded that in this and the following chapters, unless there is a specific reference provided, the source of unattributed quotations is one of the confidential interviews referred to in the Preface.

12. See, for example, Destler, *Presidents, Bureaucrats, and Foreign Policy* (Princeton: Princeton University Press, 1972), esp. "Issues as a Flow," pp. 59–61, for a discussion concerning international relations. Simeon has pointed out how "simultaneous games" are a factor as well in federal-provincial bargaining; see *Federal-Provincial Diplomacy* (Toronto: University of Toronto Press, 1972), pp. 179–80, 193.

13. *Bus and Truck Transport*, December 1968, p. 31.

14. Ibid.

15. Ibid.

16. The Coughlin case was discussed in ch. 2, pp. 18–19.

17. On the "Gabon affair," and the federal government's evident "displeasure" over Quebec's actions, see Hon. Mitchell Sharp, *Federalism and International Conferences on Education* (Ottawa: Queen's Printer, 1968), pp. 32–38.

18. Address by the Hon. J. W. Pickersgill to the ATAO, Tuesday, November 26, 1968, Toronto, p. 17.

19. The papers were prepared by Professor Ivan Feltham of Osgoode Hall Law School, Professor John Munro of Simon Fraser University, and Professor S. Trachtenberg of the Transportation Centre of the University of Manitoba. An additional paper was prepared by Dr. Derek Scrafton of the federal Department of Transport. On the use of objective information as a political resource see Simeon, *Federal-Provincial Diplomacy*, pp. 217–18.

20. Hon. Don C. Jamieson, "Opening Remarks" to the federal-provincial minister responsible for motor carrier regulation in *Advisory Council Report*, III, B. 3: 3 (henceforth *ACR*).

21. "National Transportation Act, Proclamation of Part III," ibid., B. 2, p. 1.

22. Jamieson, "Opening Remarks," p. 2 (emphasis in original).

23. Ibid.

24. Ibid., p. 3.

25. Ibid.

26. See, for example, the opening statement of Saskatchewan in *ACR*, III, B. 5. Most other provincial statements were not published but were similar to the Saskatchewan position.

27. The Ontario position is found in *ACR*, III, B. 4. Quebec's statement delivered by the deputy-minister of transportation and communications was not published.

28. On the significance of this objection as a tactic in federal-provincial bargaining, see ch. 7.

29. This is surmised from the letter of Laval Fortier, chairman of the MVTC, reconvening the Joint Technical Committee. See *ACR*, III, B. 7.

30. Ibid., B. 8.

31. Ibid., p. 2.

32. Quebec in fact had raised this concern at the Ministers' Conference. Ontario decided subsequently to make it the central argument in the negotiations. Although the concern was no doubt genuine, a senior official acknowledged in an interview that, in fact, "the phrase 'trucking and regional development' was almost cant" because he had not seen (in 1973) one example where the OHTB had used regional development as a criterion for granting licences.

33. *ACR*, I: 8.

34. The evidence suggesting informal Ontario-Quebec cooperation is found in the fact that the Quebec minister of transportation sent his Ontario counterpart the letter of reply from the federal minister of transport to the Quebec memorandum on the relationship between the Canada Labour Safety Code and Part III.

35. Simeon, *Federal-Provincial Diplomacy*, p. 229. This is a norm increasingly more honoured in the breach. Another example is the formation of a provincial consensus position on communications between 1973 and 1975.

36. British Columbia and Alberta did not send representatives to the meeting of the Joint Technical Committee.

37. "Notes from the Quebec Department of Transportation to a meeting of representatives responsible for motor carrier transportation," Ottawa, November 1, 1970, p. 9 (emphasis in original).

38. Ibid.

39. Ibid.

40. "Saskatchewan Statement to November 1, 1970 Meeting," listed as "Proposals for Discussion and Action, Provincial Representatives, November 1, 1970," *ACR*, III, B. 161.

41. "Statement by Nova Scotia Representative to Meeting of Provincial Officials, November 1, 1970," p. 3.

42. "Provincial Statement to be Read at Federal-Provincial Meeting of Administrators, Ottawa, November 2, 1970," *ACR*, III, B. 17.

43. "Chairman's Opening Statement, Second Meeting of Federal and Provincial Officials," November 2, 1970, p. 2.

44. Except where otherwise indicated, material on the proceedings of the 1970 meeting is drawn from a set of unofficial minutes prepared by the Secretary of the MVTC.

45. "Provincial Statement."

46. Ibid.

47. Ibid.

48. An explanation for the difference in federal behaviour at the 1969 and 1970 meetings is basic to an understanding of the fate of Part III. Yet, the "government-as-unitary actor" model cannot account for these differences because their cause was not to be found in the interactions between the contending governments but in the dynamics of the relationships within the federal government. The internal dynamics accounting for federal behaviour at the 1970 meeting are analysed in ch. 5.

Notes to Chapter Four

1. Irwin Haskett, Minister of Transport, Province of Ontario, to Don C. Jamieson, December 17, 1970. Mr. Haskett was acting as spokesman for the Conference of Provincial Ministers Responsible for Motor Carrier Regulation.

2. On the importance of "sites and procedures" see Richard Simeon, *Federal-Provincial Diplomacy* (Toronto: University of Toronto Press, 1972), pp. 124–45, esp. pp. 127–28.

3. Don Jamieson to Irwin Haskett, January 15, 1971. Mr. Haskett telegraphed the federal reply to the other provincial ministers.

4. Don Jamieson to provincial ministers of transport, April 14, 1971, *Advisory Council Report*, III, B. 18 (henceforth *ACR*).

5. "National Transportation Act: Implementation of Part III," *ACR*, III, B. 19.

6. Ibid., p. 3.

7. Ibid., p. 2. Province was taken to include the Yukon and Northwest Territories.

8. Ibid., p. 3.

9. Ibid.

10. The number of trucking operations affected by each stage of the federal implementation plan is as follows:

Stage 1	306
Stage 2	174
Stage 3	256
Stage 4	
Can.	827
U.S.	369
TOTAL	1,932

The data are from the information provided by the federal government with its plan of implementation.

11. Gordon Taylor to Charles MacNaughton, April 14, 1971.

12. *Queen* v. *George Smith*, [1972] S.C.R. 359. The case involved a challenge to Alberta's regulation of extraprovincial motor carriers on the grounds that because such regulation was different from that imposed on intraprovincial undertakings, it contravened the Motor Vehicle Transport Act. If the challenge were successful, the Alberta regulatory system, with its emphasis on minimal entry controls would have had to be completely revised. The court upheld the validity of the Alberta legislation.

13. "Ontario Position Paper Relative to the National Transportation Act" (April 1971), pp. 4–5.

14. Statement by the Hon. Charles MacNaughton to the Federal-Provincial Conference of Ministers Responsible for Commercial Motor Vehicle Administration, May 3, 1971, *ACR*, III, B. 20: 2.

15. "Statement by Charles MacNaughton," p. 4.

16. Statement of the Quebec Minister of Transport Relative to the Implementation of Part III of the National Transportation Act, Ottawa, May 3, 1971, p. 2.

17. Ibid.

18. The issuing of this threat supports Simeon's contentions (*Federal-Provincial Diplomacy*, p. 232) that Quebec is more prepared than the other provinces to use threats in federal-provincial negotiations. What is significant about this particular threat is that it was part of a coordinated Ontario-Quebec strategy.

19. In the Winner case, the Judicial Committee of the Privy Council noted in its decision that:

> The province has indeed authority over its own roads but that authority is a limited one and does not entitle it to interfere with connecting undertakings. It must be remembered that it is the undertaking, not the roads, which comes within the jurisdiction of the Dominion, but legislation which denies the use of provincial roads to such an undertaking or sterilizes the undertaking itself is an interference with the prerogative of the Dominion.

Richard A. Olmstead, ed., *Canadian Constitutional Decisions of the Judicial Committee* (Ottawa: Queen's Printer, 1959), III: 815.

20. The official terms of reference, found in the *ACR*, I: 2, include a negative reference to the CTC, the significance of which is discussed in ch. 6.

21. *ACR*, I: 2.

22. Press Release issued by federal Ministry of Transport after the conference, *ACR*, III, B. 21.

23. This discussion of the work of the Advisory Council is based on interviews with nine of the fifteen members of the council, as well as two official observers from the CTC. In addition, the minutes of the meetings of the council were examined.

24. *ACR*, I: 19–23.

25. Minutes of the first meeting of the Advisory Council, June 8, 1971, Ottawa, p. 3.

26. Minutes of the second meeting of the Advisory Council, July 22, 1971, Ottawa, p. 4.

27. Minutes of the third meeting of the Advisory Council, August 26–27, 1971, Halifax, p. 2.

28. Minutes of the Regulatory Structure Sub-Group, September 28–29, 1971, Toronto, p. 3.

29. David Duncan to A. L. Peel, October 4, 1971. The letter is curious in that the first section is clearly unrelated to the second, in which Duncan comments on the council's activities. It would be reasonable to suggest that the introductory part of the letter was merely a pretext to permit Duncan to raise again the propriety of the council discussing the Nova Scotia proposal. Why he would do so is the subject of some speculation in ch. 6.

30. Draft report of Regulatory Structure Chapter, Advisory Council, submitted by M. R. LeBlanc, secretary of the Regulatory Structure Sub-Group, to the members of the Advisory Council, no date (but prior to the Winnipeg meeting of the council).

31. Ibid., p. 11.

32. The following analysis is based on a verbatim transcript of the discussion at the Winnipeg meeting of the council when the federal minister's statement was read to the council. This appears to be the only instance when such a record was kept. The significance of this fact is discussed in ch. 6.

33. Don Jamieson to R. Romanow, November 24, 1971.

34. The "8 Province" proposal was the statement presented to the November 1970 meeting, of the Joint Technical Committee, calling for a majority of provincial representatives on the regulatory structure.

35. *ACR*, I: 4.

36. Ibid., pp. 4–11.

37. Ibid., p. 15.

38. Ibid., p. 16.

39. Ibid.

40. Ibid., p. 18.

41. Ibid., B. 21.

Notes to Chapter Five

1. J. W. Pickersgill, address to the Automotive Transport Association of British Columbia, Vancouver, October 20, 1967, p. 9.

2. Ibid.

3. Mr. Magee apparently had good reason for this belief. See ch. 7, p. 153.

4. Quoted by Graham Allison, *Essence of Decision* (Boston: Little Brown, 1971), p. 176.

5. Francis Rourke, *Bureaucracy, Politics and Public Policy* (Boston: Little Brown, 1969), p. 84.

6. Sayre and Kaufman, *Governing New York City*, quoted in Rourke, *Bureaucracy and Public Policy*, p. 85.

7. Ibid.

8. Harry Eckstein, *Pressure Group Politics* (Stanford: Stanford University Press, 1960), p. 23.

9. *HC Debates*, 1966–67, p. 11637. On this point, cf. Martin Westmacott, "The National Transportation Act and the Western Provinces: A Case Study in Co-operative Federalism," *Canadian Public Administration* 16 (1973): 455–56.

10. *HC Debates*, January 26, 1967, p. 12348.

11. Ibid., p. 12284.

12. Perhaps the best statement of the predominant federal approach, in theory at least, was *Federalism for the Future*, issued under Prime Minister Pearson's name in early 1968, when the negotiations on Part III were about to begin.

13. Pickersgill, Address, October 20, 1967, p. 11.

14. The policy role for the CTC is provided under Section 22 of the NTA. On this point see John W. Langford, *Transport in Transition: The Reorganization of the Federal Transport Portfolio* (Montreal: McGill-Queen's University Press and the Institute of Public Administration of Canada, 1976), pp. 37–42.

15. John W. Langford, "The Making of Transport Policies: A Case Study: The Ministry of Transport as a Policy Making Instrument," in Studnicki-Gizbert, ed., *Issues in Canadian Transport Policy* (Toronto: Macmillan, 1974), p. 410.

16. Pierre Taschereau, "Canada's National Transportation Act and the Canadian Transport Commission." Paper presented to the ninth annual meeting of the Transportation Research Forum, Kansas City, Missouri, 1968, p. 58.

17. Ibid., p. 59. For a criticism of the mixing of the regulatory and policy advisory roles see F. W. Anderson, "The Philosophy of the MacPherson Royal Commission and the National Transportation Act: A Retrospective Essay," in Studnicki-Gizbert, *Issues in Canadian Transport Policy*.

18. On the concept of "bureaucracy territoriality" see Anthony Downs, *Inside Bureaucracy* (Boston: Little Brown, 1967), pp. 212–16.

19. J. W. Pickersgill, address to the Automotive Transport Association of Ontario, Toronto, November 26, 1968, p. 21.

20. Richard Neustadt, *Presidential Power* (New York: New American Library, 1960), p. 42.

21. There was a certain degree of irony in this appointment as the individual concerned had been an adviser to the Quebec minister of transport and the Quebec representative on the Advisory Council prior to his appointment to the CTC. After his appointment, he became one of the CTC observers on the Advisory Council.

22. The estimates of the number of undertakings that would have to be licensed ranged from 2,500 to 4,000.

23. Pickersgill, Address, November 26, 1968, p. 18.

24. On this aspect of the negotiations on Part III, see ch. 7.

25. Pickersgill was not alone in thinking that Hellyer was more concerned with housing than transportation. A report on the First Canadian Urban Transportation Conference, held in February 1969, stated "there was another lament over the fact that Transport Minister Hellyer used the occasion to talk about his housing task force rather than transportation." *Bus and Truck Transport*, March 1969, p. 45.

26. On the question of the importance of industry support and the role it played in the negotiations on Part III, see ch. 7.

27. See Langford, *Transport in Transition*. In the following discussion, I am relying heavily on this study.

28. Ibid., p. 90.

29. Ibid., p. 239, n 28.

30. Ibid., pp. 160–63.

31. Ibid., p. 161. A significant omission in the reorganization of 1970 was that the minister was not given the power to direct the CTC on questions of policy. This omission was subsequently recognized when the minister of transport, in announcing a new transportation policy, emphasized that the relationship between the minister and the CTC would be further clarified and the minister given the power to issue binding directives to the CTC on questions of policy. See *HC Debates*, June 16, 1975, p. 6785.

32. For an extended discussion of the "ministry system" see Langford, *Transport and Transition*, especially pp. 15–22 and the references therein.

33. Ibid., p. 167.

34. Ibid.

35. The role of the Surface Transportation Administration caused some concern as well for the members of the DOT's Policy Planning and Major Projects section which was to be the main "policy adviser" within the ministry. As a member of this section commented: "The Surface Administration is supposed to be a parallel to the other administrations but it is completely different. The other administrations have enormous operating arms . . . The Surface Administration has no operations. It is a policy and planning group and our policy advisor on Surface Administration is competing with a group that only does policy planning."

36. "Positional policy is the term used to describe policy outcomes which have the effect of restructuring the distribution of power and influence among individuals or units within governments." Langford, *Transport in Transition*, p. 71. Cf. P. Aucoin, "Theory and Research in the Study of Policy-Making," in G. Bruce Doern and Peter Aucoin, eds., *The Structures of Policy-Making in Canada* (Toronto: Macmillan, 1971), esp. pp. 25–26.

37. "Grandfather rights" are exceptions to existing regulations based on rights granted prior to the promulgation of the regulations.

38. See ch. 4, pp. 61–62.

39. *ACR*, III, B. 19: 3.

40. Allison, *Essence of Decision*, pp. 145–46.

41. *ACR*, I: 1.

Notes to Chapter Six

1. Peter Self, *Administrative Theories and Politics* (Toronto: University of Toronto Press, 1973), p. 121. The concept is from P. Meyer, *Administrative Organizations* (London: Stevens, 1957).

2. Robert Keohane and Joseph S. Nye, "Transgovernmental Relations and International Organizations," *World Politics* 27 (October 1974): 59.

3. Two other observers were appointed subsequently, one of whom, the Quebec official who had become the managing director, Operations of the Motor Vehicle Transport Committee, was more senior. An irony of the CTC's attitude toward the Advisory Council was the fact that the CTC paid for the study of a uniform classification of accounts undertaken for the council by outside consultants.

4. For a discussion of the Nova Scotia proposal, see ch. 4, p. 70.

5. Anthony Downs, *Inside Bureaucracy* (Boston: Little Brown, 1967), pp. 212–13.

6. Ibid.

7. See ch. 4, pp. 70–71.

8. Ibid.

9. Ibid., p. 71.

10. D. M. Duncan to A. L. Peel, October 13, 1971.

11. The reference is to Peel's MBA thesis written while on study leave from the Canadian Government. The thesis was based in part on the early discussions held with the provinces in 1966–67. See A. L. Peel, "A Regulatory Structure for Canadian Motor Carriers," MBA thesis, University of California, 1967.

12. There are provincial representatives on the Canadian Saltfish Corporation, the Fresh Water Fish Marketing Board, as well as on several regulatory boards of the International Joint Commission, such as the Great Lakes Water Quality Board. The public sector panels of the Anti-Inflation Board provide the most recent precedent.

13. See Downs, *Inside Bureaucracy*, p. 190.

14. Downs defines "zealots" as officials "loyal to narrow policies or concepts. . . . They seek power both for its own sake and to effect the policies to which they are loyal." (Ibid., p. 88.) From this perspective, Peel's concern with federal regulation was his "sacred policy."

15. Apparently Ontario's representative would only speak on the original Ontario proposal, Method One. This Ontario hard line, along with the federal intransigence, was assumed to be a Pickersgill-Ontario strategy to lead to stalemate on the council. The original Ontario member of the council, David Duncan, was not at the meeting in Winnipeg. According to DOT officials present at the meeting, Duncan's representative had no authority to commit Ontario to any position. (This was subsequently confirmed in interviews with

Ontario officials.) One of the reasons given by DOT officials for this belief was the fact that the Ontario delegate continually excused himself to use the telephone. Several months after the Winnipeg meeting, the DOT submitted a bill for twenty-three dollars for telephone calls made from the airport manager's office to Duncan's office in Toronto. Additional "evidence" to support the conspiracy theory offered by DOT officials was that they apparently saw Duncan leaving the CTC offices in Ottawa just prior to the Winnipeg meeting.

There is no other evidence and a case hardly exists. Members of the commission vehemently denied any suggestion that the CTC and the Ontario government had collaborated in an effort to stop discussion of the Nova Scotia proposal. The charge, however, is interesting in that it reveals something of the state of mind of some of the federal officials concerning the CTC. Moreover, while it is highly doubtful that such collusion did take place, it is not beyond the realm of conjecture to suggest that the Ontario position in the later stages of the council's deliberations was predicated on a negative decision on the Nova Scotia proposal which the Ontario representative by his letters, I have argued, was trying to provoke. One does not need to reply on any suggestion of collusion to suggest that perhaps the Ontario government and the CTC were independently working for the same result.

16. The verbatim transcript of the discussion at Winnipeg of the minister of transport's telegram was taken so that the chairman could demonstrate that he had, in fact, followed the minister's instructions. For discussion, see ch. 4, pp. 72–74.

17. Ibid., p. 74.

18. Ibid., pp. 74–75.

19. One of the basic causes of this fear was not simply the partisan nature of Mr. Pickersgill's appointment as first president of the CTC, but was related to his actions in subsequent appearances before the House of Commons Standing Committee on Transportation and Communications when he defended the commission's estimates. See, for example, the exchange that took place on November 28, 1968, pp. 95–96, 98 of the committee's *Proceedings*.

20. It should be remembered that this assessment was offered in June 1973. Subsequently the minister of transport publicly criticized the NTA and suggested the need to change it. See the Toronto *Globe and Mail*, March 21, 1974, and *HC Debates*, March 7, 1974. Langford also mentions the unwillingness to amend the NTA to effect the reorganization into the ministry system. See Langford, *Transport in Transition* (Montreal: McGill-Queen's University Press, and the Institute of Public Administration of Canada, 1976), pp. 149–57, especially pp. 153–54. The "new" national transportation policy was announced on June 16, 1975. Of particular relevance to this study are the minister's comments on "the role of the Canadian Transport Commission and its relationship with the Ministry of Transport."

21. See note 10, above.

22. The members of the task force were: from the CTC, Vice-President Cope, Laval Fortier, chairman of the MVTC, Commissioner Magee and

Robert Martin, the managing director of operations of the MVTC; from the DOT, in addition to the senior assistant deputy minister, and Peel, John Gray, senior ministry executive legal, Charles Halton, senior ministry executive policy, planning and major projects, Roy Illing, administrator, surface administration and Homer Neilly, the policy adviser to Surface Administration in Policy Planning and Major Projects.

23. According to the proposal, offices of the CTC would be in Vancouver, Saskatoon, Toronto, Montreal, and Moncton.

24. A provincial role as proposed by the CTC would be permitted under Sections 81(1) and 42(g) of the NTA.

25. See Peel, "Regulatory Structure," pp. 91–95.

26. See ch. 7, p. 165.

27. On the significance of this argument, see John M. Munro, *Trade Liberalization and Transportation in International Trade* (Toronto: University of Toronto Press, 1969), pp. 142–51, 161.

Notes to Chapter Seven

1. "Trucking Comes of Age," *Bus and Truck Transport*, February 1967, p. 41.

2. "In Praise of Mr. Pickersgill," *Bus and Truck Transport*, February 1967, p. 5.

3. "Ottawa's Transportation Illiterates," *Motor Truck*, October 1973.

4. Morton Grodzins, "The Federal System," in A. Wildavsky, ed., *American Federalism in Perspective* (Boston: Little Brown, 1967), p. 268. For a more comprehensive statement of this thesis, see Grodzins' *The American System*, ed. D. J. Elazar (Chicago: Rand McNally, 1966).

5. These assumptions are common to American writing on group activity in federal systems. See, for example, David Truman, *The Governmental Process* (New York: Knopf, 1951), p. 323; Abraham Holtzman, *Interest Groups and Lobbying* (New York: Macmillan, 1966), p. 59; and Harmon Zeigler, *Interest Groups in American Society* (Englewood Cliffs: Prentice-Hall, 1964), p. 107. For Canadian examples where such assumptions have been made, see the Bucovetsky and Kwavnick articles in Paul Pross, ed., *Pressure Group Behaviour in Canadian Politics* (Toronto: McGraw-Hill, 1975), and ch. 7 in F. C. Engelmann and M. A. Schwartz, *Canadian Political Parties: Origin, Character, Impact* (Toronto: Prentice-Hall, 1975).

6. Grodzins, "The Federal System," p. 268.

7. Truman, *The Governmental Process*, p. 116. See also the discussion in the Dawson and Kwavnick articles in Pross, *Pressure Group Behaviour*, and in R. A. Bauer et al., *American Business and Public Policy* (New York: Atherton Press, 1963), pp. 332–40.

8. Richard Simeon, *Federal-Provincial Diplomacy* (Toronto: University of Toronto Press, 1972), p. 144.

9. Ibid., p. 282.

10. Pross discusses the support function of interest groups but not in the context of intergovernmental relations. See Pross, *Pressure Group Behaviour*, p. 6. See, however, the Dawson article in Pross which does allude to the support function.

11. A motor carrier section was included in the 1937 attempt by the federal government to establish the Board of Transport Commissioners. See ch. 2, p. 14, for a discussion.

12. One of the recurring forms for such opposition was the numerous royal commissions on transportation or related issues. The CTA appeared before the Turgeon Commission (1949), the Gordon Commission (1956), and the MacPherson Commission (1959) to emphasize its opposition to federal regulation.

13. There has been little attention in Canada paid to the judicial system as a target of interest group activity and this is surprising given the acknowledged important role the courts have played in the development of Canadian federalism. See, however, Peter H. Russell, "The Anti-Inflation Case: The Anatomy of a Constitutional Decision," *Canadian Public Administration* 10 (1977), and for a general discussion, M. L. Friedland, "Pressure Groups and the Development of the Criminal Law," in P. R. Glazebrook, ed., *Reshaping the Criminal Law* (London: Stevens, 1978).

14. "Federal Control: Dilemma Faces the Truckers," *Canadian Transportation*, December 1958, quoted in Munro, "The History of Motor Carrier Transportation and its Regulation in Canada," MBA thesis, Indiana University, 1963, p. 113.

15. Quoted by Camille Archambault in a speech to the Annual Conference of Roads and Transportation Association of Canada, Halifax, October 10, 1973, p. 5.

16. "The Need for New Federal Regulation to Control Extra-Provincial Highway Transport," submission to the Hon. J. W. Pickersgill, minister of transport, by the CTA, December 9, 1965 (hereafter, CTA 1965 submission).

17. Letter to the Hon. G. McIlraith, minister of transport, April 1963, p. 8, quoted by Paul Pross, "Dominion-Provincial Relations in the Field of Highway Regulation," M.A. thesis, Queen's University, 1963, p. 125.

18. CTA 1965 submission.

19. CTA submission to the House of Commons Standing Committee on Transport and Communications, November 3, 1966, p. 3 (hereafter, CTA 1966 submission).

20. Francis Rourke, *Bureaucracy, Politics and Public Policy* (Boston: Little Brown and Company, 1969), pp. 2–3.

21. See ch. 5, pp. 82–83.

22. See ch. 2, p. 14.

23. Robert Presthus, *Elite Accommodation in Canadian Politics* (Toronto: Macmillan, 1973), p. 226.

24. The promise was reported by the then president of the CTA in August 1967. See R. J. Lewis, in *Bus and Truck Transport*, September 1967, p. 25.

The promise was corroborated in interviews with individuals associated with both the industry and the DOT.

25. It was argued that twelve amendments proposed by CTA were accepted by the government. See *Bus and Truck Transport*, June 1967, p. 73.

26. See, for example, J. W. Pickersgill, "Canada's National Transport Policy," *Transportation Law Journal* I (1969): 85, and his address to the British Columbia and Ontario Trucking conventions on October 20, 1967, and November 26, 1968, respectively.

27. See, for example, articles in *Bus and Truck Transport*, February 1967, pp. 4, 5.

28. Truman, *The Governmental Process*, p. 159.

29. On the general question of the impact of French-Canadian nationalism on interest groups, see John Meisel and Vincent Lemieux, *Ethnic Relations in Canadian Voluntary Associations*, Royal Commission on Bilingualism and Biculturalism, Documents, no. 13 (Ottawa: Information Canada, 1972), and David Kwavnick's article in Pross, ed., *Pressure Group Behaviour*.

30. Truman, *The Governmental Process*, p. 116.

31. Quoted in "Quebec Truckers Divided Over Federal Control?" *Bus and Truck Transport*, April 1968, p. 19.

32. *Bus and Truck Transport*, May 1968, p. 45.

33. The member who introduced the various bills was Fernand LeBlanc who was at various times the auditor for the QTA.

34. *Bus and Truck Transport*, July 1969, p. 38.

35. On the concept of a "mandate" see David Kwavnick, *Organized Labour and Pressure Politics: The Canadian Labour Congress, 1956–1968* (Montreal: McGill-Queen's University Press, 1972), pp. 12–25. The mandate was initially announced in a speech by the Ontario minister of transportation and communications to the ATAO convention, November 22, 1971.

36. Rourke, *Bureaucracy*, p. 54.

37. Presthus, *Elite Accommodation*, pp. 161–62.

38. *Bus and Truck Transport*, December 1968, p. 33.

39. Minutes of meeting between members of the MVTC and representatives of CMA, February 13, 1969.

40. M. W. Donnelly, in *Bus and Truck Transport*, March 1970, p. 20.

41. The following discussion emphasizes the political role of interest groups in the negotiations. It should also be mentioned that interest groups played a technical, or functional, role in that a number of groups including CTA, CMA, the Canadian Associations of Movers, and the Canadian Industrial Traffic League were sent the draft regulations discussed at the conference and requested to comment on them.

42. M. W. Donnelly, then president of the CTA, commented to this effect in a speech to the Saskatchewan Trucking Association in Saskatoon, January 23, 1970.

43. *Bus and Truck Transport*, July 1971, p. 79.

Notes to Chapter Eight

1. Arend Lijphart, "Comparative Politics and the Comparative Method," *American Political Science Review* 65 (1971): 691–93.

2. Lawrence C. Pierce, *The Politics of Fiscal Policy Formation* (Pacific Palisades: Goodyear Publishing, 1971), p. 134.

3. Alan Cairns, "The Other Crisis of Canadian Federalism," *Canadian Public Administration* 22 (1979): 184.

4. Larry Pratt, *The Tar Sands: Syncrude and the Politics of Oil* (Edmonton: Hurtig Publishers, 1976), and M. W. Bucovetsky, "The Mining Industry and the Great Tax Reform Debate," in A. Paul Pross, ed., *Pressure Group Behaviour in Canadian Politics* (Toronto: McGraw-Hill Ryerson, 1975).

5. Richard Simeon, *Federal-Provincial Diplomacy* (Toronto: University of Toronto Press, 1972), pp. 204–13.

6. Ibid., p. 213.

7. Morton Grodzins, *The American System*, ed. D. J. Elazar (Chicago: Rand McNally, 1966).

8. Francis Rourke, *Bureaucracy, Politics and Public Policy* (Boston: Little Brown, 1969), p. 20.

9. Graham Wootton has suggested that such interactions should be conceptualized as part of a "duplex system" in the flow of influence between interest groups and their targets. See Wootton, *Interest Groups* (Englewood Cliffs: Prentice-Hall, 1970), pp. 96–98.

10. Material for the following three pages is drawn from Richard J. Schultz, *Federalism and the Regulatory Process* (Montreal: Institute for Research on Public Policy, 1979).

11. Lloyd Cutler and David R. Johnson, "Regulation and the Political Process," *Yale Law Journal* 89 (1975): 1399. See also Schultz, *Federalism and the Regulatory Process*, pp. 7–21.

12. John W. Langford, *Transport in Transition* (Montreal: McGill-Queen's University Press and the Institute of Public Administration of Canada, 1976), p. 42.

13. Schultz, *Federalism and the Regulatory Process*, pp. 29–30, 34–40. For a more comprehensive survey of the powers and functions of the CTC, see Hudson Janisch, *The Regulatory Process of the Canadian Transport Commission* (Ottawa: Law Reform Commission, 1978).

14. Janisch, *The Regulatory Process*, pp. 114–23.

15. Schultz, *Federalism and the Regulatory Process*, pp. 66–67.

16. G. Bruce Doern, "Introduction" in G. Bruce Doern, ed., *The Regulatory Process in Canada* (Toronto: Macmillan, 1978), pp. 12–13.

17. Schultz, *Federalism and the Regulatory Process*, p. 51.

18. Peter Self, *Administrative Theories and Politics* (Toronto: University of Toronto Press, 1973), p. 121.

19. G. Bruce Doern, *Science and Politics in Canada* (Montreal: McGill-Queen's University Press, 1972), p. 205.

20. See Thomas A. Hockin, ed., *Apex of Power: The Prime Minister and*

Political Leadership in Canada, 2nd ed. (Toronto: Prentice-Hall, 1977), and the literature cited in Richard D. French, "The Privy Council Office: Support for Cabinet Decision Making," in Richard Schultz et al., *The Canadian Political Process*, 3rd ed. (Toronto: Holt, Rinehart and Winston, 1979).

21. This is the comment of a senior Ontario official quoted in Simeon, *Federal-Provincial Diplomacy*, p. 37.

22. Ibid., p. 38.

23. Blair Williams, "The Transformation of the Federal Cabinet under P. E. Trudeau," paper delivered to the annual meeting of the Canadian Political Science Association, Saskatoon, May 30, 1979.

24. See, for example, Colin Campbell and George J. Szablowski, *The Super-Bureaucrats: Structure and Behaviour in Central Agencies* (Toronto: Macmillan, 1978).

25. This is the role public servants perceived themselves to be playing in the Columbia River Treaty negotiations, according to Neil A. Swainson, *Conflict over the Columbia: The Canadian Background to an Historic Treaty* (Montreal: McGill-Queen's University Press and the Institute of Public Administration of Canada, 1979), p. 302.

26. For two expressions of such concern see Canada, Office of the Auditor General, *Report, 1976*, p. 9, and Canada, Royal Commission on Financial Management and Accountability, *Final Report*, Ottawa, 1979, esp. parts one and five.

Index

Advisory Council on Motor Carrier Regulation: creation of, 65, 110–11, 113; terms of reference, 65; purpose of, 67; Regulatory Structure Sub-Group, 68; Regulations Sub-Group, 68; agreed set of principles, 68–69; and Ontario proposal, 69; and federal phasing proposal, 69–70; and Nova Scotia proposal, 70–77, 116, 117; and regional board proposal, 70, 72; and reaction to ministerial directive, 73; revised report of, 74–77; and CTC attitude towards, 114–15; and Department of Transport attitude towards, 115–16; and review of, 119–21; and Winnipeg meeting of, 122–25. *See also* Nova Scotia proposal; Peel, A. L.; Pickersgill, J. W.; Winnipeg meeting of Advisory Council

Aikin, Charles, 13

Alberta, government of: and frustration by CTC, 176

Alberta, minister of transport: and provincial strategy for Federal-Provincial Conference of Ministers (1971), 62

Allison, Graham T., 110; and bureaucratic politics model, 7–9

Allison, Graham, and Halperin, Morton, 7

Amendments to Motor Vehicle Transport Act, 129

Amendments to Part III of NTA, 128, 129

Anderson, F. W., 209n17

Assistant deputy minister, 93

Baldwin, J. R., 203n30

Benson, Hon. E. J. (president of Canadian Transport Commission), 199n3

Bill C-231 (NTA): and trucking industry approval of, 152; and minority government, 152, 153

Board of Transport commissioners, 14

Borowski, Joe, 65

British North America Act: s. 92 (10)(a), 15

Bucovetsky, M. W., 171

Bureaucratic politics model: comparison to unitary actor model, 5; nature of, 6; and intragovernmental bargaining, 6–10; and hierarchical controls, 8; and concept of signals, 9, 10; and intergovernmental negotiations, 178, 179

Cabinet: and relationship with departments, 186; and discussion of Part III of NTA, 186; and committee system, 188

Cairns, Alan, 171

Campbell, Colin and Szablowski,

219

George, 217n24
Canada Labour (Safety) Code, 37
Canadian Association of Movers, 160
Canadian Industrial Traffic League, 149, 160
Canadian Manufacturers Association, 149, 160–61
Canadian Motor Coach Association, 160
Canadian Radio-Television Commission, 135, 174, 176–77
Canadian Surface Transportation Administration: functions of, 104, 210n35. See also Highways Branch of the Canadian Surface Transportation Administration
Canadian Transport Commission (CTC): function of, 1, 21–22, 175; and Part III of NTA, 11; and provinces as interveners, 24, 25; and federal government resource, 28–29; policy advisory role of, 87–88, 103, 175–76; and relationship with Department of Transport, 87–89, 103, 176; and Joint Technical Comittee Meeting (1970), 100; and reorganization of transport folio, 102–3; policy research role of, 103; and relationship with deputy minister, 103; and fear of provincial participation on, 107, 116, 117; and court of record, 114, 119; and attitude towards Advisory Council, 114–15; 211n3; and assessment of Part III of NTA, 114; and rejection of Nova Scotia proposal, 116, 119; and report on Advisory Council report, 130, 132–34; and strategy for DOT-CTC Task Force, 136; regional proposal of, 137–38; adjudicative powers of, 175; implementation role of, 175–76. See also CTC-DOT coalition; CTC observers, DOT-CTC Task Force; Intervener; Nova Scotia proposal; Ontario, government of; Pickersgill, J. W.; Provincial participation on

regulatory agencies
CTC-DOT coalition: formation of, 92; and strategy for Federal-Provincial Conference of Ministers (1969), 92–95; and assessment of Federal-Provincial Conference of Ministers (1969), 95; and reaction to recommendations of Pickersgill, J. W., 97–98; and memorandum on Part III of NTA, 101–2; and reorganization of transport folio, 102–4; dissolution of, 107, 113; and Cabinet, 186. See also Peel, A. L.; Pickersgill, J. W.
CTC observers: and Advisory Council, 116, 117, 119, 120, 124–25. See also Pickersgill, J. W.
Canadian Trucking Associations, 14, 92, 97; and opposition to federal regulation, 139; and interest group theory, 149; and pre-1965 position on federal regulation, 149, 150–51, 214n12; and multiple crack thesis, 149–51, 167; and restricted access thesis, 150, 167; and support for Bill C-231 (NTA), 152; and representation on CTC, 152–53; and implementation of Part III of NTA, 155, 160–64; and conflict with QTA, 156–57, 164; and pressure from provincial regulators, 157–60; and role in Federal-Provincial Conference of Ministers (1969), 161; and role in Federal-Provincial Conference of Ministers (1970), 163–64; and reversion to pre-1965 position, 165; and role in intergovernmental negotiations, 171–72. See also Ontario, government of; Ontario Highway Transport Board; Quebec Trucking Association
Carr, D. W.: on intermodel competition, 17, 18
Central agencies: and power relationship with operating departments, 182–88; and manpower resources, 182–83; and informa-

timetable for implementation of Part III, 60–61; and federal proposals, 61, 65; and Ontario-Quebec common front, 63–65; and Advisory Council, 65–66

Federal-Provincial Diplomacy (by Richard Simeon), 3

Federal-Provincial Relations Office, 135, 183, 185

Fortier, Laval (chairman of Motor Vehicle Transport Committee of Canadian Transport Commission): and bureaucratic politics model, 82; and appointment of, 90

French, Richard D., 216–17n20

Friedland, M. L., 214n13

"Gabon affair," 35, 204n17

Grandfather rights, 104

Grodzins, Morton, 148, 155, 172

Hailey, A. F., 202nn12, 23

Halperin, Morton, 9

Haskett, Irwin (minister of transport, Province of Ontario), 206 nn1, 3

Hellyer, Paul (minister of transport), 92, 210n25

Hierarchical controls, 8; within DOT, 180–82; possessed by central agencies, 182–88

Highways Branch of Surface Transportation Administration: and reorganization of, 104; and reaction to recommendation of Pickersgill, J. W., 105–8; and Privy Council Office, 107–8; and attitude towards Advisory Council, 115; and assessment of Advisory Council, 125–26; and shelving of Part III of NTA, 126

Hockin, Thomas A., 216n20

Hodgetts, J. E., 11

Howe, C. D. (minister of transport), 14

Information control: and central agencies, 184

Interest groups: and unitary actor model, 4, 5; and Part III of NTA, 12; and federalism, 148–49; and multiple crack thesis, 148, 167; and restricted access thesis, 148–49, 167; and role in federal-provincial negotiations, 161, 163–64, 170–73, 215n41; and CTA, 171–72

Intergovernmental coalition, 114, 124

Intermodal competition, 17, 18, 21, 82, 89

Intervener: role of provinces in CTC, 24, 25; and Joint Technical Committee, 50. *See also* Ontario, government of; Provincial participation on regulatory agencies

Intragovernmental bargaining. *See* Bureaucratic politics model

Jamieson, Donald (federal minister of transport): and Federal-Provincial Conference of Transport Ministers (1969), 38, 39, 93; appointment of, 92; and creation of Advisory Council, 110–11. *See also* Minister of Transport

Janisch, Hudson, 216nn13, 14

Johnson, Daniel (premier of Quebec): opposition to Part III of NTA, 32–33

Joint federal-provincial committee, 61

Joint participation proposal: and Ontario Method Two proposal, 42; and renaming of Nova Scotia proposal, 75, 124

Joint Technical Committee: purpose of, 40; and Federal-Provincial Conference of Transport Ministers (1971), 63–64

Joint Technical Committee Meeting (1974): and Ontario proposal, 41, 100; and purpose of, 43–44; and federal strategy, 44–45, 54, 100; and united provincial front, 45–48, 205nn35, 36; and meeting of, 48; and federal assessment of, 52; and demand for provincial participation, 50–51; and provin-

terial directive, 72–73; and revised report of, 74–76; renamed joint participation proposal, 75; federal acceptance of, 76–77; and CTC opposition to, 116; and Ontario member on Advisory Council, 117; and review of Advisory Council, 120–21; and Winnipeg meeting, 123–25. *See also* Advisory Council; Canadian Transport Commission; CTC observers; Ontario, government of; Ontario member on Advisory Council; Peel, A. L.; Pickersgill, J. W.

Nye, Joseph, and Keohane, Robert, 114

Olmstead, Richard A., 202n9, 207 n19

Ontario delegation on Joint Technical Committee: meeting of, 49–51; and role of intervener, 59–60. *See also* Intervener; Joint Technical Committee Meeting; Provincial participation on regulatory agencies

Ontario, government of: opposition to Part III of NTA, 33, 34; and Federal-Provincial Conference of Ministers (1971), 59, 60; and common front with Quebec, 63–65, 67; and provincial participation on CTC, 107; and pressure on CTA, 158; and frustration by CTC, 176. *See also* Canadian Transport Commission, Ontario delegation on Joint Technical Committee; Ontario member on Advisory Council; Ontario proposal; Ontario-Quebec common front; Provincial participation on regulatory agencies

Ontario Highway Transport Board, 23; and pressure on CTA, 158–60, 163

Ontario Impact Study, 23, 24, 203 nn34, 35, 36

Ontario member on Advisory Council: and terms of reference for Nova Scotia proposal, 70–71,

117–18, 123, 211n15; and provincial participation on CTC, 116–17. *See also* Advisory Council; Canadian Transport Commission; Nova Scotia Proposal; Peel, A. L.; Pickersgill, J. W.

Ontario proposal, 97, 99; origin of, 40; first version, 40–41; second version, 41–42; Method One, 42, 91, 102; Method Two, 42; federal assessment of, 44, 67–68; and united provincial front, 45–47; and Joint Technical Committee meeting (1970), 48–51, 100; and Federal-Provincial Conference of Ministers (1971), 63–64; and Advisory Council, 67, 69; and CTA briefing of, 162. *See also* Ontario-Quebec common front; Peel, A. L.; Pickersgill, J. W.; Provincial participation on regulatory agencies; United provincial front

Ontario-Quebec common front: and Federal-Provincial Conference of Transport Ministers (1971), 63–65

Ontario Trucking Association, 158, 160

Ontario trucking industry: effect of Part III on, 23

Pacific Western Airlines, 176

Parliamentary system: nature of power within, 3–4, 145; and regulatory agencies, 11, 173–78; and ministerial responsibility, 11; and unitary actor model, 180; and power of central agencies, 180–89. *See also* Central agencies; Regulatory agencies

Part III of National Transportation Act (NTA): and bureaucratic politics model, 5, 11; and regulatory agencies, 11; and Canadian Transport Commission, 11; and interest groups, 12; and purpose of, 21, 22; provincial opposition to, 22–25, 32, 36, 37; and constitutional interpretation by

Quebec, 29; and federal government interpretation of, 82–83; and proclamation of, 96, 97–98, 162; and assessment by Department of Transport, 115–16; and assessment by CTC, 114; and assessment by Highways Branch of Surface Administration, 126; amendments to, 128–29. *See also* National Transportation Act

Pearson, Lester B.: and provincial discussions of Part III, 31, 32, 33

Peel, A. L. (director of Highways Branch in Department of Transport): and bureaucratic politics model, 82; and implementation of Part III of NTA, 82, 89; and Coughlin case, 83; and conspiracy, 93; and terms of reference for Advisory Council, 110–11; and reassessment of Part III of NTA, 115; and Nova Scotia proposal, 117, 119, 120, 122; and Winnipeg meeting, 123–25; and DOT-CTC Task Force, 134; and hierarchical authority, 145, 181; and drafting of Part III of NTA, 153; and CTA support, 162; and bargaining resources, 181. *See also* Jamieson, Donald, minister of transport; Nova Scotia proposal; Ontario member on Advisory Council; Pickersgill, J. W.; Pre-Part III federal actors

Philosophy of National Transportation Act (NTA): and trucking industry, 20; and Motor Vehicle Transportation Act, 21; and resource for federal government, 29; and Advisory Council report, 77; and implementation of Part III, 82; and CTA, 152, 154: and federal-provincial negotiations, 166

Pickersgill, J. W. (President of Canadian Transport Commission): rationale for including Part III in NTA, 21; and preliminary discussions to Federal-Provincial Conference of Ministers, 35; and bureaucratic politics model, 82; and implementation of Part III, 82–85, 162, 175–76; and St. Laurent government, 82; and minority government, 83; and trucking industry, 83; and resignation from government, 84; and philosophy of federalism, 85–87, 94–95; resources of, 88–89; and opposition to Federal-Provincial Conference of Ministers (1969), 90–93; and conspiracy, 93; and assessment of Federal-Provincial Conference of Ministers (1969), 96; and recommendations after 1969 Conference, 96, 98–99; and strategy at Federal-Provincial Conference of Ministers, 100–101; and recommendations on Part III implementation, 104–7; and strategy paper for Federal-Provincial Conference of Ministers (1971), 108–10; and attitude towards Advisory Council, 114–15, 211n13; and assessment of Nova Scotia proposal, 116–17, 119; and Winnipeg meeting, 122–25; and amendments to Part III of NTA, 128, 129, 212 n19; and Privy Council Office, 135–36; and CTA support, 154. *See also* Advisory Council; Canadian Transport Commission; CTC-DOT coalition; Canadian Trucking Associations; Federal-Provincial Conference of Transport Ministers (1969), (1971): Joint Technical Committee Meeting; Nova Scotia proposal; Peel, A. L.; Robertson, D. R.; Trucking industry; Winnipeg meeting

Pierce, Lawrence, 171

Pratt, Larry, 171

Premier, government of Quebec. *See* Johnson, Daniel

Premier, government of Ontario. *See* Robarts, John

Pre-Part III federal actors: original coalition, 82–84; and importance of provincial cooperation, 87;

Trudeau, Pierre Elliott, 90, 182, 183, 184, 188
Truman, David, 155, 156
Turgeon Commission, 14

Unitary actor model: nature of, 3–5; and communications process, 28; and explanation for fate of Part III of NTA, 30, 53–55; 78–80; and comparison to bureaucratic politics model, 178–79; and parliamentary system, 180. *See also* Bureaucratic politics model; Simeon, Richard
United provincial front: and Ontario proposal, 46–47; and Quebec government position, 46; Saskatchewan government position, 46; and Nova Scotia government position, 46–47; and provincial

cooperation, 45, 205nn34, 36; and demand for provincial participation, 50

Vile, M. J. C., on federalism, 2

Wamsley, G. L., 6, 8
Western Economic Opportunities Conference, 139
Wheare, K. C., 199n5
Williams, Blair, 217n23
Winner v. *S.M.T. Eastern Ltd.*: and jurisdiction over trucking industry, 14, 15, 19, 27, 39, 207n19; and CTA, 150
Winnipeg Meeting of Advisory Council, 122, 123–25
Wootton, Graham, 216n9

Zald, M. N., 6, 8